HANDBOOK
of LOGISTICS
and DISTRIBUTION
MANAGEMENT

HANDBOOK
of LOGISTICS
and DISTRIBUTION
MANAGEMENT

Alan Rushton & John Oxley

KOGAN
PAGE

First published in 1989
This paperback edition published in 1991
Reprinted 1993, 1995, 1996

Apart from any fair dealing for the purposes of research or private study, or criticism or review, as permitted under the Copyright, Designs and Patents Act, 1988, this publication may only be reproduced, stored or transmitted, in any form or by any means, with the prior permission in writing of the publishers, or in the case of reprographic reproduction in accordance with the terms of licences issued by the Copyright Licensing Agency. Enquiries concerning reproduction outside those terms should be sent to the publishers at the undermentioned address:

Kogan Page Limited
120 Pentonville Road
London N1 9JN

© Alan Rushton and John Oxley 1989, 1991

British Library Cataloguing in Publication Data

A CIP record for this book is available from the British Library.

ISBN 0 7494 0588 0

Typeset by J&L Composition Ltd, Filey, North Yorkshire
Printed and bound in Great Britain by
Biddles Ltd, Guildford and King's Lynn

Contents

Part 4: Information and Control Systems

List of Figures

List of Tables

Preface

This book has been written to fulfil a number of objectives, but perhaps the most valid is that of providing an up-to-date text at a reasonable cost. We have felt for some years that there is a significant gap in the literature between the short and generalised text and the more expansive and vastly more expensive handbook. We hope that this book will fill this gap.

A second objective has been to put together a book which provides a broad framework and offers a sound basis for a much clearer understanding of all those functions and elements related to logistics and distribution. Allied to this we have tried to include fairly equal measures of concept and practice. In some instances, due to lack of space, it has not been possible to expand into as much practical detail as we would have liked, but hopefully we have achieved a suitable balance.

Because of the very broad area covered by logistics and distribution, it has been impossible to cover all of the associated functions that we would have liked. Notable among these are purchasing and retailing, although they are considered wherever they interface with other distribution and logistics functions.

Much of the content of the book has been drawn together from material that has been developed for the Master's Course in Distribution Technology and Management run by the Distribution Studies Unit at Cranfield Institute of Technology. Also, both authors have been involved in preparing and writing courses for the Institute of Logistics and Distribution Management and the Institute of Grocery Distribution. The work at Cranfield has included basic coursework and many company-based student projects. In addition, we have been involved, with our colleagues, in undertaking many industrial short-courses and consultancy assignments. As a result of this we undoubtedly owe both our colleagues and our past graduates many thanks – and apologies where we have included some of the fruits of their labours in the text without directly acknowledging them.

The distribution and logistics industry is currently undergoing a very significant metamorphosis. There is a distinct move towards a more professional approach to planning and management, and with this has come the need for better informed and more suitably educated managers. It is hoped that this book will go some way to providing the opportunity for improved information and education with respect to distribution and logistics. It should be of interest to practising managers and supervisors, to those candidates undertaking examinations for the various professional institutes, and to undergraduate and graduate students who are reading for degrees in logistics, distribution and transport, or where these subjects are an integral part of their course.

The contents of the book are divided into five main parts which cover the concepts of distribution and logistics, warehousing and storage, transport, information and control systems, and associated factors. Each part contains a number of chapters which concentrate on the major elements within each of the main topics.

Part 1 is concerned with the overall concepts of distribution and logistics. The first chapter provides an introduction, including a discussion of various definitions, the consideration of the main elements within logistics and distribution, and a historical perspective describing the different stages of development of logistics and distribution. The overall importance of the industry is reviewed in the context of business and the economy as a whole. In Chapter 2 the emphasis is on the need for integrated logistics and distribution systems. Topics covered include the concept of total distribution and the need for a positive approach to planning. Finally, the most recent developments in integrated systems are described.

The very important aspect of customer service is considered in Chapter 3, including the means of developing a customer service policy. Chapter 4 describes the basic cost relationships in logistics and distribution, and identifies the key costs that are fundamental to the total distribution system cost. The concept of trade-off analysis is also explained. Chapter 5 reviews the various aspects associated with depot and facilities location. The different roles of depots and warehouses are described, a planned approach to facilities location analysis is outlined, and the various location techniques are indicated. In addition, the more practical aspects of site selection are discussed. The concluding chapter in Part 1 considers the alternative channels of distribution that exist. The need for and means of planning for channel selection is described. Finally, the very important developments in third party distribution services are discussed.

In Part 2, consideration is given to those factors concerned with warehousing and storage. Chapter 7 introduces the main warehousing principles and also provides an outline of warehouse planning and operations with respect to the design and layout of warehouse areas. Storage systems are considered in Chapter 8. Included here are the principles of storage as well as descriptions of the various types of storage systems that are available. Chapter 9 concentrates on the many different handling systems and equipment types that are used from fork lift trucks through to conveyors. In Chapter 10, the importance of equipment management, selection and maintenance are emphasised.

The final chapters in this part, Chapters 11 and 12, describe the many different warehouse operations. The first, and particularly important function, is that of order picking. The main principles of order picking are explained, and the various order picking methods are outlined. The significance of different information requirements and order picking efficiency are discussed. Chapter 12 concentrates on the factors related to receipt and despatch such as loading bay design and operation, and types of loading dock. In addition the implications of different vehicle types, sizes and movements are considered together with their relationship with factors such as site access, vehicle flows, vehicle manoeuvring and vehicle parking.

Part 3 concentrates on those areas of logistics and distribution specifically related to freight transport. Chapter 13 considers international distribution, comparing the different transport modes, and describing the various operational factors that need to be taken into account. A European perspective is also given, particularly with respect to the single European Market and the Channel Tunnel. The remaining chapters in this part concentrate on aspects of road freight transport. Vehicle selection factors are described in Chapter 14. Included here are the main types of vehicle and vehicle body, different operational aspects, and load types and characteristics. Vehicle acquisition options are also discussed. In Chapter 15 the various elements of vehicle and fleet costing are described.

The increasing importance of road freight transport regulations are considered in Chapter 16. There is a brief review of the major legislative landmarks followed by more detailed emphasis and explanation of the effects of transport regulations on fleet operations, the driver, the vehicle, and the load. The final part of Part 3, Chapter 17, concentrates on the planning and operational importance of vehicle routeing and scheduling. The main objectives of routeing and scheduling are indicated, and the different types of problem are described. The basic characteristics of road transport delivery are discussed, and they are related to broad data requirements. Examples of both manual and computer routeing and scheduling methods are outlined.

Various aspects related to information and control systems are described in Part 4. Chapter 18 looks at the use of information systems for the planning and control of distribution and logistics operations. A distribution or logistics audit procedure is outlined; the main functions of a distribution information system are discussed; a general procedure for the monitoring and control of operations is described. Finally, in this chapter, various operational requirements are considered. In Chapter 19 the emphasis is placed on inventory management and stock control, beginning with a summary of the reasons for holding stock and the different types of stock-holding. The implications of various stock-holding policies on other distribution functions are indicated. Different inventory replenishment systems are described, and the main principles behind the specification of reorder levels are outlined. Finally, some different forecasting methods are illustrated and some of the recent developments in inventory planning are reviewed.

Chapter 20 is concerned with the application of information technology to logistics, and it begins by outlining an evaluation process for computer hardware and software selection. The remainder of the chapter is used to describe the many different software packages and programs that have been developed for use within the logistics industry. Areas covered include distribution and logistics strategy, general applications software, storage and warehousing, transport and integrated systems.

In Part 5 a series of factors associated with distribution and logistics are included. This starts with Chapter 21, which is concerned with the organisation of distribution and logistics in the company. Initially, the interface and relationship with other corporate functions is outlined and this is followed by a discussion of the different types of distribution organisational structures that may be found. The role of the logistics and distribution manager is considered and then the relatively neglected area of payment mechanisms and incentive schemes is described. Chapter 22 deals with the product, packaging and unitisation. Different product characteristics are identified and the implications of the product life-cycle are illustrated. The packaging of products is also considered, together with the use of various unit load types.

Security and safety are identified as important areas of responsibility for distribution management, and these are discussed in Chapter 23. The book ends with a review of the trends in distribution and logistics, and these are outlined in Chapter 24. A number of external factors are discussed, and then each of the main functional areas are considered – distribution and logistics strategy, warehousing, freight transport and information technology.

PART 1

Concepts of Logistics and Distribution

Introduction to Logistics and Distribution

Introduction

Distribution has been an important feature of industrial and economic life for many years, but it has only been in the relatively recent past that it has been recognised as a major function in its own right. The main reason for this lapse has probably been the nature of distribution itself. It is a function made up of many sub-functions and sub-systems each of which can be, and is, treated as a distinct management operation.

It is now accepted by both the academic and the business world that there is a need to adopt a more global view of these different operations in order to take into account how they interrelate and interact with each other.

The appreciation of the scope and importance of distribution has led to a more scientific approach being adopted towards the subject. This approach has been aimed at the individual sub-systems and especially at the overall concept of the distribution function as a whole. Much of this approach has addressed the need for and means of planning the distribution function.

Definitions

Parallel to the growth in the importance of distribution has been the growth in the number of associated names and different definitions that are used. Some of the different names applied to the distribution function include:

- physical distribution;
- logistics;

- business logistics;
- materials management;
- physical supply;
- product flow;
- marketing logistics;
- supply chain management;

and there are several more.

There is, in reality, no 'true' name and 'true' definition that can be pedantically applied, because products differ, companies differ and systems differ. Distribution is a diverse and dynamic function which has to be flexible and has to change according to the various constraints and demands that are imposed upon it.

So these many terms are used, often interchangeably in literature and in the business world. One quite widely accepted view shows the relationship as follows:

Materials management + Distribution = Logistics

This view holds that logistics is concerned with physical and information flows from raw material through to the final distribution of the finished product. Thus materials management represents those flows into and through the production process, while distribution represents those flows from the final production point through to the customer or end user. Figure 1.1 illustrates this.

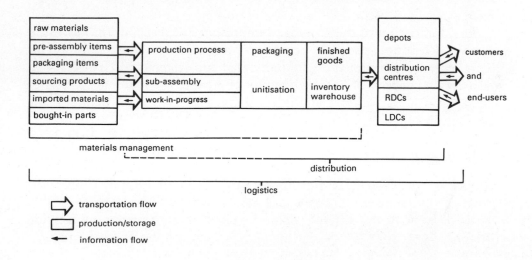

Figure 1.1 Relationship between logistics, materials management and distribution

The question of the most appropriate definition of distribution and its associated namesakes is always an interesting one. Here, the text books provide some fascinating reading. Some of the better known definitions include:

> Logistics is the Art and Science of Determining Requirements; Acquiring them; Distributing them and finally, Maintaining them in an operational ready condition for their entire life. (Stone, 1968)

> ... the management of all activities which facilitate movement and the co-ordination of supply and demand in the creation of time and place utility. (Hesket *et al.*, 1964)

> ... dispersal among consumers affected by commerce, also extent to which individuals or classes share in aggregate products of community; spreading abroad, dispersing scattered situation or arrangement; division into parts, arranging, classification. (Concise Oxford Dictionary)

> To get the goods from where they arise to the right place, in the right form, at the right time, at the right cost. (Anon)

> ... the efficient movement of finished product from the end of the production line to the consumer, and in some cases includes the movement of raw materials from the source of supply to the beginning of the production line. These activities include freight transportation, warehousing, material handling, protective packaging, inventory control, plant and warehouse site selection, order processing, marketing forecasting and customer service. (National Council of Physical Distribution Management)

It is interesting to detect the different biases – military, economic, dictionary, etc. It is not easy to determine which of the many definitions is most suitable. A more appropriate definition is perhaps, that distribution concerns the efficient transfer of goods from the place of manufacture to the place of consumption in a cost effective way whilst providing an acceptable service to the customer. This focus on cost effectiveness and customer service will be a point of emphasis throughout this book.

Elements of logistics and distribution

The NCPDM definition gives a useful list of some of the most important elements within distribution. This is a clear indication of the scope of distribution and its many facets.

This list can be 'exploded' once again to reveal the detailed aspects within the different elements. All of these functions and sub-functions need to be planned in a systematic way, both in terms of their own local environment and also in terms of the wider scope of the distribution system as a whole. A number of questions need to be asked and decisions made. The different ways of answering these questions and making these decisions will be addressed in the chapters of this book as consideration is given on how to plan and operate the distribution and logistics function.

Some examples include the following categories:

- storage, warehousing and materials handling
  - location of warehouses
  - number and size of distribution depots
  - type of operation
  - etc;
- transport
  - mode of transport
  - type of delivery operation
  - load planning
  - route schedule
  - etc;
- inventory
  - what to stock
  - where to stock
  - how much to stock
  - etc;
- information and control
  - design of systems
  - control procedures
  - forecasting
  - etc
- packaging and unitisation
  - unit load
  - protective packaging
  - handling systems
  - etc.

In addition, the total system interrelationships need to be considered and planned within the constraints of appropriate costs and service levels.

Historical perspective

The elements of distribution and logistics have, of course, always been fundamental to the manufacturing, storage and movement of goods and products. It is only relatively recently however that distribution and logistics have come to be recognised as vital functions within the business and economic environment.

There have been several distinct stages in the development of distribution and logistics in the UK.

1950s and early 1960s

In this period, distribution systems were unplanned and unformulated. Manufacturers manufactured, retailers retailed, and in some way or other the goods reached the shops. Distribution was broadly represented by the haulage industry and manufacturers' own account fleets. There was little positive control and no real liaison between the various distribution-related functions.

1960s and early 1970s

The concept of physical distribution was imported from the USA into the UK with the gradual realisation that the 'dark continent' was indeed a valid area for managerial involvement. Initially the benefits were recognised by manufacturers who developed distribution operations to reflect the flow of their product through the supply chain.

1970s

This was an important decade in the development of the distribution concept in the UK. One major change was the recognition by some companies of the need to include distribution in the functional management structure of an organisation. This decade also saw a change in the structure and control of the distribution chain. There was a decline in the power of the manufacturers and suppliers, and a marked increase in that of the major retailers. The larger retail chains developed their own distribution structures, based initially on the concept of regional or local distribution depots to supply their stores.

1980s

Fairly rapid cost increases and the clearer definition of the true costs of distribution saw a significant increase in the professionalism within distribution. With this professionalism has come a move towards longer-term planning and attempts to identify and pursue cost saving measures. These have included centralised distribution, severe reductions in stock-holding and the use of the computer to provide improved information and control. The growth of the third party distribution service industry has also been of major significance, and it is particularly here that developments in information and equipment technology are to be found. The concept of and need for integrated logistics systems is now recognised by most participants in the distribution and supply chain.

Importance of logistics and distribution

It is useful, at this point, to consider distribution in the context of the business and the economy as a whole.

Physical distribution is an important activity making extensive use of the human and material resources which affect a national economy. Several investigations have been undertaken to try to estimate the extent of the impact of physical distribution on the economy.

One such study indicated that about 30 per cent of the working population in the UK is associated with work which is related to physical distribution.

Another study, undertaken in the early 1980s (Rushton, 1983), estimated that 39 per cent of the UK gross domestic product was spent on distribution and logistics activities. For 1980, this represented £87,000 m out of a total GDP of £223,000 m.

In 1981, a study undertaken by AT Kearney indicated that, using a fairly broad definition of distribution, the associated costs in the UK were approximately 17 per cent of company sales revenue. Since then, the

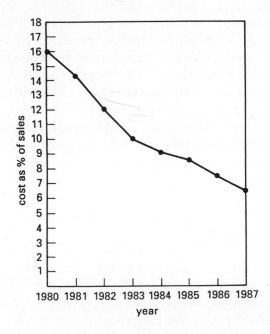

Figure 1.2 Distribution cost trend for years 1980–87, showing a steady decrease in costs as a percentage of sales

Institute of Logistics and Distribution Management (ILDM) has sponsored a series of distribution cost surveys. These have shown a steady downward trend to an overall average of 6.5 per cent of sales for 1987. Figure 1.2 is taken from the 1988 ILDM Survey results and it summarises this overall trend. The improved level of cost is due to a reduced level of inflation and also to the significant steps forward taken by the distribution industry in recent years with respect to better planning and management control.

The breakdown of the costs of the different elements within distribution has also been included in a number of surveys. A survey conducted in 1983 of American distribution costs indicated that transport was the most important element at 46 per cent, followed by storage/warehousing (22 per cent), inventory carrying cost (22 per cent) and administration (10 per cent). A comparison with the UK from the ILDM 1984 cost survey shows that transport was again out in front at 42 per cent, followed by storage (24 per cent), administration (20 per cent) and inventory (14 per cent). In both countries, therefore, the transport cost element of distribution was the major constituent part.

These broad figures are supported by a European Logistics Productivity survey produced by A T Kearney in 1988. These results, covering the major EC economies, placed transport at 41 per cent but showed the inventory carrying cost to be significantly more important at 23 per cent compared to the UK 14 per cent. Warehousing represented 21 per cent and administration 15 per cent of overall costs.

A somewhat wider view of costs was considered by the author in a survey of logistics costs undertaken in the UK in 1981. The results of this are shown in Figure 1.3. They emphasise, once again, the importance

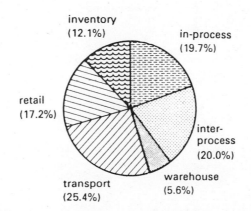

Figure 1.3 Logistics cost breakdown for the UK in 1981, showing the importance of different cost elements

material flow

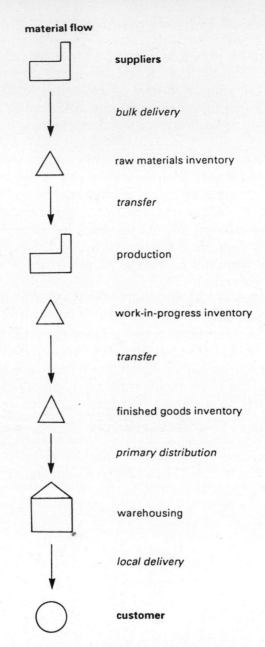

suppliers

bulk delivery

raw materials inventory

transfer

production

work-in-progress inventory

transfer

finished goods inventory

primary distribution

warehousing

local delivery

customer

Figure 1.4 Typical physical distribution flow of material from suppliers through to customer

of the cost of transport, which, in this survey also included a part of the inter-process cost element.

Logistics and distribution structure

The discussion in the previous section of this chapter has illustated quite clearly the major components within a logistics or distribution system. The fundamental characteristics of a physical distribution structure are perhaps the flow of material or product, interspersed at various points by stationary intervals. This flow is usually indicated by some form of transportation of the product. The stationary periods are usually for storage, or to allow some change to the product to take place — manufacture, assembly, packing, break bulk, etc.

A simple distribution flow is illustrated in Figure 1.4. The different types of transport (primary, local delivery, etc) and stationary functions (production, finished goods inventory, etc) are shown. It should be noted that to support these physical flows and functions, there is a complementary flow of information which allows the physical flow to occur.

There is also, of course, a cost which is incurred to enable the distribution operation to take place. The importance of this distribution or logistical cost to the final cost of the product is dependent on both the sophistication of the distribution system used and the intrinsic value of the product itself. This idea of distribution providing an 'added value' to a product has become a useful way of assessing the importance of logistics and distribution services. Figure 1.5 provides an example of this cost or added value for a typical low cost product.

Logistics structures can and do differ quite dramatically between one company and another, and one industry and another. Distribution channels can be short (ie very direct) or long (ie have many intermediate stocking points). Also, channels may be operated by manufacturers, retailers, or, as is now becoming increasingly common, by specialist third party distribution companies. These and other associated aspects are discussed in Chapter 6.

The industry and education

Logistics and distribution is now recognised as being a vital and integral part of the business and economy of a country. In recent years in the UK, for example, the industry has set out to develop a distinct professionalism to reflect this new-found importance.

The Chartered Institute of Purchasing and Supply (CIPS) is the largest professional purchasing and supply organisation in Europe. The role of distribution and logistics is fundamental to the Institute's areas of interest. Membership to the Institute is by examination, and logistics is a major element within all of the Institute's activities, including the professional examination syllabus, and the public courses and conference programmes.

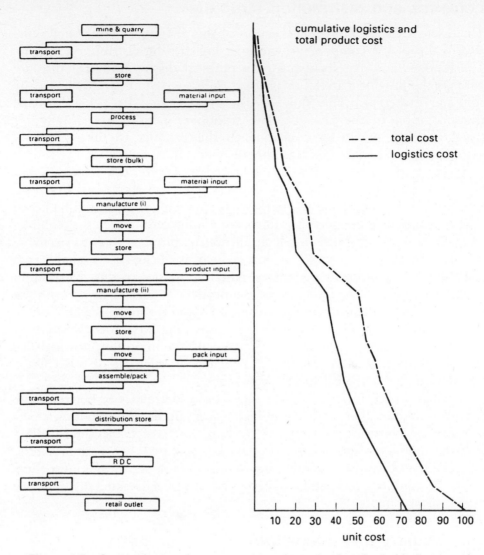

Figure 1.5 Cost make-up of a consumer product, showing the 'added' value of the logistics element in the unit cost through the logistics chain

The industry is well served by the Institute of Logistics, previously the Institute of Logistics and Distribution Management (ILDM) which evolved from the British Institute of Management, and plays a leading role in promoting logistics and distribution as a recognised profession. Membership has increased dramatically since the Institute was formed, and it continues to rise. The Institute provides a full programme of conferences and seminars in order to promote the industry.

In terms of education, there are now a number of opportunities open to the individual who chooses to make his or her career in logistics and distribution. In 1980, the Distribution Studies Unit was set up at Cranfield Institute of Technology. Now the Cranfield Centre for Logistics and Transportation (CCLT), the Centre offers a part-time Executive MSc in Distribution and Logistics and a full-time MSc in Logistics and Transportation. From the outset, these postgraduate courses have been designed specifically for the logistics and distribution industry.

Other educational developments have also taken place. The University of Huddersfield, for example, offer an undergraduate course in Transport and Distribution, while many business studies and transport courses provide options related to physical distribution and logistics. In addition, various Institutes, the Cranfield Centre for Logistics and Transportation and others offer one- to five-day short courses on various distribution related topics.

Summary

In this initial chapter, a number of subjects have been introduced. These will be expanded in subsequent chapters of the book.

The rather confusing number of associated names and different definitions were indicated and a few of the very many definitions were considered. No 'true' or definitive definition was offered, because logistics and distribution can and does differ dramatically from one industry, company, or product, to another.

The recent history of distribution in the UK was outlined, and a series of statistics served to illustrate how important logistics and distribution are to the economy in general and to individual companies. The breakdown between the constituent parts of distribution was given.

The basic structure of distribution and logistics was described, and the concepts of material and information flow and the added value of distribution were introduced. Finally, some of the opportunities for education and training were outlined.

CHAPTER 2

Integrated logistics and distribution systems

Introduction

In the previous chapter, the historical development of logistics and distribution was described and it was shown how the major distribution functions were a part of a flow process in a distribution system. In this chapter, the emphasis is on the need to integrate the various distribution functions into a complete working structure which enables the overall system to be run at the optimum. Thus, the concept of 'total distribution' is described, together with other recent developments in the planning and operation of logistics and distribution systems.

The total distribution concept

The Total Distribution Concept (TDC) is a relatively recent concept which aims to treat the many different elements that come under the broad banner of distribution as one single integrated system. It is a recognition that the interrelationships between different elements, say, transport and storage, need to be considered within the context of the broader scheme of things. Thus, the total system is considered rather than just the individual sub-systems.

An understanding of this concept is especially important where the planning of the distribution function is concerned. It is worth considering a simple, practical example to emphasise the point.

A company produces plastic toys which are packaged in cardboard boxes. These boxes are packed on to wooden pallets which are used as the basic unit load in the warehouse and on the transport vehicles for delivery to customers.

Eventually, the cardboard box is seen as an unnecessary cost, because it does not provide any significant additional protection to the quite hardy plastic toys, and it does not appear to offer any significant marketing advantage. Thus, the box is discarded, lowering the unit cost of the toy, and so providing a potential advantage in the market place.

One unforeseen result, however, is that the toys without their boxes cannot be stacked on to wooden pallets, but must be stored and moved instead in special trays. These trays are totally different to the unit load which is currently used in the warehouse and on the vehicles (ie the wooden pallet). The additional cost penalty in providing special trays and catering for another type of unit load for storage and delivery is a high one. Much higher than the savings made on the product packaging.

This example illustrates a classic case of *sub-optimisation* in a distribution system. It shows how the concept of Total Distribution can be ignored at significant cost. As the product packaging costs have been reduced, those concerned with this company function will feel that they have done their job well. The overall effect on the total distribution cost is, in fact, a negative one. The company is better served by disregarding this potential saving on the packaging side because the additional warehouse and transport costs mean that total costs increase.

This simple example of sub-optimisation emphasises the point concerning the interrelationships of the different distribution elements. A more positive viewpoint is to interpret these and other interrelationships in a planned approach to identifying and determining *cost trade-offs*. These will provide a positive benefit to the distribution system as a whole. Such a trade-off may entail additional cost in one function but will provide a greater cost saving in another. The overall achievement will be a net gain to the system.

This type of trade-off analysis is often an important part of planning in distribution. Four different levels of trade-off have been identified.

1. *Within distribution components*: those which occur within single functions. One example would be the own account or third party decision in transport planning
2. *Between distribution components*: those between the different elements in distribution. To reverse the previous packaging example, a company might increase the strength and thus the cost of packaging but find greater savings through improvements in the warehousing and storage of the product (ie block stacking rather than a requirement for racking).
3. *Between company functions*: as Figure 2.1 illustrates, there are a number of areas of interface between company functions where

trade-offs need to be made. An example is the trade-off between optimising production run lengths and the associated warehousing costs of storing the additional finished product.

4. *Between the company and external organisations*: for example, a change from the direct retail delivery of a manufacturer's product to delivery via the retailer's distribution system might lead to mutual savings for the two companies.

activity \ function	finance	production	distribution	marketing
MH equipment	✓		✓	
storage systems	✓		✓	
depot building	✓		✓	
transport	✓		✓	✓
distribution information systems		✓	✓	
inventory control	✓	✓	✓	
production control		✓	✓	
customer service		✓	✓	✓
depot location			✓	✓
order processing	✓		✓	✓
finished goods warehouse	✓	✓	✓	
packaging	✓	✓	✓	✓
unit load		✓	✓	✓
etc				

Figure 2.1 Interfaces between different company functions

These types of trade-offs are thus at the heart of the Total Distribution Concept. For the planning of the distribution function, it is important that this overall view of a distribution system and its costs is taken. The other side of the equation is, of course, the need to provide the service level that is required. The balance of total distribution cost and service level is essential to successful distribution.

Planning for distribution and logistics

In order to ensure that the concept of total distribution is put into practice, and that suitable trade-offs are achieved, it is essential that a positive planning approach is adopted. In this section, the various planning horizons with their associated distribution decisions are discussed.

Planning can be undertaken according to a certain hierarchy which reflects different planning time horizons. These are generally classified as strategic, tactical and operational. They are represented in Figure 2.2. The overlap which exists between the main planning stages should be noted. There are many planning factors which can be covered by two different stages. The choice of transport mode could, for example, be an initial strategic and a subsequent tactical decision.

The figure also indicates the interrelationship of planning and control within this hierarchy.

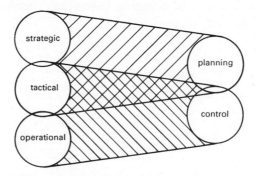

Figure 2.2   Distribution planning hierarchy

Some of the major aspects and differences between the three time horizons can be summarised as follows:

- Strategic
  - medium to long term horizon;
  - 1 to 5 years (plus) time span;
  - overall 'system' decisions are made, generally balancing and trading off between company functions or other organisations;
  - corporate financial plans and policies provide the financial basis for strategic planning;
  - developing policy decisions into a strategic plan.

- Tactical
  - short to medium term horizon;
  - 6 months to 1 year (plus) time span;
  - sub-system decisions – generally not expected to impose on other distribution components;
  - annual budgets provide the financial/cost basis;
  - the detail of the strategic plan is being put into effect.
- Operational
  - day-to-day decision making;
  - controlling the operations against expected standards and rules;
  - weekly and monthly reports provided for control purposes;
  - implementing the detail of regular operations.

The importance and relevance of these different aspects will, of course, vary according to the type and scale of business, product, etc. It is helpful to be aware of the planning horizon and the associated implications for each major decision that is made.

In terms of distribution, it is possible to identify many elements which can be categorised within this planning hierarchy. Some of these – in no particular order – are as follows:

- Strategic
  - customer service;
  - channels of distribution;
  - supply points;
  - demand points;
  - types of depot/depot configuration;
  - number of depots;
  - location and size of depots;
  - transport mode;
  - road vehicle alternatives;
  - direct delivery;
  - stock levels;
  - etc.
- Tactical – at each depot
  - transport,
    - vehicle types,
    - vehicle size,
    - vehicle numbers,
    - contract hire,
    - trunking routes,
    - fixed delivery schedules,

       support facilities,
       etc;
- depot storage,
       design,
       layout,
       space allocation,
       storage media,
       handling methods,
       truck numbers, types, etc.
       unit loads,
       etc;
- administration/information,
       monitoring procedures,
       stock control,
       stock location system,
       order processing,
       documentation,
       etc.

- Operational
  - goods receipt;
  - checking;
  - bulk storage;
  - order picking;
  - stock replenishment;
  - order marshalling;
  - load scheduling;
  - returns;
  - manpower availability;
  - stock update;
  - documentation completion;
  - vehicle maintenance;
  - vehicle workshop activity;
  - etc.

These lists serve to emphasise the complexity of distribution and logistics. In addition, they underline the need for appropriate planning and control. Distribution is not merely the transportation of goods from one point to another. There are many and varied elements that go together to produce an effective distribution and logistics operation. These elements interrelate, and they need to be planned over suitable time horizons.

It is important to be aware of the process of planning – to adopt a

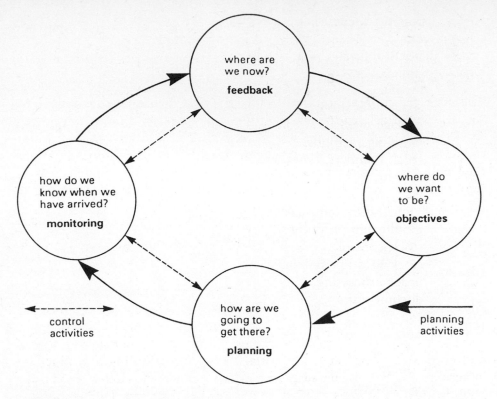

Figure 2.3 Planning and control cycle

systematic approach. This is best described in terms of a *planning framework*. One example of a fairly common framework is shown as the planning and control cycle in Figure 2.3.

The approach begins with the 'Where are we now?' question, where the aim is to provide a picture of the current position. This might be through an information feedback procedure and/or through the use of distribution audit. The second stage is to determine the objectives of the distribution process. These need to be related to such elements as customer service requirements, marketing decisions, etc.

The third stage in the cycle is the planning process which spans the strategic and operational levels previously discussed. Finally, there is a need for monitoring and control procedures to measure the effectiveness of the distribution operation compared to the plan. The cycle has then turned full circle and the process is ready to begin again. This emphasises the dynamic nature of distribution, the need for continual review and revision of plans, policies and their operations. This must be undertaken within a positive planning framework to ensure that continuity and progess is upheld.

The means of achieving these different stages of the planning and control cycle are described in detail in Chapter 18.

Integrated systems

The most recent developments in logistics and distribution systems have the concept of total distribution as their basis. Thus, quite revolutionary 'trade-offs' are now being practised. The major reason for this explosion of new ideas is twofold. The first is the realisation of the importance and the cost of logistics. The second is the progress made in the field of information technology which has enabled the type of detailed analysis to be undertaken which was previously impossible.

There are now a number of alternative integrated physical and information systems to support different distribution operations.

Direct product profitability

DPP is a technique of allocating all of the appropriate costs and allowances to a given product. All distribution costs (storage, transport, etc) are therefore assigned to a specific product rather than taking an average over a whole product range. Thus, in the same way that a budgetary system operates, the actual costs of distributing a product are monitored and are compared to a standard cost which is determined using DPP. In this way, areas of inefficiency can be identified. DPP techniques can identify the costs of specific products to individual customers and so provide invaluable information for effective marketing strategies.

Materials requirements planning (MRP) and distribution requirements planning (DRP)

MRP/DRP systems have been developed as sophisticated, computerised planning tools which aim to make the necessary materials or inventory available when needed. The concept originated with Materials Requirements Planning (MRP), an inventory control technique for determining dependent demand for manufacturing supply. Subsequently, Manufacturing Resource Planning (MRP II) was developed with the objective of improving productivity through the detailed planning and control of production resources. MRP II systems are based on an integrated approach to the whole manufacturing process from orders through production planning and control techniques to the purchasing and supply of materials. Distribution Requirements Planning (DRP) is the application of MRP II techniques to the management of the inventory and material flow — effective warehousing and transportation support.

DRP systems operate by breaking down the flow of material from the source of supply through the distribution network of depots and transportation modes. This is undertaken on a time-phased basis to ensure that the required goods 'flow' through the system and are available as and when required – at the right place, at the right time – one of the classic distribution definitions. Integrated systems of this nature require sophisticated, computerised information systems as their basis. The benefits of an effective system can be readily seen in terms of reduced freight, storage and inventory holding costs, and improved customer service.

Just in time

JIT is a new approach to manufacturing that has been successfully applied in some industries and which also has significant implications for distribution. The overall concept of JIT is to provide a production system which eliminates all activities that do not add value to the final product and which do not allow for the continuous flow of material. In simple terms, to eliminate the costly and wasteful elements within a production process. The objectives of JIT are vitally linked to distribution and logistics, including as they do:

- the production of goods the customer wants;
- the production of goods when the customer wants them;
- the production of perfect quality goods; and
- the elimination of waste (labour, inventory, movement, space, etc).

There are a number of JIT techniques which are used to a greater or lesser extent by the relatively few and generally large companies that have taken the JIT road. These techniques include:

- pull scheduling – whereby production is linked to 'demand pull' rather than 'schedule push' control systems (Thus, throughout the production and supply process, only the precise material requirements are drawn – this serves to eliminate the need for inventory);
- mixed production – this means that only the required goods need to be produced as processes can be easily switched to other products;
- fast set-up times – enabling almost continuous production of different products;
- preventative maintenance – to ensure unbroken production;
- revised plant layout – to minimise handling and movement;
- total quality control – identifying errors and defects at source;
- supplier liaison – extending JIT principles to suppliers.

An effective JIT system must be integrated throughout the manufacturing operation and must also include the supply and demand aspects of the business. It demands an effective and efficient information and physical distribution system to ensure that the major benefits can be realised.

Conclusion

The realisation of the need for the effective planning and control of distribution, coupled with the obvious interrelationships within distribution and logistics systems have led to the development of several new approaches towards integrated systems. The recent advances in information technology have made the practical application of these new approaches feasible. All in all, there has been a very positive move towards an integrated approach to distribution although for many companies, both large and small, there is still considerable scope for improvement.

The more complex and sophisticated systems such as DPP, MRP, DRP and JIT have only been adopted by a fairly limited number of very large, generally multinational companies. This is despite the clear benefits to be gained. The main reasons for this lack of progress have been highlighted in a recent survey by A T Kearney (*Logistics Productivity: The Competitive Edge in Europe*, 1988). They are:

- a lack of organisational integration that reflects the role and importance of logistics and distribution;
- a failure to develop adequate long-term plans for logistics strategy; and
- insufficiently developed information structures and support systems to provide the appropriate databases for good logistics planning and management.

For many small and medium-size companies, there is also the very pertinent factor that they need to learn to walk the distribution/logistics path before they attempt to run on it. Thus the benefit of advanced integrated systems may be many years away. But even for companies such as these, there is a great deal to be gained from taking those first few steps towards recognising that distribution should be viewed as an integrated system and that there is a strong interrelationship between the different elements of transportation, storage, information, etc. In addition, there is the need to adopt a positive approach to the planning and control of those systems.

Fortunately, in the past few years, the importance and relevance of distribution and logistics to most companies has become realised to a greater or lesser extent. Thus, organisational structures and planning policies are now beginning to reflect the integrated approach.

CHAPTER
3

Customer service

Introduction

The vast majority of companies recognise customer service as an important aspect of their business. When pressed, however, there are few companies that can readily describe or explain precisely what they mean by customer service. Traditionally, service provisions have been based on very broad assumptions of what the customer wants, rather than taking into account the precise requirements of the customer – or at least the customer's perception of what he requires.

There are several major points that need to be considered. One is the definition of customer service, another is its measurement. It is also important to recognise that customer service and customer service requirements can and will differ not just between industries and companies, but additionally between the market segments which a business might serve.

Another relevant factor is the recognition of the complexity of customer service provision. Customer service is inextricably linked to the process of distribution. With this process, there are many influences that may be important. These range from ease of ordering to stock availability to delivery reliability. Finally, there is the need to balance the level of service provided with the cost of that provision. The downfall of many a service policy is often the unrealistic and unrecognised cost of providing a service which may, in the event, be unnecessary.

The key to achieving a successful customer service policy is to develop appropriate objectives through a proper framework, and then to measure, monitor and control the procedures that have been set up.

Definition of customer service

As already stated, different companies have very different views of customer service. Some American writers have identified three distinct groups of customer service elements:

1. Pre-transaction elements, which are concerned with customer service policy. These would include such items as statements of service policy, corporate programmes, etc.
2. Transaction elements, which are concerned with those elements directly related to the physical transaction or distribution. Under this heading would be included stock availability, order cycle time, order status information, order preparation and delivery reliability
3. Post-transaction elements, which involve those elements that occur after delivery, such as after-sales service, warranty, customer complaints procedures, replacements, etc.

There are many different elements of customer service, and these will vary in their relevance according to the product and market concerned. A list of the most quoted elements is likely to include:

- stock availability;
- order status information;
- order cycle time;
- delivery reliability;
- delivery alternatives;
- delivery time;
- complete delivery of order;
- condition of goods;
- methods of ordering;
- invoicing procedures;
- invoice accuracy;
- claims procedures;
- complaints procedures; and
- order size constraints.

A customer service policy

The fact that there are so many different elements of customer service – as indicated in the list from the previous section – underlines the need for a company to have a clearly defined customer service policy. To this must be added the influence of the variety of markets and market segments that exist.

Many studies have been undertaken to measure the effects of poor customer service. These studies conclude, quite categorically, that where stock is not available or where delivery is unreliable, many buyers will readily turn to an alternative supplier's products to fulfil their requirements.

Once the positive need for a customer service policy has been recognised and accepted, it is necessary to determine the basic requirements and format of this policy. These might include:

- an understanding of the different market segments that exist
- an awareness of the customer's needs or perceived needs within this segmentation;
- the determination of clearly defined and quantifiable standards of customer service in relation to the different market segments;
- an understanding of the trade-off between the costs and levels of customer service;
- measurement of the service provided; and
- liaison with customers to ensure an understanding and appreciation of the service provided.

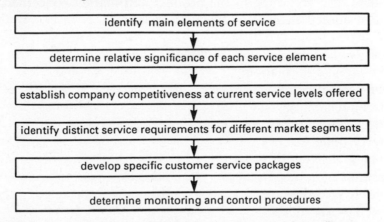

Figure 3.1 An approach to establishing a customer service policy

An approach for developing a customer service policy

It is possible to develop a logical approach to facilitate the development of a suitable customer service policy. One such approach is shown in Figure 3.1. This is a six-step plan to identify key customer service components and then to design a suitable customer service package. The main steps are as follows:

1. Identify main elements of service: As already discussed, it is important to identify those elements of service which are most highly rated by the customer. Only then can the company's resources be concentrated on these key factors. The main means of determining the key

components are by market research techniques. These processes might include:

(a) identification of the main decision maker or buyer of the product;

(b) use of personal interviews to determine the importance of customer service and the different elements within customer service; and

(c) use of group interview to determine the same.

The importance of this stage is to identify relevant measures of service which are generated by customers themselves and not imposed arbitrarily by 'best guesses' from outside.

2. Determine relative significance of each service element: Once again, there are various research techniques that can be used to measure the relative importance of the service components that are identified. For a fairly small list of components, some form of order ranking ('most' to 'least' important) or rating scale (one to ten according to importance) can be used. One relatively recent technique is that of trade-off analysis. This provides a better format for considering and measuring the relative importance of different combinations of service components.

3. Establish company competitiveness at current service levels offered: Having identified the key service components and their relative importance to the customer, the next step is to measure the company's own position compared to its competitors. This can be undertaken by means of a questionnaire which lists the key components and asks for a rating on perceived performance. A respondent is asked to rate each competing company on a separate questionnaire. The results will indicate how each competitor performs according to the key service components. This performance can then be compared to the competition and also to the most important service elements as identified in the previous stage of the study. From this information, an appropriate customer service strategy can be developed.

4. Identify distinct service requirements for different market segments: It has been recognised by some companies in recent years that customers and their needs can vary quite substantially, in terms of product quality, levels of service, etc. Within a total market, it is possible to identify distinct sub-markets.

A typical example might be the supply of stationery items. These might be supplied to retailers and to wholesalers for further distribution or to the public service or to private companies for their own consumption. Each segment of the total market may require a distinctly different level of service, or may react differently to certain deficiencies of service.

Some market segments may be quite easy to categorise – as in the previous example. In other instances, it can be far more difficult. One technique that can be used is cluster analysis, where each element is weighted according to its importance. This is done for every customer. Cluster analysis will then determine those customers that have similar requirements.

On the basis of these types of analysis, it is possible to develop a number of specific service policies to suit the different groups or segments.

5. Develop specific customer service packages: This will depend on the results obtained from the stages that have been described. It is important to be able to identify, where possible, alternative packages for the different market segments. By doing so, appropriate costs can be compared and the most suitable package determined not just by the service element, but also by the cost.

6. Determine monitoring and control procedures: It is vital to ensure that any policy that is implemented is also monitored and controlled. In practice, this is rarely carried out, firstly because companies do not have an adequate customer service policy and, secondly, because companies find it difficult to construct quantifiable standards that are capable of measurement.

The first task, then, is to identify the factors that need to be measured. These should be based on the major components identified in the early stages of the planning framework.

The second task is to produce a measure. This can be undertaken in different ways for different components, but must reflect a fair measure of the component. One example is stock availability or order fulfilment. It is possible to measure this according to:

(a) the number of orders completely satisfied – say 18 out of 20 over a period (90 per cent);

(b) the number of lines delivered from a single order – say, 75 out of the 80 lines requested (94 per cent);

(c) the number of line items or cases delivered from a single order – say, 75 out of the 80 lines requested, but only 1,400 of the 1,800 total line items (78 per cent); and

(d) the value of the order completed – say, £750 of the £900 order (83 per cent).

There are other measures that can be made. These measures might, for example, be aimed at assessing the timeliness of delivery operations. Many Express Parcels companies set great store in the speed of their delivery operations, and calculate in detail the time taken from receipt of order or parcel collection to final delivery.

It is important that the measure is a realistic representation of the component of the service that is being provided.

Levels of customer service

It has already been stressed that there is a need to balance the level of customer service with the cost of providing that service. This balance is not easy to define, although it can be described quite easily as the point where the additional revenue for each increment of service is equal to the extra cost of providing that increment.

It is seldom possible to devise a policy which is absolutely optimum in terms of the cost/service balance. Some companies adopt a cost minimisation approach where specific service objectives are laid down and met at a minimum cost. Others choose a service maximisation approach where a distribution budget is fixed, and the 'best' service supplied within this cost constraint. The approach to adopt will depend on particular product, business or market situations.

One factor which is clear is the relationship between cost and service. This is shown in Figure 3.2. The cost of providing a given service is markedly higher the nearer to the 100 per cent mark. Thus, an increase of 2 per cent in service levels will cost far more between 95 per cent and 97 per cent than between 70 per cent and 72 per cent. Also a high cost increase of the 95 per cent to 97 per cent kind may well have little, if any, impact on the customer's perception of the service that is being provided.

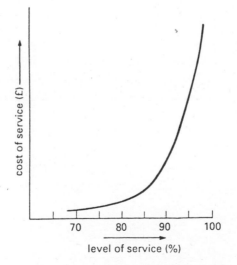

Figure 3.2 Relationship between cost and service level, showing the steep increase in cost as 100 per cent service is achieved

Summary

This chapter on Customer Service has covered the following areas:

- the definition of customer service
- the elements of customer service
- a policy for customer service
- an approach for developing a service policy
- levels and measurement of customer service

It is worth emphasising, once again, that although many companies recognise the concept of customer service, very few are able to give a precise definition of their customer service policy. Few also have detailed, accurate measures of service. Because of the vital link between physical distribution and customer service, it is crucial that distribution and logistics managers make themselves aware of the service requirements that their operations are expected to fulfil.

Basic Cost Relationships

Introduction

When planning and running a distribution operation it is important to be aware of the key costs that are involved in the total distribution system, and how these costs interact with each other. Many companies have cost information based on their conventional accounting systems, but almost always these costs are too general to allow for any detailed breakdown into the integral parts that reflect the company's distribution structure.

Without this information, and the understanding that goes with it, it is impossible to measure the effectiveness, or otherwise, of the existing operation. It is also impossible to gain the necessary insight into the distribution operation to allow for successful planning and management. The component parts of a distribution system necessarily interact with each other to form the system as a whole. Within this system, it is possible to trade-off one element with another, and so gain an overall improvement in the cost of effectiveness of the total system. An appreciation of the make-up and relationship of these key costs is thus a vital link to successful distribution planning and operations.

Key costs

The major cost relationships are outlined in this section, starting with storage and warehousing costs. The major cost breakdown is outlined below, with the percentage values indicating the approximate relative importance of the different factors based on conventional warehouses:

	%
Building costs (rent, rates, depreciation)	24
Building services (heating, lighting, etc.)	16

	%
Equipment (rental, leasing, maintenance)	13
Labour (direct)	38
Management and supervision	9

The relationship of these costs will, of course, vary under different circumstances – industry, product type, volume throughput, regional location, age of building, handling system, etc. In general, the direct labour cost is likely to be the greatest element, with the building cost likely to fluctuate from very high (new building, prime location) to very low (old building, peppercorn rent, low rates).

With respect to the cost relationship with other parts of the distribution system, the importance of storage and warehousing costs will be dependent on such factors as the size of the depot and the number of depots within the distribution network as a whole.

The effect of depot size is illustrated by the economies of scale that are experienced if larger depots are operated. It has been established that the operation of a depot and the amount of stock required to support a depot tend to be higher (per unit) for a small depot than for a large depot. This is because larger depots can often achieve better space and equipment utilisation and can benefit from spreading overhead costs over the higher throughput. As far as the stock-holding is concerned, the larger a depot, the less buffer and safety stock is required. It should be noted that, eventually, diseconomies of scale can come about, because very large depots can be adversely affected by such conditions as excessive travel distances, problems of management, etc.

The effect of a different number of warehouses or depots in a given distribution network can be seen by developing the economies of scale argument. If a distribution network is changed from one depot to two depots, then the overall depot/storage costs will increase. The change is likely to be from a single large depot to two medium-sized depots. This will not, therefore, double the costs because the change is not to two large depots. It will certainly increase costs, however, because there will be a need for more stock coverage, more storage space, more management, etc. In simple terms, this can be described by a graph, illustrated in Figure 4.1.

Thus, as the number of depots in a distribution network increases, then the total storage (depot) cost will also increase.

One point that should be appreciated is that some care must be taken over any generalisation of this nature. In practice, it will be found that each individual depot may differ in its cost structure from the other depots in a system for a variety of practical reasons. These may include, for example, high (or low) rent and rates according to the locality of the depot (ie very high in London) or high (or low) labour costs.

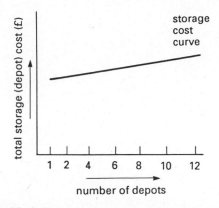

Figure 4.1 Relationship between number of depots (ie storage capacity) and total storage cost

The two most important categories of transport costs are trunking and final delivery. These are affected differently according to the number of depots in a distribution network.

Delivery transport is concerned with the delivering of orders from the depot to the customers. This can be carried out by a company using its own fleet of vehicles (such as W H Smith, Tesco) or by third party carriers (such as Lowfield Distribution, SPD). Whichever alternative is used, the cost of delivery is essentially dependent on the mileage that has to be travelled.

Delivery mileage can be divided into two types:

- 'drop' mileage, which is the mileage travelled once a drop or delivery zone has been reached; and
- 'stem' mileage, which is the mileage to and from a delivery zone.

While the 'drop' mileage remains the same whatever the distance from the supplying depot, the 'stem' mileage varies according to the number of depots in the system. The greater the number of depots, the less the stem mileage. This can be described by a graph shown in Figure 4.2.

The *trunking* or primary transport element is the supply of products in bulk (ie in full pallet loads) to the depots from the central warehouse/ production point.

Once again, the overall cost of this type of transport is affected by the number of depots in the distribution system. In this instance, the effect is not a particularly large one, but it does result in an increase in primary

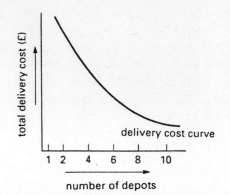

Figure 4.2 Relationship between the number of depots and total delivery costs showing a decline in delivery costs as the number of depots increases

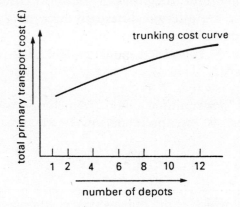

Figure 4.3 Trunking costs (total primary transport costs) as a function of the number of depots

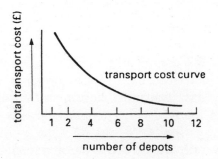

Figure 4.4 Total transport costs (delivery and trunking) as a function of the number of depots employed

transport costs as the number of depots increases. The effect is greatest where there are a smaller number of depots, as the graph of Figure 4.3 indicates.

If the cost for both delivery and trunking are taken as a *combined transport cost* then the total transport costs can be related to the different number of depots in a distribution network.

The overall effect of combining the two transport costs is that total transport costs will reduce the greater the number of depots in the system. The effect can be seen in the graph of Figure 4.4.

Another important cost that needs to be included is the *cost of holding inventory*. The main elements of inventory holding are considered in detail in Chapter 19, but the cost can be broken down into four main areas:

1. Capital cost – that is, the financing charge which is the current cost of capital to a company, and the opportunity cost of tying up capital which might otherwise be producing a return if invested elsewhere.
2. Service cost – that is, stock management and insurance.
3. Storage costs – which were considered earlier with the warehousing costs.
4. Risk costs – which occur through pilferage, deterioration, damage and obsolescence.

These costs, when taken together and measured against the number of depots in a system, can be represented as shown in Figure 4.5.

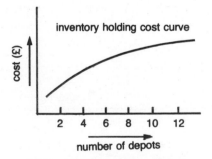
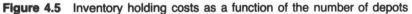

Figure 4.5 Inventory holding costs as a function of the number of depots

The final cost element for consideration is that of the *system costs*. These costs may represent a variety of information or communication aspects ranging from order processing to load assembly lists. In recent years, there has been a significant move from manual systems towards the use of the computer to provide these services. The costs are represented in the graph of Figure 4.6.

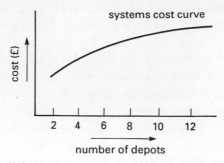

Figure 4.6 System (information or communication) costs as a function of the number of depots

Total distribution cost

By its very nature, distribution operates in a dynamic and ever-changing environment. This makes the planning of a distribution system a difficult process. By the same token, it is not an easy matter to appreciate how any changes to one of the major elements within a distribution structure will affect the system as a whole. One way of overcoming this problem is to adopt a 'total' view of the system, to try to understand and measure the system as a whole, as well as in relation to the constituent parts of the system.

Total distribution cost analysis allows this approach to be developed on a practical basis. The various costs of the different elements within the system can be built together to provide a fair representation, not just of the total distribution cost itself, but also of the ways in which any changes to the system will affect both the total system as well as the other elements within the system.

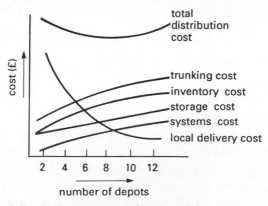

Figure 4.7 Total distribution costs as a function of the number of depots, showing the constituent cost elements that comprise the total

The total cost approach can be represented in a graphical format by building up a picture from the graphs that were used to illustrate the cost elements in the earlier section of this chapter. This is illustrated in Figure 4.7 and demonstrates how the individual distribution cost elements can be built up to give the total distribution cost. It shows, for example, the effect of a different number of depots and the related costs on the total distribution cost. In this instance, the lowest cost solution is at the minimum point on the total cost curve, somewhere between six and nine depots.

Trade-off analysis

An understanding of the total cost approach to distribution is important in order to appreciate the concept of trade-off analysis in distribution planning. It has been shown that any change in one of the major elements within a distribution system is likely to have a significant effect on the costs of both the total system and on the other elements as well. By the same token, it is often possible to create total cost savings by making savings in one element which creates additional costs in another but produces an overall cost benefit. This can be seen in Figure 4.8.

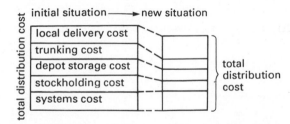

Figure 4.8 Trade-off analysis. A change in one or more cost elements, while increasing or decreasing other elements, can produce an overall reduction in total distribution costs

Here a depot rationalisation policy has been adopted whereby the number of depots in a distribution system has been reduced. Although this has led to an increase in local delivery costs, savings in some of the other main elements of distribution have produced overall cost benefits.

Cost trade-off analysis can be used as the basis for the planning and reassessing of distribution systems. Clearly, this approach is a time consuming and often daunting task, especially because of the difficulty in obtaining the appropriate data and information from within a company's accounting system.

One means of addressing the major problem of data collection and analysis is to undertake an audit of distribution operations, with a view to identifying and isolating the detailed breakdown of costs in different cost centres. An explanation of how to set up and undertake a distribution audit is given in Chapter 18. In addition, Chapter 20, on information technology, describes computer cost models that are available as an aid to determining least cost distribution strategies based on the principles of trade-off analysis.

Summary

In this chapter, the basic cost relationships within distribution have been described. Finally, these relationships have been brought together to produce a total distribution cost. It has been shown that trade-off analysis can be used to help to optimise the cost effectiveness of distribution systems, even where this may mean that individual cost elements are increased.

CHAPTER
5

Depot/Facilities Location

Introduction

In this chapter the various aspects associated with depot and facilities location are reviewed. There are both theoretical concepts and practical considerations to be taken into account. Some of the major points for discussion are:

- the role of depots and warehouses;
- cost factors;
- techniques for depot location; and
- site and building factors.

The question of number, size and location of facilities in a company's distribution system is a complex one. There are many different elements that go to make up the distribution mix, and it is necessary to take into account all of these when considering the question of facilities location.

The complexity of the location decision has led to the development of some quite sophisticated mathematical models which attempt to find the 'optimum' number of depots to serve a system. The detailed mathematical principles used as the basis for these models will not be covered, but consideration will be given to the relationships that are involved, and the approaches that can be undertaken when making location decisions.

It is worthwhile to begin the discussion on depot and warehouse location by concentrating on the most practical aspects of importance to an individual company. The main point to appreciate is that the vast majority of location studies that are undertaken are done so when the company already has a number of depots and associated delivery areas.

Thus, location studies are rarely based upon the premise that the 'best' results can be applied at the end of the day. Generally, it is necessary for a compromise to be reached between what is 'best' and what is currently in existence. The very high cost of depots and vehicle fleets is the main reason for this, as well as the high cost and great disruption involved in making any changes to existing systems.

Despite this, it is very important for companies to know how their distribution networks might be improved. Although some networks are planned from the beginning of a company's operation, this is a rare occurrence. The majority of systems are unplanned, they just evolve very much as the company evolves. This may be a steady growth (or decline), or may be in short steps or large leaps as mergers and take-overs occur. Perhaps the most common reason why distribution networks are out of balance is that of inertia, because of the great amount of work and effort that is required to make changes.

It requires a forward-looking management or a particularly significant change for a company to undertake a large scale study of this nature. The recent realisation of the importance of distribution to most companies, and the need to cut costs and improve efficiency has provided sufficient impetus for a number of companies to review their distribution system with a particular emphasis on the use and location of depots and warehouses.

The role of depots and warehouses

There are a number of reasons why depots and warehouses are required. These vary in importance depending on the nature of a company's business. In general, the main reasons are:

- to keep down production costs by allowing long production runs, thus minimising the time spent at machinery set-up;
- to help link demand requirements with production capabilities, to smooth the flow and assist in operational efficiency;
- to enable large seasonal demands to be catered for more economically;
- to provide a good customer service;
- to allow cost trade-offs with the transport system (bulk delivery, etc); and
- to facilitate order assembly.

These reasons emphasise the importance of the facilities location decision, and also give an indication of the complex nature of that decision.

It is possible to summarise the main reason for developing a distribution network as: 'the need to provide an effective service to the customer, whilst minimising the cost of that service'. The service and cost factors are thus of paramount importance when determining facilities number, size and location.

For the best possible customer service, a depot would have to be provided right next to the customer, and it would have to hold adequate stocks of all the goods which the customer might require. This would obviously be a very expensive solution.

At the other extreme, the cheapest solution would be to have just one depot (or central warehouse) and to send out a large lorry to each customer whenever his orders were sufficient to fill the vehicle so that an economic full load could be delivered. This would be a cheap alternative for the supplier, but as deliveries might then only be made to a customer once or maybe twice a year, the supplier might soon find himself losing the customer's business.

There is obviously a suitable compromise somewhere between these extremes. This will consist of the provision of a number of depots on a regional or area basis, the use of large trunk vehicles to service these, with smaller delivery vehicles to run the orders to customers.

Depot location policies are aimed at establishing this blend of storage and transport at a given customer service level. The interrelationship of the different distribution elements, and their associated costs, thus provides the basis for decision making.

Cost factors

The cost and service trade-offs within any distribution structure will, of course, vary in importance from one company to another. In the main, however, the major costs are likely to include the following:

1. *Production costs*: variable where different distribution structures require certain throughputs of products from the factory. Also related to storage and handling methods.
2. *Packaging costs*: mainly concerned with the trade-off between type of packaging and handling and transport costs. Unitisation may also be important.
3. *Information handling costs*: covering a wide area from order receipt to management information systems. The type of depot network will affect many of these costs.
4. *Lost sales costs*: which might occur due to inadequate customer service. Very relevant with respect to the proximity of the depot to the customer, together with the reliability and speed of service.
5. *Inventory costs*: including the cost of capital tied up in inventory as

well as the cost of obsolescence, etc. A fundamental relationship with the depot network in terms of the number of stockholding points and the hierarchy involved.

6. *Transport costs*: these costs are significantly affected by the number and location of depots within the distribution structure, and the associated throughputs. Both trunking and final delivery costs will be affected.

7. *Warehousing costs*: these costs vary according to the type of storage and handling systems used, together with the volume and throughput at the depot. The size of depot will thus be important, as will the location.

To plan an efficient distribution structure it is necessary to understand the interaction between these different costs – specifically as to how they vary with respect to the different depot alternatives (number, size, location), and what the overall distribution cost will be. This is best done by comparative analysis of the major alternative configurations.

For facilities location planning, the overall cost effect of a different number of depots can be explained by a graph representing the main storage and transport cost curves (shown in Figure 5.1). The top line on the graph shows the overall distribution cost in relation to the different number of depots in the network. It is obtained by adding together the storage cost and the transport cost that corresponds to each number of depots. For just a single depot, for example, there is a small storage cost to add to the large transport cost.

It can be seen from the graph that the least expensive overall distribution cost occurs at around the six to ten depot number (in this example). This lowest cost is shown by the lowest point on the overall distribution curve.

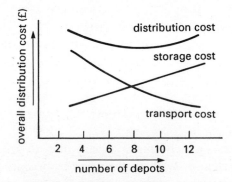

Figure 5.1 Overall distribution costs as a function of the number of depots, showing the constituent effects of storage and transport costs

The results, in practice, will depend on a number of factors – products, areas of demand, unit loads, etc.

A planned approach

It is no simple task to undertake a study or review of a company's distribution structure. The problem is a complex one. A number of important aspects need to be considered:

- current and likely future demands;
- customer service requirements;
- alternative networks to be considered;
- resources required for the different networks;
- cost of resources; and
- policy decisions (stock-holding, etc).

Thus, to determine the appropriate number, size and location of depots involves taking account of these factors and presents a monumental task with respect to the multitude of alternatives that need to be evaluated and especially to the extent of the data which has to be analysed. For this reason, the majority of studies are undertaken using some form of computer modelling techniques.

Whatever the computational means, it is important to take a structured approach to the depot location problem. One such approach is outlined in Figure 5.2. This is a generalised approach which indicates a number of steps which can be taken as a guideline to a strategic distribution study. A substantial part of such a study is the identification, collection and analysis of data.

It is also essential to ensure that the model or method of analysis is truly representative of the system that is being investigated. There is a consequent requirement during a number of these steps to check and test the appropriateness of the model and the results that are produced. This is known as model validation.

A few points with respect to the different steps are outlined below.

Define the problem and state the objectives

It is very important to take great care in defining exactly what the overall problem is. It is probably concerned with the use and location of depots within a distribution system, but it is often vital to know a number of additional factors. These might include for example.

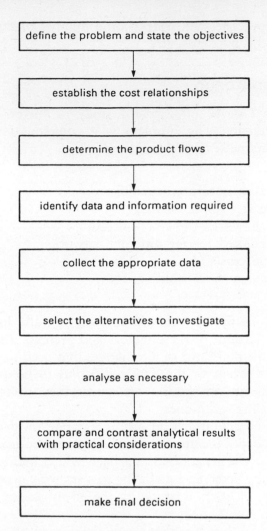

Figure 5.2 An approach for a strategic distribution study

- whether there are existing depots to be accounted for;
- whether there are any depots that must/must not be closed down; or
- whether we are concerned with the present or five, ten years into the future.

Establish the cost relationships
These will almost certainly be based around some type of cost model.

Determine the product flow
The product flow refers to the different patterns of demand and supply. Important aspects will include the type of products, the origin of these

products (factories, etc) the destination of products (shops, hospitals, factories, etc) and the amount and type of product going through the system (throughputs, etc).

Identify data and information required
There are always problems in finding and obtaining the data and information that is required. It may be necessary to make compromises over the data that is available.

Collect the appropriate data
This is often the largest part of the study. It is helpful to collect data in the way that you will finally want to use it.

Select the alternatives to investigate
It is never possible (or sensible) to investigate every alternative available. Many alternatives can be ignored (ie siting depots near to each other). It is very expensive and time-consuming to try and attempt too much analysis.

Analyse as necessary
It is important to be flexible. As analysis progresses, some of the chosen options will be seen to be irrelevant. Do not bother to analyse these, and be prepared to consider previously discarded options if they become attractive.

Compare and contrast
This final step involves the evaluation of the results of the study to select the 'best' options. It is essential at this stage to take account, once again, of all practical considerations regarding the individual depot sites.

Techniques for choosing depot location

A variety of techniques are available for determining appropriate depot location. These are categorised under the two headings of single and multi-depot location problems. Single depot location provides a more simplified case, as only the location question arises. Multi-depot location includes the problem of how many depots there should be, and how the boundaries should be drawn.

It is only possible to give a relatively simple indication of the alternative techniques and approaches that are available.

An indication of some of the general principles that apply can be described as follows.

The *Centre of Gravity method* (single depot location) or tonne-centre method was devised in the 1930s. Its basis is the analogy between the

Model of Devon, showing tonne-centre

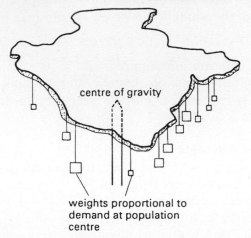

Figure 5.3   Centre of gravity single depot location method: a simple approach

centre of least cost for depot location and the centre of gravity as devised in physics.

A model of the county of Devon here is used to provide an example (see Figure 5.3). For many products, it can be assumed that customer demand is directly proportional to the size of the town or city. If the map is secured to a piece of plywood, the county boundary cut out, small holes drilled for each town, and appropriately sized weights suspended at each hole, it would be possible to balance the map at the central point. This will be the 'best' depot location, based on the tonnes of product demand at the different towns. Clearly this could only work if the plywood were of negligible weight, etc.

Although the method is crude, the principle is quite clear. It is particularly inadequate, however, because although it takes account of tonnage and distance, it does not minimise their product (ie tonnage multiplied by distance).

The *Tonne Mile Centre method* was derived to solve this problem. Using the Devon map again, if the same weights are used, but the strings are joined together by a single ring, then the ring will move to the central point which relates to the tonne-mile centre.

These are obviously very crude methods, but they do underline three of the major factors in depot location.

1. The importance of the demand for goods.
2. The importance of the distances involved.

3. The need to minimise the product of those two factors – weight (tonnes) times distance (miles).

Mathematical programming uses a number of well-known mathematical techniques (such as linear programming) that are particularly applicable to solving the depot location type of problem. Basically they use a logical step-by-step procedure to reach the optimal or 'best' solution. The main drawbacks with these techniques are:

- linear relationships are not always adequate (if linear programming is used); and
- some solutions can be 'local' optimums, that is, they are not the best from the overall point of view.

Heuristics is a Greek-based word, used to describe the method of solution which is derived on a 'rule of thumb' principle. Heuristic methods are determined by using experience and common sense to reject unlikely solutions from the outset. In this way, problems can be reduced to a more manageable size in terms of the number of alternatives that need to be tested. This type of approach is often very sensible for depot location problems, because there are always a number of locations which are totally inappropriate.

Simulation is a widely used Operational Research technique which is capable of representing complex problems and cost relationships. It is not an optimising technique, so does not produce the 'best' answers, but is used to evaluate any alternatives that are tested. The inability to produce optimal solutions has previously been seen as a drawback, but in fact a carefully derived simulation model, used with the practical expertise of a distribution specialist, is likely to result in realistic and acceptable solutions which can be readily implemented.

A number of computer programs have been written to help with the modelling of distribution systems. Initial programs concentrated on linear programming techniques to produce optimum (but sometimes impractical) solutions. In recent years, computer programs for depot location have been developed using simulation-based models. These allow for various 'what if' questions to be asked to test alternative strategies.

Site considerations

When a suitable depot location has been determined, there are various factors which should be taken into account when deciding on a particular site in a preferred general area, ie:

- size and configuration of site;
- site access;
- local authority plans;
- site details;
- financial considerations;
- legislation and local regulations; and
- building factors

These can have an influence on the overall effectiveness and operation of a depot, and on the scope of any projected future expansion.

Size and configuration of site

The proposed site clearly has to be of such a size that it can accommodate the proposed depot building, and any ancillary or other building facilities, eg:

- vehicle workshops and fuel pumps;
- vehicle wash;
- separate office, canteen or amenity blocks;
- waste disposal facilities;
- security office; and
- vehicle manoeuvre and parking.

The amount of space required for vehicle movement on site, for vehicle parking, manoeuvre and access to the depot building, is often under-estimated. This can lead to congestion and time being wasted on vehicle movement, as well as potential inconvenience to customers' and suppliers' vehicles. Estimates of space required, of course, necessitate a knowledge of the number and type of vehicles using the site. In this context, consideration has also to be given to parking for employees' private cars, and it is usual for local authorities, when giving planning permission, to insist on the provision of a minimum number of employee car parking spaces.

Note too that the local fire officer may require certain vehicular access to site buildings for fire-fighting vehicles.

Without initially having the benefit of detailed layout plans, some assessment should be made about the general shape and configuration of the site, and its consequent ability to enable a sensible layout of the depot building and other ancillary structures and site roads.

Finally, consideration should be given to the extent to which the site should also be able to accommodate future anticipated expansion.

Site access

An estimate will also be needed of the number, type and size of vehicles which will use the proposed site, including some measure of future expansion, in order to check that suitable access can be provided on to the site. This should clearly take account of the traffic characteristics for different operations, in terms of vehicle size and numbers coming on to the site, and also in terms of access for employees, whether on foot, by car, or by public transport. In this context, the external roadway system and access need to be considered as well as the likely internal site roadways. Any future plans for development of the road network in the vicinity of the site and which could possibly affect the ease of site access should be explored. Generally, goods will be arriving and leaving by road transport so that local links to the motorway network, or other major roads, are of significance.

Local authority plans

Any development of a depot will require planning permission, but checks should also be made about local development plans for the area, for adjacent land and the general environment, to ensure that there is nothing which would adversely affect depot operation in terms of such factors as:

- future plans for expansion, whether by physical growth or by extension of working times, shifts, etc;
- site access;
- availability of suitable labour; and
- overall operating environment, especially as it might affect potential customers.

Site details

A number of features relating to a potential site should be considered which can influence any proposed depot building, and also influence such aspects as construction costs, site security, and depot operation.

In general the site should be suitable in terms of soil conditions, (load bearing) slope and drainage. Such factors may exert a significant influence on construction costs in terms of piling, excavation, backfilling and similar civil engineering factors. The necessary services should be available, or planned, and accessible – power, water, sewage, telephone links.

The adjacent properties to the proposed site can also influence such considerations as site security (eg if open space adjacent) or the feasibility of working outside 'normal' day hours (eg if housing is adjacent).

Financial considerations

The cost of site acquisition, rental or other ownership costs should be established, and the probable levels of commitment for rates, insurance, or any other services or site related charges.

On the other side of the cost equation, there may be investment or other grants which apply, and which could influence the overall cost picture.

Legislation and local regulations

When occupying a site and either putting up new buildings or taking over existing buildings or facilities, there will be legislation and local regulations and planning requirements to be considered, and to be met.

When considering the site, some typical constraints are:

- a requirement for a minimum number of employee car parking spaces;
- a requirement for access for fire tenders;
- an upper limit on the height of any building to be put up on the site; and
- limits to the type of building to be constructed or to other factors which determine the external appearance.

Building factors

It is not infrequent for a warehouse or depot operation to be set up in an existing building not specifically designed for the operation it is to accommodate. This applies typically on industrial and trading estates where the buildings have been put up by a developer.

In this sort of situation a number of factors relating to the building, and which can influence depot operation, need to be considered.

1. Type and size of building:
   (a) clear space between stanchions or other obstructions;
   (b) clear working height;
   (c) total working area;
   (d) configurations of the working space – length: width.
2. Building access for incoming and outgoing goods including the number and size of access doors, raised or level vehicle loading docks.
3. Quality and strength of floor for fork lift truck operation.
4. Availability of required services.
5. Security factors:
   (a) car park outside the security fence;
   (b) facility to segregate drivers and warehouse operations.
6. Other available facilities:
   (a) offices;
   (b) cold/chill store;
   (c) fork truck maintenance bay;
   (d) fork truck battery charging area;
   (e) canteen and amenities.

Summary

In this chapter, the major discussion point has been the planning of depot and facilities location. A number of different aspects have been covered, and it has been emphasised that the problem is a complex one, involving a great deal of data manipulation and the need for quite sophisticated modelling techniques.

The various roles of depots and warehouses were discussed, and once again the influence of the different elements within the distribution system was noted. The major cost factors were outlined.

A formal, planned approach for any depot location study was recommended, and a straightforward example was discussed. In addition, the main techniques for depot location were described.

In the final section, a number of factors were put forward for consideration when a preferred general area of location had been identified. These factors are all influential in ensuring the effective operation of a depot or warehouse.

CHAPTER
6
Channels of Distribution

Introduction

Physical distribution channel is the term used to describe the method and means by which a product or a group of products are physically transferred, or distributed, from their point of production to the point at which they are made available to the final customer. In general, this end point is a retail outlet or shop or factory, but it may also be the customer's house, because some channels by-pass the shop and go direct to the consumer.

In addition to the physical distribution channel, another type of channel exists. This is known as the *trading or transaction channel*. The trading channel is also concerned with the product, and with the fact that it is being transferred from the point of production to the point of consumption. The trading channel, however, is the term that is used to describe the nonphysical aspects of this transfer. These aspects concern the sequence of negotiation, the buying and selling of the product, and the ownership of the goods as they are transferred through the various distribution systems.

One of the more fundamental issues of distribution planning is regarding the choice and selection of these channels. The question that arises, both on the physical and the trading side, concerns the decision of whether the producer should transfer the product directly to the consumer, or whether intermediaries should be used. These intermediaries are, at the final stage, very likely to be retailers, but other links in the supply chain are now often provided by some type of third party operation.

Channel types and structure

There are several alternative channels of distribution that can be used, and a combination of these may be incorporated within a channel structure.

The diagram in Figure 6.1 indicates the main alternative channels for a single product being transferred from a manufacturer's production point to a retail store.

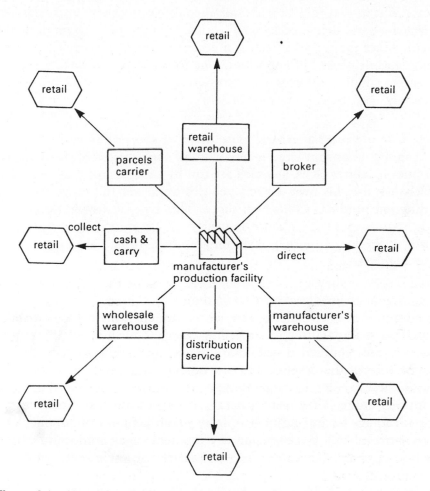

Figure 6.1 Alternative distribution channels from manufacturer's product through to retail distribution point

These channels are described below:

Manufacturer direct to retail shop
The manufacturer or supplier delivers direct from the production point to the retail shop. As a general rule, this channel is only used when full vehicle loads are being sent.

Manufacturer via manufacturer's warehouse to retail shop
This is the classic physical distribution channel, and the most common channel for many years. Here, the manufacturer or supplier holds his products either in a central warehouse/depot or in a series of regional warehouses/depots. The products are trunked in large vehicles to the depots, where they are stored and then broken down into individual orders which are delivered to retail shops on the supplier's retail delivery vehicles. Since the early 1970s, the use of this type of physical distribution channel has decreased in importance due to a number of developments in alternative channels of physical distribution. This type of channel is still commonly used by the brewery industry.

Manufacturer via retailer warehouse to retail shop or store
This channel consists of the manufacturers supplying central or regional distribution centres (RDCs) which are run by the retail organisations. The retailer then uses his own delivery vehicles to deliver full lorry loads of all the different products to his own shops. This type of distribution channel has grown in importance since the early 1970s as a direct result of the growth of the large multiple retail organisations which are now a feature of the high street.

Manufacturer to wholesaler to retail shop
The existence of wholesalers, who act as 'middlemen' in the distribution chain from manufacturer to shop, has been established for many years. However, this physical distribution channel has changed recently. This change concerns the development of wholesale organisations or voluntary chains. These wholesaler organisations are known as 'symbol' groups in the grocery trade. They were generally begun on the basis of securing a price advantage by buying in bulk from manufacturers or suppliers. One consequence of this has been the development of an important physical distribution channel because the wholesalers use their own warehouses and vehicle fleets.

Manufacturer to cash and carry wholesaler to retail shop
Another important development in wholesaling has been the introduction of cash and carry business. This is usually built around a wholesale organisation and it consists of small independent shops collecting their orders from regional wholesalers, rather than having them delivered. The increase in cash and carry facilities has arisen because many suppliers will not deliver direct to small shops because the order quantities are very small.

Manufacturer via distribution service to retail shop
Third party distribution or the distribution service industry has grown
very rapidly indeed in recent years. The industry has grown for a number
of reasons, the main ones being the extensive rise in distribution costs and
the constantly changing and more restrictive legislation that has occurred.
Thus, a number of companies have developed a particular expertise in
warehousing and distribution. These consist of general distribution services as well as companies that concentrate on providing a 'specialist'
service for one type of product (ie china and glass, hanging garments).
Typical examples include SPD, Lowfield Distribution, National Carriers, etc.

Manufacturer via small parcels carrier to retail shop
Very similar to the previous physical distribution channel, these companies provide a 'specialist' distribution service where the 'product' is any
small parcel. There has been an explosion in the 1980s of small parcels
companies, specialising particularly in 'next day' delivery. The competition generated by these companies has been quite fierce.

Manufacturer via broker to retail shop
This is a relatively rare type of channel, and may sometimes be a trading
channel and *not* a physical distribution channel. A broker is similar to a
wholesaler in that he acts as a 'middleman' between manufacturer and
retailer. His role is different, however, because he is often more concerned
with the marketing of a series of products, and not really with their
physical distribution. Thus a broker may use third party distributors, or
he may have his own warehouse and delivery system. The broker can
provide an alternative physical distribution channel.

The main alternative physical distribution channels described above
refer to movement from the manufacturer to the retail shop. There are
two additional channels which are concerned with recent developments in
selling which have necessitated new distribution channels. They are not
included in the diagram because they by-pass the retail shop.

Mail order
The use of mail order or catalogue shopping has become very popular.
Goods are ordered by catalogue, and are delivered to the home by post or
by parcels carrier. The physical distribution channel is thus from manufacturer to mail order house, and then to the consumer's home, by-passing
the retail store.

Factory direct to home
The direct factory to home channel is a relatively rare alternative. It can
occur by direct selling methods – often as a result of newspaper advertising.

It is also commonly used for 'one-off' special products that are specially made and do not need to be stocked in a warehouse to provide a particular level of service to the customer.

It can be seen from the list of alternative channels that the channel structures can differ very markedly from one firm to another. The main differences are:

- the types of intermediaries (as shown above);
- the number of levels of intermediaries (how many firms handle the product); and
- the intensity of distribution at each level (ie are all or just selective intermediaries or outlets used at the different levels?).

The large number of variable factors and elements that are possible within a channel structure make it difficult to summarise effectively. The diagram of Figure 6.2, however, gives a fair representation of a typical channel structure. Note the different physical and trading channels.

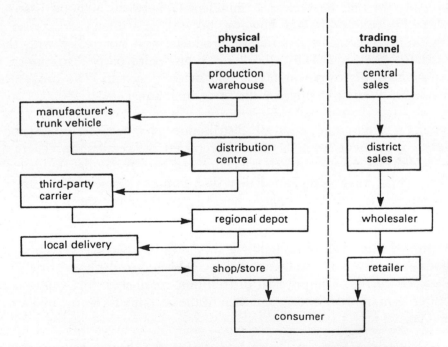

Figure 6.2 Typical channel of distribution, showing the different physical and trading routes to the consumer

Channel selection

Channel objectives will necessarily differ from one company to another, but it is possible to define a number of general points that are likely to be relevant. These should normally be considered by a company in the course of its distribution planning process to ensure that the most appropriate channel structure is developed. The main points are as follows:

To make the product readily available to the market consumers at which it is aimed
Perhaps the most important factor here is to ensure that the product is represented in the right type of retail store. Having identified the correct 'market place' for the goods, the company must make certain that the appropriate physical distribution channel is selected to achieve this objective.

To enhance the prospect of sales being made
This can be achieved in a number of ways. The most appropriate for each product or type of retail store will be reflected in the choice of channel. The general aims are to get good positions and displays in the store, and to gain the active support of the retail salesman, if necessary. The product should be 'visible, accessible and attractively displayed'. Channel choice is affected by this objective in a number of ways.

- Does the deliverer arrange the merchandise in the shop?
- Are special displays used?
- Does the product need to be demonstrated or explained?
- Is there a special promotion of the product?

To achieve co-operation with regard to any relevant distribution factors
These factors may be from the supplier's *or* the receiver's point of view, and include minimum order sizes, unit load types, product handling characteristics, materials handling aids, delivery access (ie vehicle size) and delivery time constraints, etc.

To achieve a given level of service
Once again, from both the supplier's and the retailer's viewpoints, a specified level of service should be estabished and maintained.

To minimise the costs of the system
Clearly, the cost aspects are very important, as they are reflected in the final price of the product. The system cost must be assessed in relation to the type of product and the level of service that is to be provided.

To receive fast and accurate feedback of information
This flow of information is essential for providing an efficient distribution service. It will include sales trends, inventory levels, damage reports, service levels, cost monitoring, etc.

The type of objectives which a company needs to clarify when determining the most appropriate physical distribution channels to use have been outlined above. A number of important factors become apparent from these objectives. These factors clearly affect the decisions which need to be made when designing a channel or channels that are used in a distribution system. They can be summarised with respect to the following general characteristics.

Market characteristics
The important consideration here is to use the channels and types of outlet which customers and potential customers will use. The size and spread of the market is also important. If a market is a very large one which is widely spread from a geographic point of view, then it is usual to use 'long' channels. A long channel is one where there are several different movement and storage points for the product as it goes from its production point to the final customer.

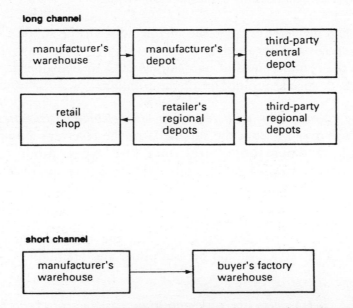

Figure 6.3 'Long' and 'short' distribution channels. Long channels are best employed for demand over large geographical areas; short channels are best used for few buyers in limited areas

Where a market has only a very few buyers in a limited geographical area, then short channels are used. Examples of these channels are illustrated in Figure 6.3.

Product characteristics

The importance of the product itself when determining channel choice should not be underestimated. This is because the product may well impose constraints on the number of channels which can be considered. For example:

- high priced items are easier to sell direct (short channel) because the high gross profit margins can more easily cover sales and distribution costs (also, the security aspects of highly priced items makes a short channel much more attractive – eg jewellery, watches, records, etc);
- complex products often require direct selling because any middleman may not be able to explain the product (ie how it works) to the potential customers – eg micro- and mini-computers;
- new products may have to be marketed directly or by mail order because traditional outlets may be reluctant to stock the product;
- products with a time constraint need a 'fast' channel, for obvious reasons – eg bread, cakes, newspapers, etc; and
- products with a handling constraint may require a specialist physical distribution channel – eg frozen food, china and glass, hanging garments.

Channel characteristics

As well as taking account of market and product characteristics, another important aspect concerns the characteristics of the channel itself. There are two different factors which need to be considered.

1. Does the channel which is chosen serve or supply the customer in the way that is required? A simple example might be a new grocery product which needs to be demonstrated or tested in the shop. There would be no point in distributing this product through a small self-service store where no facilities can be provided for a demonstration.
2. This factor follows once the type of channel has been chosen. At this stage the final decision on the detailed choice should depend on the efficiency of each alternative compared with the others. Efficiency may include a number of different features such as the size of orders that are placed, the sales potential in the outlets that are served, etc.

Competitive characteristics

These concern the activities of any competitors who are selling a similar product. Typical decisions are whether to sell the product alongside these

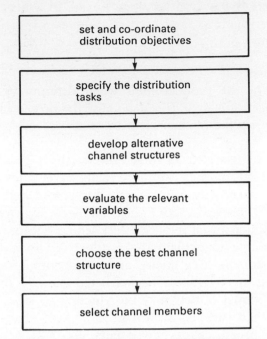

Figure 6.4 Designing a channel structure; a formalised approach

similar products, or whether to try for different, exclusive outlets for the product to avoid the competition. It may well be that the consumer preference for a wide choice necessitates the same outlets being supplied. Good examples include confectionery and most grocery items.

Company resources
In the final analysis, it is often the size and the financial strength of the company which is most important in determining channel strategy. Only a fairly large company can afford to set up a distribution structure which includes its own warehousing and transport facilities. With these, the company can provide the service which it thinks its customers require. Smaller and less financially secure companies may have to use inter-mediaries or third party organisations to perform their distribution function. In these instances, it may be less easy to ensure the provision of the service which they feel their customers would like.

These factors will all need to be taken into account when designing a channel structure and selecting the appropriate channel members.

A *formalised approach* which might be adopted when undertaking the design of a channel structure is set out in Figure 6.4.

Third-party versus own-account distribution

The most common channel decision for those operating in physical distribution is whether to use a third-party distribution service, or whether to run an own-account distribution system. The increase in the importance of third-party distribution is such that it is estimated that in 1988 probably 27 per cent of the UK road freight distribution market was moved by third-party operators.

The own-account/third-party decision is rarely a straightforward one, especially as there are a number of different types of distribution services that are available. The main ones include the following:

Exclusive distribution service
This is a distribution service provided by a third-party company which devotes all of its resources exclusively to a single client, on a national or regional basis. These resources include warehouses, depots, transport fleets, managers, etc. These are obviously confined to very large companies. Typical examples are BOC Transhield, Transcare, Salserve and Fashionflow, which provide exclusive services for the Marks and Spencer range of products. This type of service is becoming very common in the UK.

Consortium distribution service
The consortium distribution service is similar to the exclusive service, the principal difference being that a small group of client companies are catered for, rather than just a single client. One of the characteristics of this type of service is that the clients are all manufacturers or suppliers of goods and that their products are all delivered to the same retail outlets — for example, grocery products to grocery stores, supermarkets, catering establishments, etc.

Special product/specialist distribution services
These distribution services have become quite common in the past few years. They are used for the storage and movement of products which require special facilities or services, and the distribution operation run by the third-party company is especially tailored to suit these needs. There are several examples. One is the frozen food distribution service run by companies such as Christian Salvesen. Other examples are Tibbet and Britten (hanging garments) and Chinaflow (china and glass).

Regional multi-client distribution services
These services are provided for any number of clients, and for most product types. They are the 'general' third-party distributors who have

probably started as very small operations and have grown into a regional service (ie East Anglia, North-West, etc).

National multi-client distribution services

This category is very similar to the previous one, a service being provided for any number of clients and product types. The main difference relates to the size of the operation. This is nationwide, and would include a trunking operation between the companies' depots, so that if necessary, a client company can have a retail delivery service to anywhere in the country (for example BRS).

Own-account plus third-party

Some companies with their own distribution system also offer a service to certain other companies. This is quite rare, and generally occurs when a company has unnecessary slack in its distribution system. High Street Transport developed in this way from its origins with the Burton Group.

Transit services

These are systems where the operator is not storing any products for the manufacturer, but is only providing a collect, break bulk and delivery service. Thus, no unordered stocks are held, although some minor stock-holding may occur for a limited number of product lines.

The choice between own-account and third-party distribution needs to be carefully quantified and analysed. This should be undertaken with a structured approach similar to that outlined previously in Figure 6.4.

Third-party distribution has developed rapidly over the past decade and has become a very competitive and dynamic industry. There has been a significant growth in both the number and size of companies. The result of this fast growth and robust competition has been that many distribution and distribution-related services are now offered by third-party companies.

The basic service can vary from contract hire — the provision of single vehicles or a fleet of vehicles — to fully dedicated operations, including storage, primary and secondary transport, management services, order processing and stock control. The results of a survey of 47 of the major UK third-party distribution companies recently undertaken by the Distribution Studies Unit at Cranfield, showed that the following services were offered:

- trunking;
- collection;
- break-bulk;

- fleet management;
- tele-sales;
- management information;
- local delivery;
- stock-holding warehouse;
- transhipment;
- order picking;
- inventory management;
- general management;
- contract hire;
- home delivery;
- production inspection;
- training;
- packing; and
- merchandising.

The histogram of Figure 6.5 illustrates the popularity of these different services with local delivery, break-bulk, collection, trunking, transhipment and inventory management all being offered by over two-thirds of the companies in the survey.

There are a number of different types of contract agreement made between distribution companies and their clients. These can be broadly categorised as follows.

Unit price or fixed price agreements
An agreed unit price is paid for the services provided. This might be cost per case, cost per mile, cost per drop, etc or a combination of these costs, dependent on the services being offered. This is the more traditional method of third-party payment.

Hybrid unit price agreements
These are based on a unit price but also include guarantees on such matters as volume throughput, resource usage, etc. This ensures that the contractor is not penalised by seasonal effects or unexpected demand fluctuations.

Cost-plus arrangements
These provide for the payment of an agreed fee for the facilities to be used and services to be provided. A pre-set profit margin for the contractor is added to this.

Open-book contracts
As it suggests, an open-book contract is where the client company pays for the entire operation plus a management fee to the contractor. This

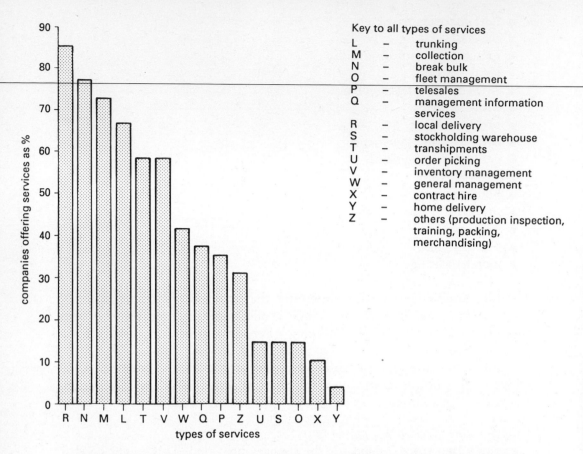

Figure 6.5 Third-party services; percentage of different specific services offered to clients

type of arrangement can only be used for completely dedicated operations. Performance is monitored against a budget which is agreed between the contractor and the client.

The length of contracts can vary from six months to six years. Longer contracts have become the norm for dedicated operations because of the amount of capital required for set-up purposes.

The recent Distribution Studies Unit survey asked third-party companies what they thought were the major benefits that their client companies gained from using their services. The results were weighted according to popularity, and they showed quite categorically that the third-party companies saw financial and service considerations as being overwhelmingly important. Figure 6.6 illustrates this, and shows that control, management and flexibility were also seen as being beneficial. A small

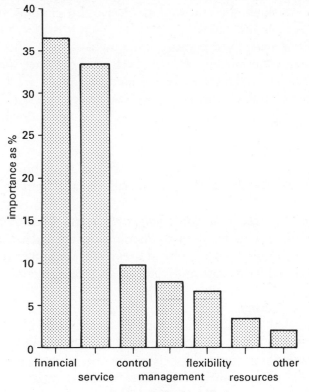

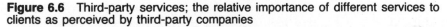

Figure 6.6 Third-party services; the relative importance of different services to clients as perceived by third-party companies

survey of user companies emphasised the importance of financial and service benefits but also highlighted factors such as the flattening of peaks for seasonally affected products, relief from industrial relation problems and as a benchmark for in-house distribution services.

In summary, there are a large number of advantages and disadvantages claimed for and against both third-party and own-account distribution. Some of these can be objectively assessed. Others are subjective, relating more to historical convention and personal preference than to anything else. The major points of discussion can be split into three broad categories covering cost, organisational and physical factors.

Cost factors

There are *capital cost* advantages claimed for third-party distribution because the client does not have to buy vehicles as he might for his own fleet. Thus, the capital can be invested in other areas of the business, such as new production machinery, retail stores, etc.

There are day-to-day or *operating cost* savings – ie more efficient operation – although these advantages are often claimed by both third-party and own-account users.

Economies of scale exist because some own-account operations are too small to be run economically. If they are linked together with other small operations, then the larger system which results is likely to be more economic. For example, only one warehouse may be necessary instead of three or four. This is, in effect, what happens when third-party systems are used.

For individual client companies, there is a likely *cost lag* or *cushion effect* as increased costs are delayed before the third-party company can pass them on to the client. This is particularly apparent in times of high inflation.

It may be the case that the *changeover costs* of moving from own account distribution to third-party distribution are such that it does not make good economic sense. Problem areas are the sunk costs of existing own depots, fixed low rents and vehicles and equipment.

Organisational factors

It is claimed that the use of third-party distribution leads to a loss of control over the delivery operation. Any lack of control can be minimised, however, by buying the right service at the outset, and by carefully monitoring the performance of the distribution company in terms of the service that they are actually providing.

There may also be a loss of control over the company's logistical variables if a third party is used. This means that the company is no longer in a position to define the number, type or size of warehouses, or vehicle types and sizes etc. Once again, if this is important, the company must choose the third-party system which suits it the best.

Third-party distribution companies are said to be less sophisticated than own-account operators in terms of their management ability, vehicle and warehouse utilisation, service levels, etc. With the advent of much greater professionalism in distribution management within third-party companies this is not now the case.

Third-party distribution companies are said to lack the experience of client companies' products and markets. The growth in specialist distribution companies has helped to change this point of view.

It is thought that service levels are poorer among third-party distributors than own-account operators. This is not necessarily true because many third-party distributors make frequent and regular deliveries to high street outlets. In addition, in remote rural areas, the use of a third party can greatly improve service levels.

There can be a problem trying to co-ordinate third-party delivery service with a client company's sales service. For example, the salesman may make his call and an order may be placed, but the delivery of that order may not be completed for some time afterwards. This potential problem can often be overcome by a system of fixed day delivery.

The use of a third party can often mean the loss of direct influence within shops because the driver is delivering a number of different companies' products. This can be avoided if a salesman is used as a contact point.

The value of advertising on a vehicle may be thought to be important. Using a third party means that the company does not have its own livery and name on a vehicle. For vehicle contract distribution the livery can be and is used.

There may be a problem of confidentiality when using a third-party distribution service. This may arise because products can be mixed with those of competitors.

Physical factors

Most obviously, there may be channel differences in the way that the product is distributed, in particular, at the point of delivery. If this is important then a more suitable distribution service may be necessary.

The *drop characteristics* of some products may be incompatible for some third-party systems. This may relate to the frequency of deliveries that are required (ie a large number of small drops for high value items) or the nature of the product itself. It is likely that some form of specialist distribution system can provide an appropriate alternative.

Vehicle characteristics and requirements can differ between products and product ranges. Vehicle size, body quality, equipment and unit load specifications may all be relevant dependent on weight/volume ratios and any 'special' product features. Once again, the use of a specialist third-party company could be appropriate.

Basic delivery systems may be incompatible. This particularly applies to the options of pre-selected orders against van sales, and also the need for a 'mate' to help unloading.

Some products may be incompatible – the particular problem being the danger of contamination. Many third-party companies get around the problem by the use of special sections in vehicles, and contamination is rare.

Summary

This chapter has been concerned with channel choice and selection, the main aspects covering:

- the physical and the trading channel;
- alternative channels of physical distribution;
- channel objectives;
- factors affecting channel selection;
- designing a channel structure;
- different types of distribution service;
- services offered by third party companies;
- third party contract arrangements; and
- advantages and disadvantages of third party versus own-account distribution.

Channel choice and selection, and particularly the increased use and sophistication of third-party distribution services are all very important aspects of modern day logistics. This is an exciting area of change within the industry and there is ample scope and opportunity for growth and development in the future.

PART 2

Warehousing and Storage

Warehousing Principles and Planning

Introduction

Warehouses are set up for various industrial and commercial operations: component stores, commodity warehouses, shipping warehouses, finished goods warehouses, bonded stores, wholesale warehouses, and cash and carry warehouses.

Sizes vary from small stores of a few hundred square metres with modest stock and throughput levels, to units covering more than 100,000 square metres handling thousands of pallets per day.

Warehouse and storage systems should provide facilities for holding specified materials in the appropriate quantities, in a suitable environment, at minimum overall system cost.

The reasons for holding stock include the following:

- as a buffer stock between supply and demand;
- to hold stock from long production runs;
- to hold stock between production operations (work in progress);
- safety stock to cover unplanned interruptions in supply;
- as a cover for seasonal fluctuations; and
- as strategic reserve, eg against a planned shutdown.

Warehouses should be operated to meet defined objectives, which may be to achieve any or a combination of such things as:

- a defined level of customer service;
- a given throughput level;
- a given stock level; or
- a minimum cost of operation.

Meeting such objectives requires the appropriate storage and handling methods and equipment in a properly planned and controlled system of operation, and an appropriate and secure environment.

Outline of warehouse operations

Warehousing is not just a matter of putting goods into store and then retrieving them – it encompasses a range of activities, all monitored and controlled, including some or all of the following.

Goods in
- Receipt – unload, temporary hold.
- Check – correct goods received, grade, package;
      – quantity, quality, damage or shortages.
- Record receipts and discrepancies.
- Unpack, repack if necessary.
- Decide where goods are to be located.

Main store – reserve stock
- Locate goods in reserve storage area.
- Confirm goods location to control function.
- Issue goods to replenish order picking stock.

Order picking – forward stock
- Select goods from order picking stock to meet customer orders.
- Pack and check.
- Packaging material store.

Marshalling
- Assemble goods by customer, or by vehicle load.

Goods out
- Load – loading facilities for vehicles
- Despatch – vehicle schedules.

Separating reserve stocks from order picking is basic to the design and operation of some warehouses. For warehouses with high stock volumes and throughputs, the separation of picking stock, in sufficient quantities for immediate needs – say one or two days' worth of stock for all items – reduces the area in which the order picking staff work and, hence, the total travel distance to access the stock.

Picking stock is replenished, often as whole pallet-loads, as required. Without this separation, the order pickers would have to traverse the whole warehouse area to access the product lines required. The ratio of reserve to picking stock locations varies in different applications, from about 2:1 up to 6:1 or more, so the reserve storage area is normally much larger than the order picking area.

Note that one pallet replenishment from reserve stock to order picking may be equivalent to 20 or more separate order picking accessions, so it pays to keep the picking area small – consistent with minimum congestion.

Principles of warehouse layout and operation

When considering the planning, layout, and operation of any warehouse system, there are fundamental principles which embody a general philosophy of good practice. These can be summarised under six headings.

- using the most suitable unit load(s);
- making the best use of space;
- minimising movement;
- controlling movement and location;
- providing safe, secure and environmentally sound conditions; and
- all at minimum overall system cost.

Load unitisation
A unit load is defined as: 'An assembly of individual items or packages, usually of a like kind, to enable convenient composite movement', whether mechanical or manual movement.

Typical unit loads are various sizes of wooden pallets, roll cage pallets, tote bins, post and cage pallets, and ISO containers.

The advantages of using the most appropriate unit load for a given handling and storage application include:

- moving a greater quantity of goods per journey and so reducing the number of journeys required, and hence the handling time and cost;
- enabling better use to be made of warehouse space;
- enabling the use of standard handling and storage equipment;
- speeding the loading and unloading of transport; and
- minimising the risk of damage and pilferage.

The choice of unit load – type and size – is fundamental when setting up a handling and storage system. It influences the type and amount of handling and storage equipment required, the manning, and the overall system cost.

Different types of unitisation can be illustrated by considering tinned food. The consumer buys the food in tins. The retailer buys and handles in shrink-wrapped cardboard trays containing a number of tins. The wholesaler, and the producer, probably handle and store as full pallets, each pallet stacked with trays.

Load unitisation is dealt with in more detail in Chapter 22.

Use of space

The cost of a warehouse building, calculated on an annual basis, can be up to 25 per cent of the total operating cost of the warehouse. Maintenance and service costs can add a further 15 per cent so up to 40 per cent of warehousing cost can be for having and using the building. This is why storage and handling equipment is designed to improve the utilisation of cubic capacity, and why it is important to make the best use of space when planning and operating a warehouse. Effective space utilisation makes good use of total building volume, and not merely the floor area.

Considerations for good space utilisation include:

- not holding obsolete stock;
- minimising total stock, compatible with customer service;
- fully utilising head room;
- using mezzanine floors;
- minimising gangways – number and width – compatible with safe movement and access to stock;
- careful positioning of services, pipes etc; and
- using, where possible, random stock location systems rather than fixed (see later).

The history of fork lift truck development, from the counterbalance truck, through reach trucks and very narrow aisle stackers, has enabled height to be used, at the same time as reducing the aisle widths required for truck operation. Both factors improve the utilisation of space.

Minimise movement

System planning and operation should aim to minimise movement and movement costs. Ways of achieving this, include:

- locating close together those parts of a system between which there is a lot of movement;
- locating the most popular stock lines (the fastest moving ones) to minimise travel distance, eg popularity storage;
- separating order picking stock from reserve stock;

- using appropriate unit loads;
- using equipment designed to eliminate personnel movement, eg carousel storage, etc; and
- using computerised techniques for determining goods and people movements.

When deciding on a layout, there may have to be a compromise between minimising movement and minimising congestion, with its consequent risk of accident or of slowing down the operation.

Control

Control is very important in warehousing. It is concerned with movement, and with awareness of where material is located within a system, and the status (eg in use/empty etc) and location of handling and storage equipment. The ability to control a system, and to have rapid and accurate data on locations and system status enable management to run a warehouse effectively, and to respond quickly to changing situations and customer requests. Accurate and fast information processing and transmission systems are becoming more and more available on mini- and microcomputers and PCs, which is enabling significant improvements in control.

The flow of material in warehousing and storage can be planned and laid out in different ways, and it is worth mentioning the two broad approaches.

'U' flow for internal movement

'U' flow occurs when the goods receipt and despatch functions are located at the same end of a warehouse building (see Figure 7.1).

It enables popularity storage systems to be used to minimise movement by locating fast-moving product lines close to the loading bays.

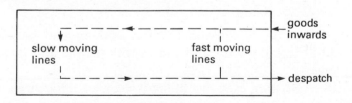

Figure 7.1   'U' flow in a warehouse

Positioning the goods-inwards and the despatch functions adjacent to each other gives further benefits such as better utilisation of dock space and associated handling equipment, possibly less total area required than with separate load/unloading areas, more flexibility, and better control of security and of environment.

Through flow for internal movement

Through flow happens when separate loading bay facilities for goods inwards and despatch are provided, often at opposite ends of a warehouse (see Figure 7.2). It necessitates all goods travelling the full length of the building, can be environmentally less easy to control, and be less flexible both operationally and in the event of the need for future building expansion.

However, for some operations, eg where there is risk of interference/confusion between goods in and goods out, or where the goods inward vehicles and despatch vehicles are very different (eg platform height, nature of unit load), or where a warehouse is connected to a production plant it may be better to adopt through flow.

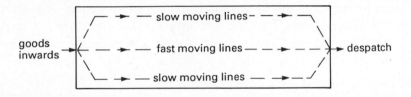

Figure 7.2   Through flow in a warehouse

External flows

In warehouse layout and operation it is important to plan and control material, vehicle, and personnel movements external to a building, as well as the internal flows.

Safety, security and environment

Safety

Warehousing operations involve mechanical and manual handling, and movement and lifting of goods, and can expose people and goods to the risk of accidents.

Hazards can result from excessive lifting (weight or frequency), awkward lifting and handling, and from maloperation or malfunction of equipment. Fork lift trucks can be driven too fast, be overloaded, can overturn — goods can fall, or be knocked over, people and trucks can collide, and so on.

Safe operation requires careful planning and layout of warehouse operations, effective management of those operations, and good supervision and training of operators.

Fire, too, is an all too present hazard in warehouses. Recently there have been a number of multi-million pound losses from warehouse fires. Warehouse planning, location, and operation should all take account of fire risk, and wherever warehouse design, relocation or building change of use are being considered, the insurers and the local area fire officer should be consulted.

Product security

In warehousing, goods are at risk — in transit, on loading docks, collated in large quantities, and they are often readily accessible. Where high value goods are involved, security should be given particular attention. The objective must be to minimise damage, loss within the system or theft.

Environment

Working environment is important for operator comfort, for product preservation and for equipment operation.

Relevant factors include:

- working temperature, and humidity;
- ventilation, if required, for engine fumes (gas or diesel fork lift trucks), fumes from shrink wrapping, or to remove hydrogen gas released during truck battery charging;
- lighting levels for operators to make out colour codes, product and location identification letters and numbers — often high up in storage racking, and for safe truck driving and general movement.

Minimum total cost

Annual surveys by the Institute of Logistics and Distribution Management (1982 to 1990) indicated the cost of storage as a percentage of total distribution cost (storage + inventory + transport + administration etc) varying in the range 22 to 32 per cent.

Analysis of the costs of grocery warehousing by the National Materials Handling Centre at Cranfield suggest that the two highest cost elements are the cost of having and operating the building (building + services) which can be up to 40 per cent of the total warehouse cost, and direct labour, which can be up to 45 per cent of the total cost. Although these figures relate to one industry, and a limited number of warehouses, they do indicate where the major costs occur.

Analysis by warehouse function instead of by cost element, shows order picking as over 40 per cent of the total cost, reserve storage just under 30 per cent, and the remaining costs evenly divided between goods inwards and despatch.

The figures quoted do not constitute a norm against which to measure performance, but they do stress the significance of building and labour costs, and the proportion of total costs taken up by the order picking function.

Warehouse planning and layout – outside factors

There are various external factors that will influence the design and layout of a proposed warehouse operation and that must be taken into account to achieve an optimum overall system. For example, the concentration of customers and/or the location of suppliers may have implications for setting up a warehouse in a particular area. These factors are discussed in detail in Chapter 5 (see pages 47–50) but it is appropriate to mention them here:

- size and configuration of the site – must be adequate to accommodate the required facilities and vehicle movements.
- site access – must be adequate for the types of vehicle and volume of traffic using the site.
- local authority plans – are there local development plans which could affect the proposed warehouse?
- site details – what are the ground and drainage characteristics?
- financial considerations – what are the rates and rent? Are there any other costs of ownership? Are investment grants available?
- legislation and local regulations.
- building factors – if there is already a building on site, can this be used as a warehouse?

Warehouse planning and layout – inside factors

The internal layout has a dominant influence on how effectively a warehouse can be operated.

The factors which may be relevant include:

- the flow of goods through the system, eg 'U' flow or through flow;
- the movement of people and equipment/trucks;
- access to stock and the need to minimise congestion;
- identification of stock;
- stock location, location and identification codes;
- stock rotation – first in first out (FIFO);
- stock checking requirements;
- stock replenishment;

- the handling of goods into and out of the warehouse;
- supervision;
- safety; and
- stock security.

Warehouse aisles and gangways should be laid out in rectilinear plan, of adequate width for the movements occurring there. Aisle widths are always a compromise between allowing enough space for movement of people and equipment, while at the same time making best use of available space. Aisle widths are often determined by the physical characteristics — turning circles etc — of the handling equipment. Ideally there should be separate doors for people on foot and for fork lift trucks.

When planning a warehouse it is easy to concentrate on the important and major aspects and then have to fit in some of the less prominent ones as after-thoughts — and it is this which often results in congestion and poor control. The features and areas which may have to be incorporated include some or all of those described at the beginning of this chapter and in addition where appropriate, the following items:

- quality control;
- 'quarantine' area;
- chill/cold store;
- pallet and/or trolley store and repair area;
- returned goods area;
- waste disposal;
- battery charging area;
- maintenance shop;
- fuel supply;
- services area — heating, lighting, ventilation;
- offices — administration, management, etc;
- amenities
  - rest room
  - cloak rooms
  - toilet and wash
  - canteen
  - first aid;
- security; and
- special data link/communication lines.

Analysis of handling and storage systems

When a warehouse is being set up or indeed if a warehouse system is being analysed to establish whether improvements can be made, it is necessary to obtain certain basic data about the goods being warehoused and the nature of the warehousing operation.

Typically the sort of data relevant to such analysis includes the following factors.

Material handled
- Number of product lines.
- Handling and storage characteristics and constraints (eg shelf life, weight, size, hazards, unit load types).
- Throughput levels
  - maximum, minimum, average
  - seasonal variations
  - growth trends
  - order characteristics
  - receipt and despatch patterns of movement.
- Stock levels
  - maximum, minimum, average,

Facilities
- Options for different storage and handling equipment and their characteristics.
- Services
  - heating, lighting, ventilation
  - temperature control – chill stores.
- Site and building factors.
- Maintenance.

Staffing
- Skills required and availability.
- Shift patterns.
- Operating (time) data.

Management and control
- Information systems.
- Costing methods and constraints.
- Safety and fire considerations.
- Security.
- Insurance.
- Legal and planning requirements or constraints.

A useful analytical tool in materials handling and warehouse/storage systems analysis is the Pareto Analysis, (see Figure 7.3) also known as the 80:20 rule or the P/Q curve (Product/Quantity).

In any series of elements to be controlled, a selected small fraction in terms of the number of elements always accounts for a large fraction in terms of effect.

In nearly every case 20 per cent of the 'elements' account for about 80 per cent of the effect – eg analysing warehouse stocks, line by line, in descending order of stock quantity, usually shows a relationship as shown in Figure 7.3.

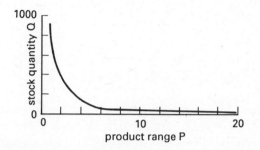

Figure 7.3 Example of the Pareto (80/20) effect. In a product range of 20 items with 2,000 units of stock, the 'top' 20 per cent of the product range (ie 4 types of items) account for 80 per cent (1,600 units) of stock

In this simple example of 20 product lines, the total stock is about 2,000 units and the top 20 per cent of the products have stock:

Product	Stock
1	910
2	350
3	200
4	140
	1,600 = 80 per cent of total stock

The general statement is:

- The top 20 per cent of products account for about 80 per cent of total stock.
- The next 30 per cent of products account for another 15 per cent of total stock.
- The final 50 per cent of products account for the remaining 5 per cent of total stock.

This relationship can be shown graphically, but for large product ranges, it is usually produced as a computer print-out, the products ranked in descending order of stock quantity.

Note that the example was based on stock levels. In practice, similar types of analysis for throughput quantities, picking accessions, occupied volume, product sales value, order sizes, etc, are of great help in analysing handling and storage situations.

Data analysed in this way, can be used to help decisions on, eg:

- warehouse layouts to minimise movement;
- location of stock in a warehouse; and
- the most appropriate type of storage/handling equipment for different parts of the product range and the most appropriate break points. (Fast moving lines may be handled and stored using different methods and equipment from those appropriate to the slower lines.)

In such an analysis, however, any unusual or special items (eg very large or small, difficult to handle, etc) which do not conform to the general pattern, should not be allowed to determine the operating methods or equipment, but should be treated separately, ie do not let the tail wag the dog.

CHAPTER
8
Storage Systems

Storage principles

Choice of storage equipment

Selecting the appropriate storage system for an application involves matching storage and throughput requirements to the equipment characteristics, and there may have to be a compromise between maximising the use of space and the need for easy and quick access to the stored goods.

In general, a well designed storage system should:

- make good use of building volume, by choice of appropriate storage system, by careful layout, by minimising aisle widths and by using headroom;
- provide good access to stored goods, minimise travel distance, and facilitate throughput of goods;
- incorporate systems such as stock records and location, and stock movement control and replenishment;
- provide security against fire, damage and theft; and
- provide an environment to prevent deterioration or contamination of stock.

The choice of storage medium for a particular application will depend on at least, the following:

- physical characteristics of goods stocked, ie weight, shape, size, strength, (can it stack?), package and unit load weight, shape and size;
- contamination risks – odours;

- hazard factors – fire, noxious gases;
- deterioration factors – product life, is First-in-First-out (FIFO) necessary?;
- value of the goods;
- number of line items;
- stocks and throughput levels – max, min, average and seasonal fluctuations;
- capital availability; and
- characteristics of the available storage methods and equipments.

Access to stock

Storage methods which give random access to every item stocked, eg shelving, drawer units, adjustable pallet racking, narrow aisle racking and high bay, should be distinguished from those which do not, eg block storage, drive-in racking, live storage, double deep racking. In the latter category, only the stock at the front of the storage medium is readily accessible, ie, would not require double handling to reach it.

Fixed and random location

The holding capacity of a given storage installation is influenced by whether each stock line is held in a fixed location, or is randomly located. In fixed location, any given location within the store is only used to hold a specified product line, and never for any other item. Consequently, the store/warehouse has to be designed so that there is enough capacity to accommodate the maximum stock of every product line.

In random location, when a given location becomes empty, it can then be used to hold any other product line, ie when the next receipts arrive they can be put into whatever locations are empty at that time. With this method, total average stocks plus an allowance (say 10 per cent) can be used for calculating how much storage capacity is required.

Random location is frequently used for reserve storage – the largest area of a warehouse, and fixed location for order picking. This enables order pickers to become familiar with product locations.

Whatever location system is used, the utilisation of space in storage will always be less than 100 per cent. Because of the movement of material in and out there will always be some empty locations.

Storage systems and equipment – palletised storage

Block stacking

In block stacking, loaded pallets are placed directly on to the floor and built up in stacks, in rows (see Figure 8.1). Ideally, any one row of pallets

the part empty rows
in block stacking
are referred to as
'honeycombing'

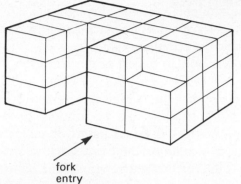

fork
entry

Figure 8.1 Block stacking of pallets. Loaded pallets are placed directly on the floor and built up in stacks, by row

should only contain pallets of the same product to avoid double handling and to simplify stock location records.

The block stacking technique is used with plain palletised loads, and also with post pallets, pallet converters and similar load protection devices which are used if the load itself is not strong enough or flat enough to permit safe stacking.

When setting out simple block stacking, clearances should be incorporated to facilitate fork truck movement (see Figure 8.2).

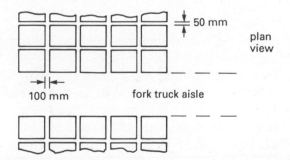

50 mm

plan
view

100 mm   fork truck aisle

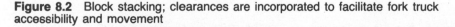

Figure 8.2 Block stacking; clearances are incorporated to facilitate fork truck accessibility and movement

It is good practice to empty a row completely before putting any more stock into that row, and it is important to maintain stock location records to ensure stock discipline.

The technique is suitable where there is a limited number of product lines, each of which has a comparatively high stock level.

The advantages of block stacking are: lower capital costs; no storage equipment needed; good use of area though not necessarily of height; simple to control; and suitable for high throughputs.

Potential disadvantages are: limits on stack height which can restrict the use of building height; honeycombing which reduces storage capacity; no strict FIFO; free access is only to pallets at the front/top of each row; and fire risk.

Lines painted on the floor help to maintain layout discipline.

Stock location in block stacking can be random by row, or fixed by row, but cannot go down to individual pallet or pallet stack, since free access is limited to the top pallet on the front stack in any individual row.

Pallet stack height is limited by the strength of the pallet load to support the imposed weights, by stack stability, and by the strength and condition of the floor.

Block stacking layout will be determined by the number of pallets to be held, the allowable height of stack, and the depth of rows. The depth of row for safe fork truck driving into the stack is generally not more than six pallets (ie a block of 12 deep, back to back), the actual depth being dictated by typical stock levels. Most layouts are likely to incorporate different lengths of row for different product stock levels, but it is good practice to have straight access aisles and to use both sides of every aisle. If four-way entry pallets are used, it is worth trying layouts at both pallet orientations to determine which gives the best layout and space utilisation.

Adjustable pallet racking (APR)
Adjustable pallet racking is probably the most commonly used palletised storage equipment (see Figure 8.3).

Racking construction consists of end frames and horizontal beams, and the height of the beams can be adjusted to suit the height of the pallet loads to be stored.

The basic design of APR is for flat pallets, but accessories are available for storing particular types of unit load, such as drum supports – to prevent rolling, decking – converts APR to shelving, and channel supports for post pallets, etc.

APR can be set out in single or in back-to-back rows. The horizontal spacing of uprights and the vertical spacing of beams should allow adequate clearances for safe movement of pallets in and out of the racking. Guidelines are given in the Storage Equipment Manufacturers Association (SEMA) codes of practice.

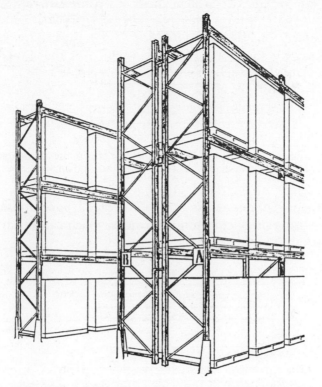

Figure 8.3 Adjustable pallet racking; the most commonly used form of racking

Typically, when accessed by fork reach trucks, APR can go up to heights of about 8 metres.

The advantages of APR are that it is fairly inexpensive, beam height is adjustable for different pallet load heights, it can be dismantled and moved, there is random access to every pallet location, damaged parts are easily replaced, and simple positive location recording systems can be used.

The disadvantages of APR are that one fork truck aisle gives access to only two rows of racking, so the building space utilisation is low, and at racking heights above 8 m a specially flat floor is needed, to reduce risks of hitting the racking with the load when the mast is raised.

Double deep pallet racking
Conventional APR provides poor utilisation of space because an aisle is needed between every second row of racking (see Figure 8.4).

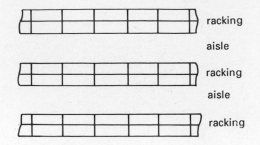

Figure 8.4 Adjustable pallet racking (plan view); conventional configuration is wasteful of space requiring aisles between every second racking row

If some loss of random access can be accepted, space utilisation can be improved, by using double deep reach trucks which can reach two pallets deep into racking (see Figure 8.5)

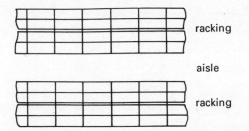

Figure 8.5 Double-deep pallet racking (plan view); double reach trucks can be used with this racking configuration which provides improved space utilisation

The bottom pallets are supported on beams, rather than on the floor, so that the legs of the double reach truck can fit under the racking structure (see Figure 8.6)

This system is suitable for line items having at least two pallets-worth of stock, the advantage being enhanced space utilisation. The disadvantages include the need to have double reach trucks, loss of absolute FIFO and poor visibility for the truck drivers when accessing the rear locations.

Drive-in and drive-through racking

This racking has vertical support frames, tied at the top, with cantilever pallet support beams at different heights (see Figure 8.7). Fork trucks enter the racking between the vertical members, to access the pallets. If the access is from one end, the term 'drive-in' is used. Racking accessed from either end is called 'drive-through'.

Operationally, this racking is similar to simple block stacking – first in

Courtesy of Link 51

Figure 8.6 Double-deep pallet racking; the bottom pallets are supported on beams, clear of the floor, to enable access by double reach trucks

Courtesy of Link 51

Figure 8.7 Drive-in racking; access by counterbalanced fork lift truck from either end

last out (FILO), only one product line per row, and suitable for a small number of high stock product lines.

The pallet loads do not have to carry the weight of the pallets above them, so the height of the installation is not limited by the strength of the palletised goods.

The cantilever supports have to be narrower than the pallets, so aisle clearances are tight, and pallets have to be moved in a raised position. Driver strain, therefore, is a factor to be taken into account. Because pallets are only supported at the edge, pallet condition is important and the types of pallets which are suitable is also limited.

This racking is not as rigid as APR, there being no beams joining the uprights along the face of the racking, so it is more susceptible to damage.

Construction of the racking, and the laying of the floor must be carried out to tight tolerances, to minimise the risk of truck masts striking the structure.

It can be built to about 10 m high, but the maximum front to back depth for safe operation is about six pallets or twelve deep if accessed from both sides.

Palletised live storage

This is made up from inclined gravity roll conveyors, side by side and at a number of vertical levels (see Figure 8.8). Pallets are fed in at the higher end, and taken out when required at the lower end. The system imposes FIFO and any one lane should only contain pallets of the same product.

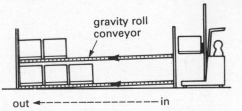

gravity roll conveyor

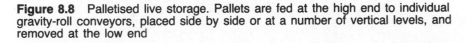

out ←————————————— in

Figure 8.8 Palletised live storage. Pallets are fed at the high end to individual gravity-roll conveyors, placed side by side or at a number of vertical levels, and removed at the low end

The incline in these installations is critical and is usually established by trial and error. They are not, therefore, always suitable where there is a wide variation in load weights. Braking devices are usually fitted in the lanes with stops at the off-take ends. To limit pallet speed and for space utilisation (honeycombing), lengths above about 20 metres are not generally practical.

Live storage systems can be appropriate where there is a high through-put per line item. A typical application is where the output face is used for order picking and this gives separation between order picking and stock replenishment, but a facility for removing empty pallets from the picking face should be incorporated.

Live storage is expensive, pallet space utilisation within the system is not always good, special pallets or even slave pallets may be needed, and stock location and control may need particular attention.

Powered live storage for pallets can also be used, and has similar operational characteristics to gravity systems, without the potential problems of setting a safe incline. They are very costly but lend themselves to automated control.

Powered mobile storage

This consists of sections of back-to-back adjustable pallet racking on electrically powered base frames which move along rails set into the floor (see Figure 8.9). Space for only one aisle is needed for fork truck access, and the racks are moved to open up an aisle as required for access to specific pallet locations.

Courtesy of Link 51

Figure 8.9 Powered mobile storage; back-to-back adjustable pallet racking mounted on electrically-powered base frames which move along rails set in the floor

The layout usually consists of a number of mobile sections working between fixed end racks. Safety mechanisms are fitted to prevent rack movement in the event of obstruction.

Mobile racking provides good space utilisation and random access to every pallet. It is suitable for stock which does not move very fast – where the number of line items is high but frequency of accessions per line is low.

Mobile racking is expensive, though this cost may be offset by a reduced building cost, consequent on the better space utilisation. Floor loadings are high, probably requiring reinforcement. Control of movement is important to reduce queuing if a number of fork trucks are working the racking at the same time.

High rack narrow aisle racking

This is basically adjustable pallet racking, accessed by narrow aisle free path stackers, equipped with rotating or sliding pallet handling mechanisms on the mast, and which do not have to turn through 90 degrees in the aisle to pick up or set down a pallet load (see Figure 8.10). Hence the aisles are narrower than for installations accessed by reach

Courtesy of Boss Warehouse Systems

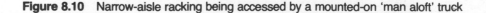

Figure 8.10   Narrow-aisle racking being accessed by a mounted-on 'man aloft' truck

trucks or counterbalance trucks. There is free access to every pallet location.

The trucks, sometimes called 'turret trucks', can operate up to 12 metres high so space utilisation is quite good – narrower aisles and use of height. Aisle widths can be as little as:

load width + side clearances (say 100 mm)

A free path truck, working up to 12 metres high, requires a high quality of floor flatness and finish, and guide rails or electrical wire guidance are used to constrain and guide the trucks.

Turret trucks are expensive – twice or more the cost of a reach truck of similar capacity.

Narrow aisle installations usually require pick-up and deposit stations (P and D) for the feeder trucks, eg reach trucks, to bring the pallet loads to and from the storage installation.

High bay

'High bay' warehousing describes pallet racking up to heights of 30 to 35 metres, in which the pallet movement is by means of stacker cranes, giving free access to all pallet locations. Aisle widths can be as narrow as load width plus side clearances.

Because of the height, conventional APR is not generally strong enough to carry the imposed loads so structural steel is usually adopted. The racking structure may then be used to support the walls and roof of the building, ie it becomes the building structure, hence the terms 'roof-on rack' and 'clad rack'.

Because pallets are accessed by a stacker crane running on floor-mounted rails, the floor surface and flatness are not critical, although floor strength clearly is.

Space utilisation is high – the use of height and narrow access aisles. Special fire sprinkler systems may be required.

Stacker cranes can move very quickly. They can be manually or automatically controlled, hence they are very suitable for automated warehouses.

High bay storage systems are expensive to build, and the design should be carefully based since, once built, there is little flexibility for subsequent change.

Storage systems and equipment – small item storage

In addition to the factors noted earlier under storage principles, small item storage systems should be modular to allow different storage components to be grouped together, be subdivisible to allow for different sized stock items, incorporate facilities for product and location identification, and minimise the manual effort in lifting and handling.

Some small parts storage systems are described.

Shelving

Shelving is usually made from mild steel, in standard component sizes, to various heights, vertical shelf spacing and shelf depth. There is a limited range of standard widths for the modules (see Figure 8.11).

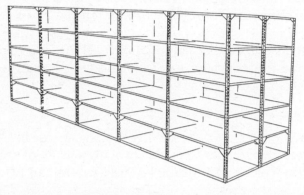

Courtesy of Link 51

Figure 8.11 Basic shelving used for small-parts storage

Courtesy of Link 51

Figure 8.12 Two-tier shelving showing upper level access from flooring suspended from the upper levels

Shelving can be as 'short span', usually 1 metre wide, and 'long span', 3 metres or more in width.

Shelving is comparatively inexpensive, gives random access to stock, is modular, interchangeable and is easily moved.

Adjustment to shelf heights is not always easy after a period in use. Separation of small quantities can restrict access, eg hand access between vertical shelf partitions spaced 50 mm apart is limited.

Another common design of shelving, called cantilever shelving, is supported from the back and sides, giving totally clear access from the front, which enables very good utilisation of shelf space.

Shelving can be installed at multiple levels (Figure 8.12), and the upper levels can be accessed from flooring suspended from the shelving structure, or by using free path, or fixed path trucks or order picking cranes.

Tote pans and bins

There are various designs of totes, produced in different materials, eg galvanised steel, polypropylene, fibreboard, and wire mesh.

Generally, totes are made in modular sizes in submultiples of standard dimensions, have the facility to nest, or to stack, incorporate label holders, and subdividers – cross or lengthways, and can be fitted to louvre panels.

Courtesy of Link 51

8.13 Louvre panels; plastic and other containers can be attached

Louvre panel systems

Louvre panels are used in stores, and also mounted on to trolleys for movement, eg between storage and assembly operations. They can be used to hold tote pans, and also other attachments for more awkwardly shaped items such as gaskets, vee belts, tool holders, etc, using spigots (see Figure 8.13 at the top).

Cabinets and drawer units

Cabinets and drawer units can be free-standing, or incorporated into shelving modules. They make good use of space, are compact and give good access with a clean, secure environment. They can be fitted with subdividers, and special inserts for protecting delicate components, eg electronic parts.

Both cabinets and drawer units can be incorporated into stores issue counters, giving excellent access for the stores staff.

Dynamic systems

As for pallets, there are small item storage systems using mobile shelving, and gravity conveyors – live storage. The characteristics are similar to those for the comparable palletised systems.

Mechanised systems

Carousel units consist of shelving or bins, supported from chains, driven electrically, which bring the stock to the operators' location as required, and so help to reduce operator movement. They can give good order picking rates, ready acces to stock but also good security, and are readily put on to computer control. There are two types, ie vertical and horizontal.

In the vertical carousel (see Figure 8.14), a series of shelves suspended between two continuous chains are driven through supporting sprockets to move the trays up or down as required. Operator access to the stock is at a fixed level, and the carousels can be built to make use of available building height.

In the horizontal carousel, shelved storage 'baskets' are suspended from a continuous overhead chain which is driven forwards or backwards to bring the required stock to the operator.

Another mechanised small parts storage system, known as the mini-trieve, also suitable for computer control, brings the goods to the operator, using a mini-stacker crane mechanism operating in a central aisle between shelving.

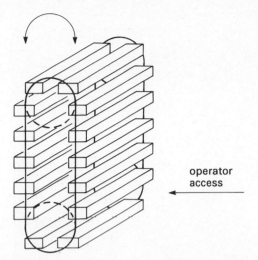

Figure 8.14 Vertical carousel; operator access to moving shelves is at fixed level

Other types of storage

Other types of storage equipment are available designed for material not suitable for the equipment described so far.

Long loads

Long loads such as carpets, linoleum, and engineering materials such as rods, bars and tubes, require special storage and handling.

Bars can be held in vertical racking but this can involve manual handling of the bars into position. Access to the stock is comparatively easy.

Horizontal storage for long rigid items uses the cantilever principle to stack goods at different levels.

Mechanical handling is usually by means of side-loaders, four directional reach trucks or overhead crane, which enable access without requiring especially wide aisles (see Figure 9.11).

Pigeon hole racking gives good access and protection to the stock. The gangway area in front of the racking must be wider than the length of the items being stocked, which reduces overall space utilisation (see Figure 8.15).

There are also various systems for mechanised storage of long loads.

Metal plate and sheet

Plate can be stacked horizontally, the layers being separated by baulks of timber. This does not give good access and can distort the metal.

Vertical storage in 'toast rack' frames to support and separate the material is more usual.

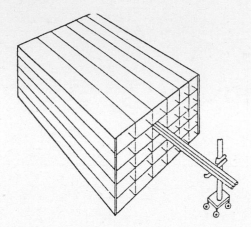

Figure 8.15 Pigeon-hole racking with mobile, variable height trolley for in/out access

CHAPTER
9

Handling Systems

Industrial trucks and attachments

Industrial trucks used in warehousing are primarily for the movement of goods, over comparatively short distances, for lifting goods into and out of storage, and for vehicle loading and unloading.

The use of trucks also facilitates load unitisation and larger loads so reducing the frequency of movement, it enables quicker movement, and also the use of height for storage purposes.

Industrial trucks can be manually powered and operated or they can be motor (electric) or engine driven. Some powered trucks are designed for pedestrian control, some for control by the operator standing or sitting on the truck. Many trucks have a (fork) lift capacity, and there are attachments designed for handling loads of specific shapes.

The main types of truck encountered in warehousing and similar types of operation are:

- manual trolleys;
- pallet trucks – manual and powered;
- fork lift trucks
  - counterbalanced truck
  - stacker truck
  - reach truck – and double reach truck
  - narrow aisle stackers
  - side loaders;
- order picking trucks;
- tugs and tractors;
- straddle carriers; and

- crane units
  - stacker cranes and order picking cranes which run on bottom rails and are rail guided at the top.

Power source
Counterbalanced fork lift trucks can be driven by:

- internal combustion engine – liquefied petroleum gas (LPG), or petrol (not common);
- compression ignition engine – diesel; and
- electric motor.

Side loaders used outdoors in timber yards, etc tend to be engine driven.

Generally, powered pallet trucks, reach trucks, stacker trucks, high rise stackers, and driverless trucks, are electrically powered. This is clean, quiet, reliable and compact, gives high initial acceleration, and is suitable for intermittent working, although traction batteries are heavy.

Battery charging areas should incorporate facilities to deal with accidental spillage of acid, and be ventilated. Hydrogen gas, given off during charging, can be explosive when mixed with air. Battery power 'fade' can occur towards the end of a shift, if the truck has been on continuous duty with a lot of lifting. Electric trucks for continuous use over more than an eight hour shift usually require additional batteries with one set on charge while the other is in use.

Note that most fork lift trucks have rear wheel steering.

Lifting capacity
The capacity of a fork lift truck is usually quoted as a maximum load weight when the load centre of gravity (CG) is at a specified distance (load centre) from the heel of the forks (see Figure 9.1).

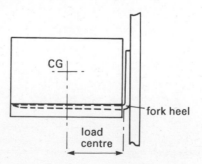

Figure 9.1 Fork-lift-truck load; load centre is defined as the distance between the centre of gravity and the heel of forks

If the load has a longer load centre than specified, the weight that can safely be carried must be reduced, to avoid the risk of truck overturn. Makers' technical literature usually states how much 'de-rating' should be applied. Most trucks also de-rate if the load is lifted above a specified height, because the higher the load the less stable the truck, eg:

Reach truck normal rated capacity	1,350 kg
lift above 4.8m	1,250 kg
lift above 5.4 kg	1,000 kg

Masts
There are three standard fork lift masts, ie single stage, two stage (duplex) and three stage (triplex). The more stages in a mast, the higher the potential lift and the lower will be the closed height of the mast. When the forks begin to rise, the mast begins to extend.

A variation called 'free lift' enables some lift of the forks without any mast height increase – a valuable facility when stacking pallets into container vehicles, or working in a low headroom environment.

With full free lift the fork carriage can rise to the top of the mast closed height before the mast starts to rise. 'Partial' free lift allows a part lift before the mast extends.

Masts can be tilted forward (about 5 degrees) to facilitate picking up and setting down pallets. Backwards tilt (to about 12 degrees) helps to stabilise the load during horizontal movement.

Non-lift trucks

Trolleys
There are various types of non-powered trucks and trolleys, often designed for particular applications. Two examples are shown in Figure 9.2.

Pallet trucks
The most commonly used truck for horizontal movement of pallets is the hand pallet truck (see Figure 9.3).

Cranking the steering arm pumps up the hydraulic system which lowers the front wheels so raising the load sufficiently to allow horizontal movement. Capacities go up to 2,000 kg, ideally for use only on good condition horizontal floors.

For frequent or inclined moves, electric pallet trucks are preferable. These can be pedestrian or rider controlled, with capacities up to about 3,000 kg (see Figure 9.4).

(a)

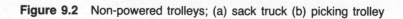

(b)

Figure 9.2 Non-powered trolleys; (a) sack truck (b) picking trolley

Figure 9.3 Hand pallet truck

Courtesy of Lansing Bagnall Ltd

Figure 9.4 Pedestrian-controlled electric pallet truck

Courtesy of Boss Warehouse Systems

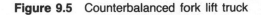

Figure 9.5 Counterbalanced fork lift truck

Tugs and tractors

For long horizontal movement tugs may be more economic and appropriate than fork lift trucks, the payloads being carried on platforms or trailers.

Lift trucks

Counterbalanced fork lift trucks (CBFLT)

These are robust and fast machines (see Figure 9.5), with capacities ranging between 1,000 kg and about 45,000 kg (container handling).

Some small capacity models (1,000/1,500 kg) have three wheels rather than four, giving better manoeuvrability. There are also pedestrian controlled models in the smaller sizes.

Generally these trucks are used to lift and stack to heights up to about 5 metres.

The load is carried forward of the front wheels, which tends to tip the truck forward, so a counterbalance weight is built into the rear of the machine.

The truck length necessitates a wide turning area. Trucks of 2,000/3,000 kg capacity require a 90 degree turning aisle (for putting pallets in/out of stock) of about 4 metres (see Figure 9.6).

For comparison, reach trucks, pedestrian stacker trucks, and high rack stackers would require about 2.5, 2 to 2.5, and 1.5 metres respectively, depending on the size of load being handled.

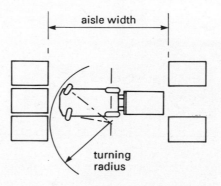

Figure 9.6 Turning pattern for counterbalanced fork lift truck

Electric trucks, used for indoor work to avoid fumes, are made in capacities up to about 5,000 kg with travel speeds up to 20/25 km per hour.

Diesel and LPG engine trucks, more suitable for outdoor work, are faster and more robust.

Reach trucks

Reach trucks are driven electrically. During horizontal movement the load is carried partially within the area enclosed by the truck wheels (see Figure 9.7). This means a shorter overall length than the CBFLT, and eliminates

Courtesy of Lansing Bagnall Ltd

Figure 9.7 Reach truck

the need for a counterbalance weight. When picking up or setting down a load, the whole mast slides forward in channels in the truck legs, so bringing the forks forward to a position where they can access the load.

The capacity range for reach trucks is from 1,000 kg to about 3,500 kg, and with maximum fork lift to about 8 metres.

Horizontal travel speed does not usually exceed 10 to 12 km/hour. A typical 90 degree stacking aisle width would be in the region of 2.5 metres, depending on truck size.

A reach mechanism more used in the USA than in the UK, has a fixed mast and a pantograph (scissor) mechanism on the fork carriage to obtain the necessary reach.

Double deep reach truck
A variation on the reach truck principle uses a pantograph for accessing double deep racking, and for loading flat bed road vehicles, (loading from one side of the vehicle).

Double reach is achieved on some lighter weight trucks by use of telescopic forks mounted on a basic truck design (as shown in Figure 8.6).

Four directional reach trucks (4D)

A further variant of the basic reach truck enables the front wheels to be turned through 90 degrees, effectively converting the truck into a side loader. This is especially useful when long loads have to be moved and stored.

Stacker trucks

These are lightweight trucks, with maximum capacities up to about 2,000 kg, and can be pedestrian controlled, stand-on, and rider versions (see Figure 9.8).

They have outrigger legs, but no reach facility, so any storage medium accessed must have space to accommodate the outriggers.

There are two designs for achieving this. One has the outrigger legs running under the storage medium (narrow track stacker), for example pallet racking with the bottom pallets sitting on a beam rather than on the floor. Note that perimeter based pallets cannot be used with narrow track stackers.

The other design has the outrigger legs wide spaced to straddle the payload (wide track stacker).

The 90 degree minimum stacking aisle width for these trucks is from 2 to 2.5 metres.

Courtesy of Lansing Bagnall Ltd

Figure 9.8 Stacker truck

Courtesy of Boss Warehouse Systems

Figure 9.9 Side loader operating in timber yard

Side loaders

The side loader has a mast which reaches at 90 degrees to the direction of truck travel, and is used for loads up to 6/7 metres long handled in narrow aisles, or in outdoor stock areas (see Figure 9.9).

To access stock on one side of a storage aisle, the truck enters the aisle with the reach mechanism on the appropriate side. To access the other side the truck comes out of the aisle to turn. The length of the truck and load requires cross aisles of about 7 metres.

Free path high rack stackers

These trucks, up to 2 tonnes capacity, lift to about 12 metres. They work in very narrow aisles between guide rails, with a mechanism on the mast which accesses stock to either side of an aisle. Since the truck does not have to turn to access the racking, the aisle width need be only slightly wider than the payload – typically 1.5 metres in pallet racking. Some models have the operator at ground level. In others, a rising cab raises the operator to working level.

Because of the lift height and narrow aisles, floor flatness is important to avoid collision with the racking. For the same reasons there are devices which will position the forks at pre-selected heights. The trucks can move between aisles, but movement of goods up to and away from the racking are normally by reach or other trucks. An example of this sort of truck, with rising cab is shown in Figure 8.10.

Other designs of narrow aisle stacker are equipped with a rotating mast to access the payload to left or to right (see Figure 9.10).

Courtesy of Boss Warehouse Systems

9.10 Very narrow aisle-free path stacker with rotating mast

Stacker cranes

Stacker cranes run between a floor mounted rail, and an overhead rail (see Figure 9.11). They can be single or twin mast (for heavier loads), with a rising carriage for lifting and lowering the load to the required height and for transferring the load into and out of the racking on either side of the crane aisle. They can have a rising cab for the operator, but they lend themselves to remote computer control. Drive is by an electric motor, fed by suspended or reeled power cable.

Aisle widths should be just greater than the unit load carried, and operating speeds are high.

A stacker crane can be dedicated to one specific aisle, but if transfer from one aisle to another is required a transfer car and cross aisle (see Figure 9.12) or special transfer rails have to be provided.

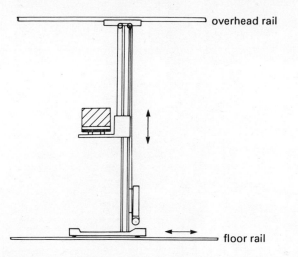

Figure 9.11 Single-mast stacker crane; these operate between floormounted rail and overhead rails

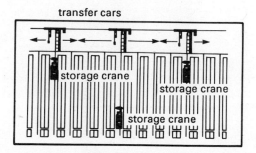

Figure 9.12 Stacker crane; transfer cars are used for transfer from one aisle to another

Generally, stacker cranes cannot pick up or set down loads directly at floor level and the usual practice is to have pick-up and deposit stations (P & D) at the end of the aisles. The linking AGV, conveyor or fork truck system bringing the loads to and from the stacker crane storage system picks up or sets down the loads at these slightly raised stations.

Order picking trucks

Free path trucks for order picking are available for low level, intermediate, and for high level picking.

Courtesy of Boss Warehouse Systems

9.13 Multi-level-free-path order picking truck

Pallet trucks are often used for case picking at ground level, in addition to various types of pedestrian trolleys, and roll cage pallets.

For intermediate levels, there are trucks with a small step for the operator to reach up, and other designs which have a limited lift platform.

Multi-level order picking trucks, with lifts up to about 6/7 metres, enable an operator to pick from about four pallet levels high. The truck shown in Figure 9.13 has forks which can be raised or lowered relative to the cab, to maintain the working level at which the operator is placing picked goods.

There are versions of high rack stackers fitted with rising cabs for picking from pallets in high level racking up to 9/10 metres high (see Figure 9.14).

Courtesy of Boss Warehouse Systems

Figure 9.14 High-rack stacker truck with rising cab

For higher rates of small item picking at high levels, fixed path picking cranes can be used which run on bottom rails, guided by a top rail. The order picker is in a rising cab. Cranes can transfer between aisles, but this is an expensive option and it is more usual to dedicate cranes to aisles.

Truck attachments

There are various fork lift truck attachments for handling loads which cannot be handled with forks, or for providing additional degrees of movement.

Clamps
These are operated from the fork truck hydraulic system with movable and sometimes shaped side arms for handling cartons, bales, reels and drums, etc. A pressure relief valve limits the compressive force exerted by the clamps.

Side shift
This enables forks or other attachments to be shifted laterally by about ± 75mm, and is for accurate positioning of loads, eg in containers.

Rotating head

This device changes the orientation of a load, eg reels of newsprint delivered horizontally, and to be stacked vertically in a warehouse.

Load push-pull

This mechanism handles loads assembled on skid sheets. The load, on a cardboard or plastic skid sheet is carried on a steel platen and is pulled or pushed on and off by a pantograph mechanism which grips a protruding lip on the skid sheet (see Figure 9.15).

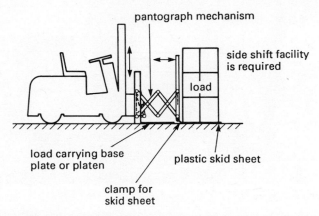

9.15 Load push-pull fork truck attachment. This device handles loads assembled on skid sheets

Non-powered attachments

Booms or poles, fitted in place of forks, are used for carrying loads such as carpets, linoleum, reels and coils.

There are also clamp attachments for carrying drums and small coils, etc.

All attachments have weight and this should be added in when calculating truck payload, ie attachments can de-rate a truck and a higher capacity truck may be needed to compensate.

Conveyors

Conveyor systems are used for moving material between specified points, for holding material (buffer capacity), for sortation, and for process purposes, eg cooling.

Characteristics

- High throughputs on fixed routes.
- Comparatively low power usage but high equipment cost.

- Manning required only for feed and discharge.
- Usable where other handling systems cannot be used, eg across uneven floors, in confined spaces, between floors.
- For intermittent or continuous movement.
- Easy to control flows, fast response.
- Suitable for fixed routes; not easy to alter routes or start/finish positions.
- Can obstruct other flows and activities.

Choice of conveyors or trucks

Consideration of the most appropriate movement system – conveyors or industrial trucks – for a particular application should take account of the material to be moved, the quantity and length of movement, the numbers of pick-up points and destinations, the nature of the route, speed of movement, required flexibility of the system, and cost.

Types of conveyor

The range of types of conveyor is wide, and each has its particular operating characteristics. Warehousing conveyor applications are usually for unit loads – cases, pallets, cartons, etc, as distinct from bulk solids, handling of granules, powders, or lump material.

Gravity conveyor systems

Gravity systems are simple in concept, not requiring power supplies, motors and switch gear. However, control of speed can be a problem, and inclines should always be tested when designing such systems.

Chutes

Gravity chutes, especially spiral chutes, require very careful design of inclines and configuration, to account for possible variable coefficients of friction and package shapes and surfaces.

Gravity roller conveyors

This is probably the most common type of conveyor. A wide range of loads can be carried from small boxes up to pallets, but the bottom of the load should be flat, smooth and firm and the rollers should be pitched to keep at least three rollers in contact with the load at all times.

The critical aspect is the incline, which should not allow dangerous speeds to be reached. The supporting legs can be adjusted to set the angle, ideally using the actual loads to be carried. Even so, there can be problems if handling different load weights on the same system. Stops are usually fitted at the discharge end of gravity roller conveyors.

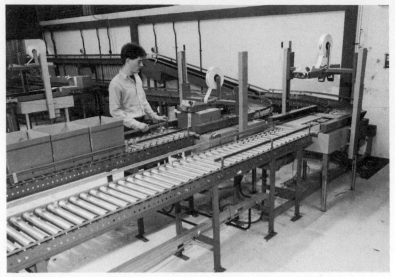

Courtesy of Link 51

Figure 9.16 Combined gravity and powered-roller conveyor system

Gravity rollers, incorporated as part of a display, are illustrated in Figure 9.16.

Skate wheel conveyors

Skate wheel conveyors consist of discs fitted on to spindles which are mounted between side channels and the conveyed loads travel along the discs. These conveyors are suitable for light loads with rigid bases. They track better than roller conveyors, especially at bends, and tend to be faster – so requiring less incline.

They are sometimes used for vehicle loading or unloading, set into a pantograph framework which allows the conveyor to be extended or shortened during use.

Powered conveyors

Powered-roller conveyors

These are available in a wide range of sizes, from about 200 mm wide, to 1,500 mm wide, and capacities from 5 to 1,500 kg/metre. The load should be smooth and firmly based with three rollers in contact at all times. Inclines are not recommended, and for changes of height a flat belt conveyor may be more suitable.

Loads can be taken off conveyors by deflecting ploughs, by push mechanisms acting from the sides, or by skate wheels which 'pop up' through the rollers at right angles. There are various other mechanisms, eg for merging two conveyors into one, for splitting one conveyor stream into two or more, for right angle switching – change of direction, for preventing jams at intersections – 'policeman units', and so on.

Accumulation

Unpowered-roller conveyors can be used to accumulate loads to form a queue on a line. If the line is inclined, the pressure between one load and the next – known as 'line pressure' can become excessive, especially when it comes to removing the end load.

Ways of overcoming this include a 'pop-up' stop located one load's length back from the end stop.

Powered-roller accumulation can be achieved by using rollers with friction clutches which slip if the loads are stopped, eg by an end stop.

An alternative is to fit rollers into a powered chain conveyor. When the loads are moving the rollers do not rotate, but if the loads are stopped, the chain continues to move, with the rollers rotating in their bearings.

Flat belt conveyors

These consist of continuous belting carried on rollers, and are used for moving comparatively light cartons or cases. They can be made from rubber, plastic, fabric, composites of these, steel and steel mesh.

They handle goods gently, are quiet, can be inclined, and can operate at high throughputs. They tend to be cheaper than powered-roller installations. They do not enable accumulation, except for special steel belts.

Slat conveyors

Slat conveyors can operate horizontally and inclined, and handle heavier or more awkwardly shaped items than belt conveyors.

Parallel side chains carry cross slats, which may be flat, shaped, hinged or overlapping, to provide a firm, rigid carrying surface. Slats can be wood or steel and are easily replaced.

These conveyors are more robust than belts, but tend to be slow, noisy and with a high power usage.

Chain conveyors

These conveyors carry the load on two or more sets of parallel roller chains, and are for heavy loads which are not suitable for roller conveyors – crates, pallets, etc with uneven bases. They are also used as transfer conveyors between roller conveyor systems.

An extension of this concept is to bridge a set of parallel chains with flight bars at regular intervals, running over a smooth bed along which the loads are pushed by the flight bars. These can be used up quite steep inclines – 40–45 degrees.

Tilt tray and tilt slat conveyors

Tilt conveying is by means of a continuous conveyor chain, usually in horizontal carousel configuration (though some are vertical). A series of trays or slats, attached to the chain can be tilted left or right to tip the loads off at any of a number of designated points.

Slats can be tilted singly or in multiples so that a range of different loads sizes can be handled.

Tilt conveyors are used for high speed sortation in post offices, mail order businesses, and parcels distribution, often utilising bar code techniques for coding the loads and actuating the tilt mechanisms.

Overhead chain conveyors

These consist of a continuous chain running on or in an overhead track, with the loads on carriers suspended from the track and moved by the chain.

An installation may include horizontal and inclined track and bends, motor drive unit, speed controls, and chain tensioning devices.

Overhead conveyors do not obstruct working floor areas, can provide accumulation, but they do take up headroom and require support off the roof or building structure.

The carriers are designed to fit the load and can incorporate features such as auto-trip discharge, swivel and rotating heads, and various indexing devices.

Overhead conveyors are used in production for moving materials through assembly operations, paint plants, drying and baking ovens and dip tanks. They are also used for hanging garments in clothing manufacture and warehousing.

Power and free conveyors

In this type of conveyor there are two tracks, one above the other. The top track carries a conveyor chain and the lower track supports load-carrying trolleys. Pushers on the conveyor chain act on the trolleys and move them along the bottom track.

Spurs can be taken off the bottom track to 'shunt' the carriers into holding zones for accumulation, or on to other conveyor circuits, either mechanically or electrically, and by manual or automatic control.

Under-floor conveyors

These comprise continuous motor driven chains running inside floor channels. Loads are carried on trolleys which engage with the conveyor chain by retractable pins or hooks.

Systems can incorporate side/parking spurs, or transfer spurs to other conveyor circuits. Trolleys are 'addressable' – they can be directed to specific destinations by pins which act on limit switches which activate the appropriate routeing controls.

Because the floor channel has a narrow top slot there is no interruption to flow of other traffic over the floor.

These systems are suitable for fixed routes between fixed points – there is no flexibility for easily changing circuits.

Trolleys have bumper bars to disengage the chain drive in the event of contacting an obstruction.

Automated guided vehicles

These are suitable for frequent movement on set routes. They are powered driverless trolleys which are guided by following an under-floor wire which carries an electric signal, or by optically following a painted or plastic tape track laid on the floor. They are addressable, and also highly suitable for computer control. Recent developments are towards radio control which allows the vehicles to be guided anywhere within the defined radio zone, and eliminates the need for following predetermined routes.

Lifting

Introduction

Cranes and hoists are generally for raising and moving material, on an intermittent basis, within an area which is defined by the equipment configuration (the exception is mobile cranes). Installations are therefore less flexible than, for example, fork lift trucks, though for regular lifting within a defined area, and for heavy loads, may be much more suitable. Because they lift overhead, they do not require aisles for horizontal movement of material.

Crane and hoist systems, once installed are not readily modified, and should be carefully planned in advance of installation.

Types of lifting equipment

There are various types of lifting equipment, in a great range of sizes and capacities. Small equipment can be manually operated, but for regular or heavy lifts powered equipment is appropriate.

The equipment types includes hoists – hand and power operated, jib cranes, overhead travelling cranes, gantry cranes, attachments, and other devices.

Hoists

Hoists are devices for raising or lowering items carried by a hook from a chain or wire rope. They can be hand operated, electrically powered or compressed air powered, and can be suspended from a fixed point, from a slewing jib, from an overhead runway system or from a travelling crane. Capacities range up to 25 tonnes SWL.

They cover a wide range of uses from production shop machine loading/unloading to vehicle loading/unloading. They are flexible in operation and comparatively inexpensive.

Generally speaking, for lower weights and heights of lift, chain hoists will be cheaper than wire rope.

For extended and heavy lifts, wire rope is more appropriate – it can be reeled on to a hoist drum. However, the condition of the wire rope should be watched for broken strands, cuts, kinks, etc.

Jib cranes

Slewing jib cranes are fixed units which have been used for many years, particularly in engineering production.

Such a crane consists of a pivoted slewing arm along which a hoist can travel radially in or out. It can be totally hand operated, or can have powered lift, or powered lift and radial racking. For very heavy loads even the slewing action can be power operated.

The slewing arm can be mounted on a free-standing pillar, which must be very securely base plated and bolted to the floor to carry the considerable bending movements imposed. An alternative is the wall mounted slewing jib, and in this case the loads imposed on the wall should be carefully calculated. The wall mounted version is restricted in radial movement by the wall, eg if mounted along a flat wall the slewing arc would be just short of 180 degrees.

The power supply for powered hoists is provided by cable, or air line, slung from some form of pendant along the slewing arm, which does not restrict radial movement of the hoist. Control for powered hoists is usually by pendant control box.

Overhead travelling cranes

An overhead travelling crane consists of a bridge made up of one or more beams, carried on end carriages, which drive along a pair of parallel high level rails. A trolley incorporating a hoist, travels on rails on the bridge structure. Thus the load can be moved as follows:

- Longitudinal – by bridge driving on raised rails.
- Cross Traverse – by hoist trolley along the bridge.
- Vertical – by hoist.

Some light duty cranes are hand operated, but most OH travelling cranes are electrically powered. Uses include heavy, large, long loads such as items of machinery, bundles of bar and tube, metal plate, fabrications, girders, etc. With modification, these cranes are also used for pallet and long load handling in warehouses.

The loads can be moved within an area slightly less than that enclosed by the length and span of the overhead rails, and the floor area underneath can be fully utilised. They can be operated from a cab, or by pendant or radio control.

The disadvantages are a possible need for reinforced building frames, slow operation, confined to a defined/limited area, and risks of queuing.

Gantry cranes

Gantry cranes are used for very heavy loads and consist of a bridge section supported by legs at each end, the legs running in floor-mounted rail tracks.

They tend to be slower in operation than OH travelling cranes due to generally heavier but less rigid construction, but for outdoor use they may well be cheaper since they do not require an elevated support structure.

Gantry crane capacities run from about 20 tonnes up to shipbuilding cranes capable of lifting prefabricated ship sections to 1,500 tonnes.

There are designs of gantry crane which cantilever out from the sides and allow lifting outside the area within the travel rails.

'Semi-gantry' cranes are a cross between full gantry and the OH travelling crane. They can be used outdoors, one side running along a ground rail and the other running on a building supported high rail.

Gantry cranes, in the lower lift capacities up to about 50 tonnes, can be designed for running on pneumatic tyres, usually with four legs straddling the load. These units offer mobility and can operate in different areas over uneven ground surfaces. They have limited lift and span widths and are used for moving general cargo and containers in docks and rail yards.

Crane attachments

There is a wide variety of attachments for use with cranes, depending on the type of load being lifted. Effective attachments should be easy to use, ie quick fit and quick release, and they should be safe. The range includes:

- simple hooks;
- safety hooks, ie with safety catches;
- slings
  - wire rope
  - chain
  - synthetic fibre – nylon, polypropylene etc.
  - wire mesh;
- mechanical clamps and grippers;
- forks;
- spreaderbeams, eg used with ISO containers;
- magnetic lifting heads – battery and mains energised;
- vacuum lifting heads; and
- grabs.

Scissor lifts

Scissor lifts consist of a 'table', on which the payload is placed, and a hydraulically actuated scissor mechanism under the table which raises or lowers it. Capacities range from 2/300 kg up to 200 tonnes.

When designed as work platforms, models are available giving safe lifting to 12/13 metres above ground level.

Scissor lifts are comparatively slow in operation and are suitable for infrequent movement, eg moving a fork lift truck from ground level to loading dock level ready for lorry loading. They are used extensively in production for positioning items at suitable heights for working, and for machine feeding. For the higher lifts double scissor legs are used.

CHAPTER
10

Equipment Management

Choosing the most appropriate type of equipment for any particular application is important for getting the most productive and cost effective working of the system, and time spent on equipment specification and selection is time well spent.

Once equipment is installed and working, management has the responsibility to maintain and operate it in the most effective way to suit system objectives, including optimum productivity, cost, and safe working.

Equipment selection

The selection of handling or storage equipment should be carried out systematically and a possible approach would be:

- Define what the equipment will have to achieve.
- Specify possible equipment types.
- Initial equipment evaluation against what is required – technical and cost factors.
- Obtain detailed design of possible equipment configurations.
- Obtain detailed assessment and evaluation.
- Decide on the equipment needed.
- Purchase the equipment and install it.

Definition

The definition of what the equipment will have to achieve, ie the equipment tasks, will include:

- material being handled/stored
  - unit load/package

    – weight and dimensions
    – quantity/frequency/trends
    – operating speeds required
    – distances and heights of moves;
● operating hours
    – day work, shifts;
● equipment use
    – intermittent, continuous
    – indoors, outdoors
    – floor surface.

Constraints should also be taken into account, such as space limitations on area or height, integration with adjacent systems, power source limitations, eg no diesel indoors, level of equipment availability required, safety, noise and environmental requirements, and level and type of control.

Equipment types

Specifying possible equipment types will involve reviewing the available equipment which could possibly meet the requirements, and understanding the operating and performance characteristics.

Initial evaluation

The initial evaluation will set out to equate the identified possible equipment and its characteristics with the defined requirements, and then take account of the factors appropriate to the application.

These factors will include such things as costs – capital and operating, space requirements, manning requirements, flexibility and scope for expansion, and equipment life.

This information is most likely to be obtained from manufacturers' budget quotations and technical literature.

Detailed design

The detailed design of possible equipment configurations will involve more detailed technical and cost data, based on a specification giving the equipment requirements and based on tenders from potential suppliers. The suppliers should be provided with data on system requirements and asked to formulate detailed proposals to meet those requirements – equipment types, equipment numbers, equipment operating characteristics – speeds, capacities, dimensions, etc, costs.

When going out to potential suppliers for tender, it is good practice to obtain a minimum of three tenders, and for major investments possibly more. Part of the evaluation of short listed equipment tenders can include getting the suppliers to arrange for visits to other users of the equipment, to obtain their operating experience on such factors as: reliability, ease of maintenance, suppliers' back-up service, spare parts availability, and operational performance of the equipment.

Detailed assessment and evaluation – decision

Detailed assessment of possible equipment configurations, and the decision on which to adopt, will depend on the broad factors already mentioned, and more detailed considerations as follows:

- Costs
  - capital, and possible resale value
  - operating – personnel
  - energy
  - maintenance and downtime
  - management
  - space
  - savings resulting from the use of the equipment;
- space required;
- manning levels required;
- reliability and ease of maintenance;
- service back up from manufacturer – spares, callout time, operator training;
- standardisation;
- compatibility with existing equipment;
- level of control;
- scope for expansion;
- safety;
- power source;
- ergonomic factors – ease of operation, access, visibility, whether operators like it.

Purchase and installation

Contract documents will often specify the supplier's obligations for installation of equipment, and for minimum performance levels. Clearly these should be monitored to achieve a final system which meets the original system and equipment requirements.

Maintenance

The reason for maintaining equipment is primarily to keep it available for use at specified levels of performance, during specified times, and in a safe condition.

Maintenance is mainly associated with equipment which moves or has moving parts, but even static equipment will require attention from time to time. Pallet racking does get hit by fork trucks.

The requirement placed on maintainers is to carry out maintenance at minimum cost, ie minimum system cost. To illustrate the point, by increasing the resource allocated to maintenance on a particular piece of equipment, thereby increasing maintenance costs, it can be that equipment availability is increased with consequent increased production – less downtime, and the overall system loss/cost may be reduced. The difficulty can be to identify what is the optimum level of maintenance. In practice maintenance levels are often determined initially by following manufacturers' recommendations for servicing, and then building up an operating history as a guide to optimum maintenance levels.

Maintenance activities
Maintenance consists of a number of different activities, some planned and others unplanned.

Inspection
This is to establish the condition of specified components, usually carried out at regular intervals (of time, or distance) on mechanical equipment. Components to be inspected can be determined by maker's recommendation and by operating experience. Any necessary repair/replacement work can be carried out at the next service or as dictated by the nature of the identified fault.

Servicing
This is also a routine activity to take specified action to prolong equipment life. Typical examples are oil changes, lubrication, oil filter changes. Makers usually provide a suggested servicing schedule for mechanical equipment. Other faults identified during inspection may also be rectified during routine servicing.

Note that some inspections and servicing can be carried out by operating staff – drivers, etc.

Planned repairs
Inspections, and normal operational reporting systems, will sometimes identify necessary items of repair work which, if not carried out, could lead to equipment breakdown. These can often be planned into a maintenance programme to suit operational and maintenance requirements.

Breakdown repairs
Despite inspections and servicing there will be occasions when components fail in service and have to be repaired or replaced before the

equipment can continue to be used. This usually has to be fitted into the maintenance time plan, and the timing can also be influenced by the availability of spare parts.

Maintenance planning

Effective maintenance is not just a matter of carrying out routine inspections and servicing, together with repairing breakdowns as they occur. It should be based on a philosophy of preventing breakdowns from occurring, partly by the routines of inspection and servicing, but also by monitoring equipment performance so that any failure trends, any warning signs of impending failure, can be recognised before failure occurs. The maintenance work can then be planned and structured in such a way as to minimise unscheduled breakdowns and maintenance work.

A planned maintenance approach is therefore likely to be based on a plan which sets out inspections, lubrication and minor adjustments, planned repairs and overhauls, on a monitoring scheme to check that the plan is adhered to, and on a recording system of work done on each significant item of equipment.

A planned maintenance scheme will also have to be flexible to cope with unplanned maintenance and breakdowns, which will always occur to some extent.

Maintenance records

Effective planning of maintenance activities implies sufficient knowledge to be able to:

- identify what needs to be done;
- sort maintenance tasks in priority order;
- direct maintenance effort where it is most needed;
- plan, schedule (time) and determine how the maintenance tasks are to be done;
- allocate resources – people and equipment;
- monitor the quality of the work done; and
- establish the cost of the maintenance work done – labour, materials, equipment.

A planned maintenance scheme should provide information to show up any areas of consistent failure, ie identify trends, which might point to inadequate maintenance, eg frequency of servicing, wrong method or poor quality of repair, or to inherent design or manufacturing weakness. This should also give pointers to possible reasons for high failure rates, high maintenance cost, excessive downtime, etc.

The above highlight the need for a good system of maintenance records, which should be kept for each significant item of equipment, eg each individual fork lift truck. Recording for groups of items will not show up if any one individual item is consistently giving trouble.

The data which it is appropriate to record, includes:

- Basic equipment description, capacity, etc. and manufacturer's references and drawing(s) numbers.
- Type and frequency of servicing and inspections.
- Reference to any relevant standard repair job and inspection and servicing descriptions.
- A history of all work carried out, including for each task:
  - planned date;
  - nature of fault – where relevant;
  - description of work done;
  - reason for the work – schedule, breakdown, etc;
  - date completed;
  - hours worked;
  - materials/parts used; and
  - hours machine/plant item off work.

Analysis of the maintenance data will show: areas/equipments of high failure rate, areas of high cost, whether routine inspections/servicing need changing in nature or frequency, reasons for failure, and areas of excess maintenance, eg unnecessarily frequent inspections or lubrication.

The data can also be used to derive detailed analysis of maintenance costs, which in turn help in equipment replacement decisions.

Maintenance stores

Spare parts are initially purchased on equipment makers' recommendations and inventory levels modified in the light of operating experience. Maintenance engineers like to have adequate spares since lack of a component can keep a piece of equipment out of use. On the other hand, spares represent money tied up. The maintenance records are used to indicate what spares it is advisable to keep, and the appropriate stock levels.

Many organisations contract out their equipment maintenance, eg to the equipment manufacturers who then take on the responsibility for parts availability and for the necessary maintenance skills.

Personnel considerations

Increasing equipment sophistication in recent years has implications for equipment operators/users and for maintainers.

It is important that operators are adequately trained in the use of equipment, since an obvious potential cause of equipment damage is maloperation. Manufacturers of handling equipment generally provide some training as part of their service in supplying the equipment.

The use of electronic, solid state, etc components in modern equipment imposes a need for additional skills on the maintainers, and it is important to recognise those required to maintain any particular equipment. As noted under 'Maintenance Stores', it may be appropriate to contract out all or part of equipment maintenance to the appropriate specialists.

CHAPTER
11

Warehouse Operations – Order Picking

Order picking re-arranges the form of a product as held in a warehouse into a form acceptable to the customer, at the service level demanded, and at minimum cost.

The labour cost for order picking can be up to 50 per cent of the total direct labour cost, hence picking systems should be properly designed and operated.

In a typical order picking and replenishment operation, full pallets of goods are held in reserve storage, and transferred to order picking stock locations as they require replenishment. Order picking, to assemble customer orders, would be in case quantities selected from the pallets in the order picking stock locations.

Principles

The principles for good order picking are as follows. Note that there can be conflict between some of them:

- There should be at least one location for every product line handled, but within the smallest possible area.
- Movement of picking staff and replenishment staff should be kept to a minimum.
- Congestion should be minimised.
- The order picking and replenishment operations should be separated to minimise congestion and for safe operation.
- There should be no stock-outs.
- Required service levels should be achieved.

Number of locations

It can be appropriate to have multiple picking locations for those (few) 'popular' products in the total product range which are accessed very frequently. This reduces congestion and the risk of stock-out.

The number of locations in a picking face comes from such questions as 'how many days' (or hours') worth of stock should there be at the picking face?' ie what is a reasonable interval between replenishment? This is also influenced by the size of unit load in reserve storage, eg a pallet, and whether the same unit load is used in the picking face.

Minimise movement

Order pickers' movement can be a high proportion of their total time, eg one survey of simple picking systems gave a time breakdown of:

- movement – walking between pick locations – 38 per cent;
- paperwork – picking lists, etc – 27 per cent;
- non-productive time – waiting instruction, waiting replenishment, etc – 23 per cent;
- picking – 12 per cent.

Clearly anything which reduces the amount of movement is going to be beneficial.

Separation of reserve and picking stock

Movement and interference between pickers and replenishers can be reduced by separating order picking and reserve stock. This concentrates picking stock into a smaller area, but entails double-handling, ie goods-in to reserve stock, followed by replenishment from reserve to the picking face. Congestion at the picking face can occur unless care is taken in planning and sizing the picking face.

The separation of reserve and picking stock can be vertical, eg reserve stock in the upper levels of racking, with picking stock at the lower levels (see Figure 11.1).

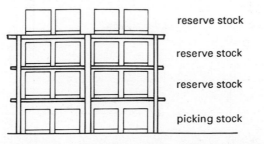

reserve stock

reserve stock

reserve stock

picking stock

Figure 11.1   Reserve and order-picking stock; vertical separation

Separation can also be horizontal, ie keeping reserve and picking as two separate, if adjacent, areas of the warehouse (see Figure 11.2).

plan view of pallet racking

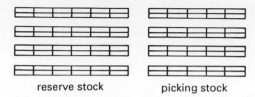

reserve stock   picking stock

Figure 11.2 Reserve and order-picking stock; horizontal separation

Order-picking system and stock layout

The order-picking system also influences the amount of picker movement.

A simple and obvious example is when a number of orders can be 'batched' and picked in a single circuit of the picking face, rather than picking only one order per circuit. The benefit is reduced total travel time, but clearly such an approach depends on the size of orders being picked, and the capacity of the trolley, etc being used for the picking.

Within the picking face, movement can be reduced by locating nearest to the order marshalling area those product lines which are accessed most frequently, ie 'popularity storage' (see Figure 11.3). The corollary is that products which need to be visited least often should be positioned furthest away. The ability to lay stock out in this way requires having data on accession frequencies for the whole product range, ie a Pareto analysis. Note that a high throughput for one product line may not be associated with high accession frequency – perhaps it goes out as whole pallet loads. Indeed a lower throughput as numbers of pallets used per week may be associated with a very high frequency of location visits (accessions), each one of which is small in quantity terms. Mechanised order picking, eg using carousels where the equipment moves the goods to the picker, rather

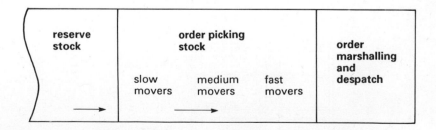

Figure 11.3 Popularity storage; fast moving stock is placed nearest to order marshalling and despatch areas

than the picker travelling to the goods, also minimises travel time and movement.

In general, the optimum layout for picking will be determined by the nature of the goods, the pick frequencies, and order sizes. Different parts of the range of products may well be held in different types of storage layout and equipment – APR, live storage, single row racking, etc.

Minimise congestion

Congestion can be reduced by ensuring adequate picking locations in the picking face, possibly by having more than one location for high access frequency products. Congestion can be reduced further by separating such locations, ie not adjacent, or even by having duplicate picking faces (see Figure 11.4).

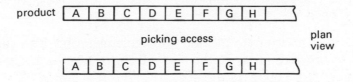

Figure 11.4 Duplicate order-picking locations; congestion is reduced by using multiple-pick locations and duplicating access for popular products

If an aisle contains fast accession rate products, and so has a high frequency of picking visits and a high replenishment rate, there can be congestion. Hence, separation of picking from replenishment reduces congestion, especially for the 'popular' product lines. One way of achieving this is to have rows of single deep racking in which every other aisle is for picking, the adjacent aisles being for replenishment (see Figure 11.5). This is a compromise between minimising congestion and achieving good space utilisation, and would be applicable to fast-moving lines, but not generally to the whole product range.

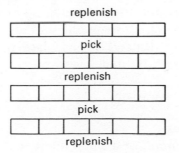

Figure 11.5 Separation, by aisle, of order-picking and replenishment operations to minimise congestion

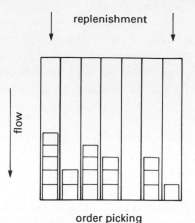

Figure 11.6 Separation of order-picking and replenishment using live storage (gravity rolls) for fast-moving products

Another way to separate picking and replenishment, also suitable for fast-moving product lines, is the use of short lengths of live storage (gravity rolls) (see Figure 11.6).

As one pallet or case is used up, the next one rolls forward by gravity to replace it. Such systems should always incorporate ways of removing empty (used) cases or pallets.

Separation or partial separation of picking and replenishment can also be achieved by off-set or separate working shifts, eg replenishers start say 1 hour ahead of the order pickers.

Avoid stock-out

This is achieved by ensuring adequate stocks at the picking face, and by an effective system of stock replenishment.

Replenishment can be planned, by calculating (usually by computer) when a picking location becomes empty. Alternatively, it can be by request from pickers, as a location becomes empty, or by replenishers noting empty locations, and then bringing up replacement stock. Radio communications systems are also used. Another approach uses the next working period picking demand to calculate the requirement for that period, and then replenish on that basis.

Methods of order picking

Consignee order picking

In this approach, one order, or a small number of small orders, is picked on each picking circuit. At the end of the circuit the order or orders are in separate containers ready for checking and despatch.

Batch picking or summary picking

For small sized orders, movement and handling can be reduced by picking a number of orders simultaneously during one picking circuit, followed by a secondary pick into individual orders. The increased length of picking circuit is more than offset by the reduction in the number of picking circuits required.

The secondary pick can be carried out immediately following the order picking, but can also, depending on such factors as the number of product lines per order, and per batch of orders, be carried out on the delivery vehicle at the customer premises.

Zone picking

This method applies where there is a large product range and high throughput. Each order is split down by picking zone and each part of the order is picked in that zone for subsequent collation before despatch. Goods can be laid out in popularity sequence within each zone to minimise movement.

Order picking information

The minimum information required by an order picker to complete the work is:

- picking stock location;
- the quantity of each product to be picked;
- the destination of the picked goods;
- action in the event of shortage/stock-out; and
- the next location to visit.

The processing and transmission to the pickers of customer order information can influence the efficiency of order picking.

Easily read and understood information should be provided, either as a paper picking list, or via a VDU mounted on the picking truck, or via a hand held data terminal. The sequence of routeing the picker to the picking locations should minimise the total movement required, eg the picking list in pick location sequence (possibly different from the sequence in which products are listed on a multi-product order). Location codes/ references should be understandable and unambiguous. Clerical work required of the picker should be minimal, if any at all, eg mobile terminals can eliminate clerical work. There should be no delays in the information systems – this can 'starve' pickers of picking instructions.

Bar code techniques also help to reduce error in order picking, and speed up the information processing by the picker.

Order picking efficiency

Order picking represents a significant part of warehouse/store operating (labour) costs.

The efficiency of order picking is measured by such parameters as:

- the pick rate – the number of picks per hour;
- order throughput/case throughput/pallet throughput;
- service levels; and
- the amount of stock-outs.

The importance of movement, stock layout, picking methods, congestion, replenishment and information processing has been emphasised. Other points include elimination of waiting time and balancing of work loads, eg between picking zones, minimising checking, optimising packaging operations downstream of picking, ensuring a smooth flow of work, and eliminating clerical work.

Space utilisation in order picking is not usually high. When a picking location is replenished the space is then fully utilised. As the stock is used the utilisation falls, eventually to zero, when the location is replenished again. If the usage of stock is fairly steady, and assuming no back-up stock (eg as in a live storage system), then the average utilisation of space, within the picking stock holding equipment, will not be more than 50 per cent.

CHAPTER 12

Warehouse Operations – Receipt and Despatch

This section deals with the goods inwards and despatch areas of a warehouse, where handling and movement take place both inside and outside the building.

There is potential for congestion unless the planning and operation are carefully thought out. Safety and security are also important at the loading bay.

Factors in loading bay design and operation

The main factors which influence what is required and how best to operate are:

- material and unit loads handled, and quantities;
- vehicle types and sizes, and vehicle movements;
- site access, and site roads and flows;
- areas for vehicle manoeuvre and parking;
- loading dock types;
- environment;
- control and security;
- loading bay equipment; and
- separate or combined goods-in and despatch areas.

Material handled

The material handled through a warehouse, the packaging, and the unit loads, all influence the requirements for:

- type of handling equipment for vehicle loading/unloading;
- space for palletising, depalletising, re-palletising and for empty pallets, roll cages, etc;
- space for marshalling vehicle loads prior to despatch; and
- quality control/check facilities.

The quantity of material passing through loading/unloading will influence the number of handling devices required, the manning levels, and how much space should be allocated for material movement, temporary holding areas – checking, marshalling and quality control.

Vehicle types and sizes and movements

Loading dock layout and capacity are influenced by the types and sizes of vehicle using the dock, and whether they are side or end loading.

The dimensions including platform height and turning characteristics are important.

These details can influence the type of dock – raised or floor level, the height and size of dock, the area required for vehicle turning, manoeuvre and parking, and road bearing capacity.

Possible future changes in vehicle size should be taken into account – hauliers and fleet operators will always tend to use the largest possible vehicles.

There is no 'formula' for calculating the number of dock locations required to meet a particular duty, but for a realistic assessment the numbers of vehicles using the dock facility, and the patterns of arrival/departure should be established.

For example, if a warehouse takes on average thirty vehicles per day for offloading, the requirements will be very different if the vehicles arrive evenly throughout the day, than if they all arrive, say, between 2 pm and 5 pm. Similarly, the peak figures, and expected growth trends for the future, would affect the requirements.

The more vehicle loading bays in a warehouse, the higher the building cost, and, depending on traffic movement, there can be a 'trade-off' between the number of loading bays required and the size of the vehicle marshalling area for vehicles awaiting loading or unloading.

Site access, site roads and flows

The required site access – turning in area, gate sizes etc – is influenced by the type and size of vehicles using the site, and by the nature of the access roadway to the site.

Site roads should be constructed for the size of vehicles and intensity of movements at maximum anticipated levels.

Blind reversing and cross flows should be avoided and flows should be controlled – white lines, mirrors for restricted visibility points, speed limits, and no parking on the main site circuit.

Pedestrian and vehicle traffic should be separated by pavements, barriers or separate routes.

In the UK, vehicle drivers are on the right side of the cab and site circuits should be clockwise, so that any reversing from the circuit back to the face of a building allows the driver to see back to the area into which he is reversing.

Vehicle manoeuvre, marshalling and parking areas

The amount of space required for these activities depends on the numbers and patterns of vehicle arrival, ie how much queuing will there be, the number of vehicle parking locations required, eg overnight.

It can be useful to allow for temporary marshalling of vehicles during document processing before and after loading/unloading. The vehicles to be accounted for include: own, suppliers', customers', and third party vehicles.

For all areas of vehicle holding and manoeuvre the use of marked lanes helps vehicle discipline and vehicles can be marshalled, or parked in various ways depending on site constraints, eg 90 degrees, angled, etc.

Types of loading docks

There are two basic dock types, ie raised or level docks. In general, raised docks are most suitable for vehicles which are loaded/unloaded over the end – box vans, swap body or ISO containers – because raised docks enable access for handling equipment into the back of the vehicle.

For flat bed or other vehicles loaded over the side, a ground level dock can be used.

Other factors are cost – raised docks cost more; safety – raised docks are potentially more hazardous; and site features – a sloping site can make it easier to incorporate a raised dock.

Ninety degree raised docks
Vehicles reverse up to the building face for loading/unloading over the tail of the vehicle.

The sideways spacing between vehicles determines how many can be positioned along the building. With close spacing, more vehicles can be accommodated, but the material movement on the dock face is more congested, and manoeuvring of the road vehicles requires more care. In addition, room has to be allowed in front of the vehicles for them to draw forward before turning, to avoid collision with adjacent vehicles as they pull out and turn (see Figure 12.1).

Angled-raised docks

If the space in front of a warehouse is insufficient for vehicles to manoeuvre up at 90 degrees, the requirement can be reduced by angling the dock face, although for a given length of building face, this accommodates fewer vehicles than a 90 degree dock. It also requires a saw tooth dock face (see Figure 12.2).

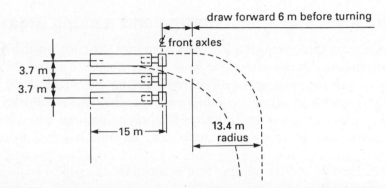

Figure 12.1 Parking of vehicles in loading docks. Reversed vehicles are parked at 90 degrees to the loading docks with sufficient room left in front of the cab for turning.

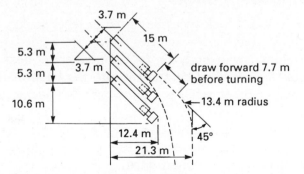

Figure 12.2 Angle-raised dock parking. In conditions of limited space angled parking is used with saw tooth dock configuration.

Level docks

The main point in setting out the area for a level dock, which is usually associated with side loading of vehicles, is to allow sufficient space for fork trucks to manoeuvre up to and away from the vehicle being loaded/unloaded.

Environmental factors

The loading dock is at the interface between the warehouse and the outside world, and the position of the loading dock should ideally take account of the prevailing wind, and on whether the site slope simplifies construction of a raised dock.

Enclosed loading bays
These are expensive and take up a large area of building just to house vehicles. They may need ventilation (vehicle fumes) and inevitably some dirt comes in from outside. The advantages are operator comfort and security.

Canopied loading bays
If canopies are built onto a warehouse, it is usual to provide five or six metres of cover, preferably translucent (for illumination). They should be at least 5 m high for containers, but higher clearances may be required for special box vans. The canopy should fall towards the building, to avoid water running on to the vehicle below.

Sunken vehicle access
If the dock access is set below ground level, to avoid the need for a raised dock, road slope should not exceed 10 degrees and a flat section should be allowed by the dock face so that vehicles are level when at the dock face. Drainage should be provided.

For specially cold conditions it may be appropriate to install heating wires, or non-slip surfaces in sloping road sections to prevent skidding.

Dock shelters
Totally enclosed docks and canopies are expensive. Where end-loading predominates, it is usual to fit a dock shelter at each door to form a weather seal. When the door to the building is opened the inside of the vehicle becomes effectively an extension to the building.

Various types of dock shelter/dock seal are available including sprung plastic 'plates' which seal by closing on the vehicle sides and top, and inflatable bags which seal on inflation. Dock shelters are only appropriate for box vehicles.

Other dock fittings
Dock access should always have lockable doors, which can be roll shutter – chain or power operated, sliding doors, or folding doors. Dock

bumpers can be fitted to the face of a loading dock to protect dock and vehicles. There are also devices which give drivers audible or visual warning of the closeness of the rear of the vehicle to the dock face during reversing.

Control and security

Loading bay operations involve movement – of goods, vehicles, handling equipment, people – both inside and outside the building.

There may be own employees, suppliers, hauliers' drivers, and collecting customers on site. Control is important.

Facilities can include supervisor's office with views to both inside and outside working areas, separate facilities for drivers to report in, with access to amenities but controlled access to the warehouse, and marshalling areas for vehicles in sight of the building.

Loading bay equipment

There is a wide range of equipment for loading and unloading operations. Examples include:

- devices for bridging between vehicle and raised dock including bridge plates and dock levellers;
- devices for access to vehicles from ground level – loading platforms – ramps – fixed or mobile;
- handling equipment – fork trucks various – conveyors various – cranes;
- mobile unit loads – rollcage pallets; and
- vehicle mounted aids – tail lifts – floor mounted conveyors – cranes – fork trucks.

Separate or combined goods-in and despatch areas

In general terms, if the areas for goods-in and despatch can be integrated, there are benefits in terms of potentially less total required area, common use of loading bay equipment, closer control, more flexible use of staff, better environment (only one end of building open to outside) and tighter security. It is often the case that vehicles delivering to a warehouse are there at different times from vehicles taking goods out, so a combined dock can provide more flexible and effective use of dock resources.

However, a combined operation can give problems of security and confusion between incoming and out-going goods, and would not be suitable if the sizes and types of goods-in vehicles are significantly different from the goods-out vehicles.

PART 3

Transport

CHAPTER
13

International Distribution: Modal Choice

Introduction

Within the UK, the transportation element of physical distribution is very heavily weighted towards the use of road transport as against the various other modes of transport. The trend towards the use of road transport has continued for many years and there is no indication that the importance of road freight transport is likely to diminish in the near future. Rail freight has continued to decline. Water transport, in the form of coastal shipping, continues to be significant. The use of pipelines has increased for certain specialised movements. Table 13.1, adapted from recent HMSO statistics, indicates the relative importance of the different modes for goods transportation in the UK.

Table 13.1: The importance of different modes of freight transport in the UK

Mode	Tonnes lifted (percentage)	Tonnes–kilometres moved (percentage)
Road	82.6	58.4
Rail	8.5	9.9
Water	4.1	25.9
Pipeline	4.8	5.8

For the movement of goods internationally, however, the different modes continue to be important. The selection of the most appropriate transport mode is still a fundamental decision for international distribution, the main criterion being the need to balance costs with customer service. There are very significant trade-offs to be made when examining the alternatives available between the different distribution factors and the different transport modes.

This chapter is concerned with the means of determining the choice of transport mode within the distribution environment. This covers the important operational factors that impose on the choice of mode, the characteristics of the different modes, and an approach or method for selection. Finally, with 1992 in mind, there is some comment on a European perspective of distribution.

Operational factors

Encompassing the many operational factors that may need to be considered are those that can be categorised as external to the direct distribution related factors. These are particularly relevant when contemplating the international context of modal choice because from country to country these factors can vary significantly. These include:

- basic infrastructure;
- trade barriers (customs duty, import quotas, etc);
- export controls and licences;
- law and taxation;
- financial institutions and services, economic conditons (exchange rate stability, inflation, etc);
- communications systems;
- culture; and
- climate.

This list can be a long one, and the relevant inclusions will vary according to the country under consideration.

The particular customer characteristics may also have a significant effect on the choice of transport mode. Most of the characteristics will need to be considered for both national and international modal choice, that is, they are not specific to overseas distribution. The main characteristics to consider are:

- service level/type of service location;
- delivery point constraints (access, equipment, etc);
- after-sales service needs;
- credit rating;
- terms of sale preference (CIF/FOB);
- order size preference;

- customer importance; and
- product knowledge.

From the modal choice standpoint, these characteristics can be classified into two broad areas – those related to customer service (speed, reliability, etc) and those related to physical attributes (order/drop size, location, delivery constraints, etc).

One categorisation of characteristics that is discussed in more detail in Chapter 22 is that of the product itself. Clearly, the physical nature of the product is of paramount importance in determining modal choice as well as other distribution functions. The main factors include:

- volume to weight ratio;
- value to weight ratio;
- substitutability (product alternatives, etc);
- special characteristics (hazard, fragility, perishability, time constraints, security).

The final series of important characteristics that need to be considered when determining modal choice concerns the company. In any distribution plan there will be a number of factors that are fixed or unchangeable – and others that are at least seen as sacrosanct by certain sections of the company. These factors need to be known. There is no point in designing a system or choosing a mode that fails to allow for these 'fixed' factors. Even so, it is important to be aware of the constraints that these factors impose on any newly devised system, as the cost implications may well indicate that a trade-off would produce a better overall solution. The main characteristics may include:

- product locations;
- supply points;
- warehouse/storage/facilities;
- own transport;
- marketing plans/policies;
- financial situation; and
- existing delivery system.

Transport mode characteristics

The decision so far has been concerned with the various operational factors that might need to be taken into account when determining modal choice. From the opposite perspective, it is necessary to be aware of the various attributes of the different modes. It is not possible to describe here the detailed operations of the different modes, but it is important to indicate their major attributes – specifically in relation to the factors described in the previous sections and also with respect to cost, service and the other distribution-related functions.

Of the main alternative types of sea freight, the conventional load and the unit load are the most relevant. The unit load (container) is considered later. For conventional sea freight, the main points are:

1. Cost economies – for some products, the most economic means of carriage remains that of conventional sea freight. This particularly applies to bulk goods and to large packaged consignments that are going long distances. Where speed of service is completely unimportant, then the cheapness of sea freight makes it very competitive.

2. Flexibility – there are very many liners and tramp ships, and very many ports, both large and small. In addition to this, sailings are quite frequent, so that sea transport is very flexible in terms of the number of alternatives that are open.

3. Availability – liner services are widely advertised, extensively categorised and most types of cargo can be accommodated.

4. Speed – sea freight tends to be very slow for several reasons. These include the fact that the turnaround time in port is still quite slow, as is the actual voyage time.

5. Need for double-handling – conventional sea freight is disadvantaged by the inefficient handling methods that still have to be used. This is especially true when compared with the more competitive 'through transport' systems with which sea freight must compete. The problem is particularly apparent on some of the short sea routes.

6. Delay problems – there are three major delay factors that can lead to bad and irregular services, as well as helping to slow up the transport time itself. These are over and above the journey time. They are pre-shipment delays, delays at the discharge port and unexpected delays due to bad weather, missed tides, etc.

7. Damage – the need to double-handle cargo on conventional ships tends to make this mode more prone to damage for both products and packaging.

As already indicated, road freight transport is the most important mode within the UK. In the context of international distribution, road freight transport is also important, particularly for the UK in terms of the use of roll-on/roll-off (RORO) ferry services. This form of transport consists of the through transport of goods from factory or warehouse direct to customers' premises abroad.

Compared with the other forms of international freight transport, the major advantages and disadvantages of these services are as follows:

1. They can provide a very quick service, if ferry schedules are carefully timed into the route plans.
2. For complete unit-loads, with single origin and destination points, they can be very competitive from the cost viewpoint.
3. There is a greatly reduced need to double-handle and tranship goods and packages, so saving time and minimising the likelihood of damage.
4. There is a great flexibility for through-movement as a unit load. This is so because the system combines the large routeing choice provided by a road vehicle with the short ferry crossings.
5. Packaging cost can be kept to a minimum because loads are not subject to the extreme transit 'shocks' that other modes can cause.
6. The system can provide regular, scheduled services due to frequent ferry sailings, and due to the flexibility of road vehicle scheduling.
7. The RORO system loses many of its advantages when used for less than lorry-sized loads. These entail groupage and so involve double-handling (at both ends of the journey), additional packaging and time delay.
8. Problems and delays can arise because paperwork systems are often unable to keep pace with the speed of the RORO through-transport system itself.

There have been recent developments in rail freight systems, including the development of containerised systems, using ISO containers as the basic unit load; the regular scheduling of rail wagon services; and the introduction of the swap body concept of transferrable road-rail units. The ISO container system has the particular attributes of all container systems as discussed later. More conventional rail freight systems have the major benefit of being a relatively cheap form of transport. This is particularly true for bulky and heavy consignments that require movement over medium to long distances and where speed is not vital. The principal disadvantages of conventional rail freight are as follows:

- Shunting shocks can cause damage.
- There is a need to 'double-handle' many loads because the first and last leg of a 'through' journey often needs to be by road transport.
- There are a limited number of railheads in the UK – many companies with railway sidings on their premises have closed them down.
- In general, rail transport is a very slow means of carriage.

- Rail freight transport is also very unreliable. Batches of wagons may arrive at irregular intervals. This can cause further delays for international traffic if a complete shipment is on a single customs document.

The use of air freight as an alternative transport mode has grown rapidly in recent years. Major developments in the areas of integrated unit loads, improved handling systems and additional cargo space, together with the proliferation of scheduled cargo flights have increased the competitiveness and service capability of air freight.

The major attributes of air freight are as follows:

1. Air freight compares very well with other transport modes over longer international movements. This is because it has very rapid transit times over these longer distances.
2. It is a very fast mode of transport. There can be delays at airports, however, and this factor can often make a significant difference to overall journey times.
3. One particular advantage is known as 'lead-time economy'. This is where the ability to move goods (and particularly spare parts) very quickly over long distances means that it is unnecessary to hold stocks of these items in the countries in question. The short lead-time that is required between the ordering and receiving of goods, and the resultant saving in inventory holding costs, gives this benefit its name of 'lead-time economy'.
4. The air freighting of products allows for a great deal of market flexibility, because any number of countries and markets can be reached very quickly and easily. This is particularly advantageous for a company that wishes either to test a product in a given area, or launch a new product. The flexibility of air freight means that the company need not necessarily set up extensive stock-holding networks in these areas.
5. The movement of goods by air freight can result in a marked reduction in packaging requirements. The air freight mode is not one which experiences severe conditions, and so its consignments are not prone to damage and breakages.
6. Air freight transport is very advantageous for certain ranges of goods, compared to many of the alternative modes. This includes those commodities with high value to weight ratios (a lot of money is tied up, therefore an expensive freight on-cost is not significant); perishables (where speed is vital); fashion goods (which tend to be both expensive and have a short 'shelf life'); emergency supplies

(speed again is vital); and, finally, spare parts (the lack of which may be holding up the operation of a multi-million pound project).

7. For the vast majority of products, air freight is a very expensive form of transport. This is by far its greatest disadvantage. In some instances, and for some products, cost is of very little consequence, and it is for these types of goods that air freight tends to be used.

8. Although air freight is very quick from airport to airport, there is a tendency for this factor to become less of an advantage because a great deal of time can be lost due to airport congestion and handling and paperwork delays.

9. Air freighting has suffered, in recent years, from having quite severe lapses in the security of the goods that are moved.

Container systems can be viewed as a specialised mode of freight transport, although the container is now a fundamental feature of all the major national and international transport modes – road, rail, sea and air. Containerisation makes possible the development of what is known as the 'intermodal' system of freight transport, enabling the uncomplicated movement of goods in bulk from one transport mode to another.

The main attributes of containers and container systems are as follows:

1. They enable a number of small packages to be consolidated into large single unit loads.

2. There is a reduction in the handling of goods as they are distributed from their point of origin to point of destination.

3. There is a reduction in individual packaging requirements – dependent on the load within the container.

4. There is a reduction in damage to products that might have been caused by other cargo.

5. Insurance charges are lower due to the reduced damage potential.

6. Handling costs at the docks and at other modal interfaces are reduced.

7. There is a quicker turnaround for all the types of transport that are used. Port utilisation also improves.

8. The all-round delivery time is speedier, so raises service levels.

9. Documentation is much simpler – this applies both to company and customs documentation.

10. The concept of 'through transit' becomes feasible, and allows for a truly integrated transport system to be developed.

11. In the early days of containerisation, the systems that were developed tended not to be well integrated across the different transport modes. This has considerably improved in recent years.

12. There is a need for special facilities and equipment, and these are

very costly. Thus, there are a limited number of transfer points available.

13. The initial cost of the containers themselves is very high.

14. The return of empty containers can often be an expensive problem. Trade is seldom evenly balanced so that return loads may not be available.

15. Containers may leak, thereby causing damage due to rain or sea water.

16. Loads may be affected by their position of stow, ie above or below deck, etc.

Method of selection

A fairly straightforward approach can be adopted as a method of modal selection. This is based on the factors previously discussed and is outlined in Figure 13.1.

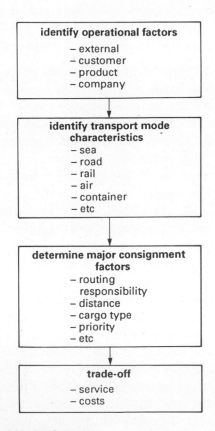

Figure 13.1 Method of Modal Selection

The major consignment or route factors are those that affect the decisions relating to the shipment in question. Often only a few of these will apply, but sometimes several need to be taken into account. The main ones include those noted below – together with examples of some of the more important questions to consider:

1. *Routeing and through transit responsibility*
   - Is a direct route stipulated?
   - Who is concerned with the through transit?
2. *Distance*
   - What is the distance to be moved?
3. *Type of cargo*
   - If bulk or general cargo, will a certain type of route be best?
4. *Quantity*
   - Full load, part load, etc.
5. *Unit size*
   - Small or large?
   - Will unitisation help?
   - Is groupage an alternative?
6. *Priority*
   - How soon must the goods reach their destination?
   - Does urgent! really mean urgent!?
7. *Commodity value*
   - How important is the transport cost element?
   - If import/export, how is the commodity rated?
8. *Regular shipments*
   - How often will these shipments be made?

The final decision is the customary distribution trade-off between cost and service. This must be undertaken in relation to the relevant operational factors, transport mode characteristics and consignments factors that have been outlined above.

European perspective

This is a particularly exciting period for the European logistics and distribution industry because of two major changes that are due in the next few years. The first of these is the Single European Market in 1992, and the second is the Channel Tunnel which was planned to open in 1993. Clearly, these two events will have a significant influence on the structure of distribution and logistics systems throughout Europe as trade barriers are broken down and new transport networks are initiated.

The relative importance of the different modes of inland freight transport is summarised in Figure 13.2. This illustrates the importance of road transport within Europe, but also shows that other modes are significant. The significance of these other modes would be much more emphatic if tonnes moved (tonne-kilometres) had been considered rather than tonnes lifted (tonnes). Nevertheless, Figure 13.2 demonstrates that both rail and inland waterways play a very vital part in European freight movement.

	rail	road	inland waterways	others
Belgium	14	64	19	3
France	12	78	4.5	5.5
W Germany	10	80	8	2
Italy	11	84	0.2	5
Holland	3	58	35	4
Spain	9	88	–	3
UK	9	87	0.6	3

Source: United Nations 1985

Figure 13.2 Relative importance of modes of inland freight transport for Europe (percentage of tonnes lifted)

The creation of a single European economy was one of the original intentions of the Treaty of Rome when the Community was established. Although some progress has been made towards this end – no tariffs between member states, common competition laws – there remain many barriers that prevent the complete flow of trade across EC internal boundaries. Progress towards an integrated single market has continued, however, and the Single European Act 1987 has put the target of 1992 into Community law as the date for the completion of this process. It is likely that companies of all types and sizes will be affected by the achievement of a Single European Market, such factors as economies of scale, larger sales volumes, and reduced product life cycle being just a few of the likely consequences.

The major barriers of trade that remain to be overcome include:

1. Physical barriers: removal of customs control and introduction of the Single Administrative Document; removal of immigration and passport control; harmonisation of public health standards.
2. Technical barriers: removal of all barriers in trade between member states; free movement of goods, capital, services and workers; harmonisation of technical standards; common protection

for intellectual and industrial property; opening up of public procurement.
3. Fiscal barriers: approximation of indirect taxation (VAT, excise duties); consequent removal of fiscal frontier checks.

Those provisions that are particularly relevant to distribution can be summarised as:

- goods and services can be bought anywhere in the community;
- customs barriers virtually abolished;
- simplified and standardised documentation;
- removal of operating (transport) permit restrictions;
- testing standards acceptable in all community states;
- free movement of capital; and
- harmonisation of indirect taxation.

There are clearly some significant opportunities for transport and distribution companies that will result from the Single European Act. These should encourage companies to develop the scope of their services across the community as a whole. These will include the following:

- more competition between third party companies due to the increased market;
- transport and third party distribution companies can give a more comprehensive European-wide service;
- the easier and faster movement of goods across borders;
- distribution and transport can be bought in any country – there will be more cross trading and cabotage (transport companies moving goods in other member states);
- there will be an incentive for joint ventures with other European hauliers to enable a European-wide integrated distribution structure to be realised; and
- new depot locations and consequent transport flows can be determined to suit both sources and markets.

Linked with these new opportunities for transport and distribution that the Single European Market will provide are the effects that the Channel Tunnel may have. The Tunnel should have the effect of stimulating and encouraging rail freight transport because of the new direct transport link between the UK and the rest of Europe. There is the potential for a reduction in the length of land transit times and also a reduction in costs. The possibilities for long hauls are significant especially with the use of ISO containers and road/rail swap bodies. The inauguration of the Tunnel should be an added bonus to the integration of the UK into the total European market.

Although new, purpose-built rail depots are to be constructed by the railway companies, there are some areas of concern over the extent of the effect that the Tunnel may have. Currently rail freight in the UK is a very small percentage of the total, and the UK road lobby is a powerful one. Additionally, the reputation of UK and continental rail companies is not good with respect to the efficiency and service provided by rail freight systems. Improvements in organisation, but more particularly in major capital investment in the rail infrastructure are essential if the Tunnel is to have a significantly beneficial effect for freight transport.

In summary, it can be said that the Single European Market and, to a lesser extent, the Channel Tunnel will provide important new opportunities for transport and distribution companies.

Summary

In this chapter the very broad area of transport modal choice has been covered although limited space has made it impossible to describe the detailed operations of the different modes of transport. Emphasis has thus been given to the decision-making process involved in modal choice, covering the following aspects.

- Operational factors relating to:
  - external environment;
  - customer characteristics;
  - the product; and
  - the company.
- Transport mode characteristics covering:
  - sea freight;
  - road freight;
  - rail freight;
  - air freight; and
  - container systems.
- Method of modal selection, indicating an approach which takes into account the main consignment or route factors.

From the viewpoint of the different modes of transport it seems likely that the higher productivity and adaptability of road freight transport together with the increasing demands on service levels will put additional pressure on rail, and strengthen the already strong position of road transport.

If concepts such as just-in-time continue to flourish with the requirement for regular, frequent deliveries, flexibility and reduced stock levels, then it will be less easy for rail and water transport to compete. The railway companies need to develop their intermodal systems to offer flexibility and cost advantages comparable to road freight transport and container services. For long distance movement, rail should be able to compete with road. Computerised systems should enable improvements in reliability and transit times.

CHAPTER 14

Road Transport: Vehicle Selection

Introduction

As with most of the decisions that have to be taken in physical distribution, there are a number of aspects that need to be considered when trying to make the most appropriate choice of vehicle for a vehicle fleet. Vehicle selection decisions should not be made in isolation. It is essential that all the various aspects should be considered together before any final conclusions are drawn.

There are three primary areas that need to be carefully assessed – efficiency, economy and legality.

Efficiency, in this context, means the most effective way to do the job, based on a number of important factors. These factors concern:

- the types of operation, ie the distance to be travelled, the types of terrain, etc;
- the type of load, ie physical features, weight, etc;
- the type of vehicle, ie chassis, body, etc.

The area of *economy* is concerned with the prices and costs of the different types of vehicle. There are a number of points that should be taken into account. These should be analysed and compared with the costs and performance of the various alternative vehicles. The main points concerning economy are:

- the fixed cost of a vehicle, ie the vehicle, the licences, etc;
- the variable cost of a vehicle, ie the fuel, the tyres, maintenance, etc;
- the utilisation factors, ie miles per gallon, cost per mile, etc; and

- the ways of acquiring a vehicle, ie buy, hire, etc.

The third and final area for consideration in vehicle selection is that of *legality*. This emphasises the need to ensure that vehicles are selected and operated within the existing transport legislation. Transport law is complicated and ever changing so constant awareness is imperative. The major factors concern:

- operator's licences;
- construction and use regulations;
- weights and dimensions of vehicles;
- drivers' hours; and
- drivers' records.

In this and the following two chapters, these various aspects are considered in some detail. This chapter is concerned with those aspects of vehicle selection which relate to the physical effectiveness of the vehicle for the particular job in hand.

Main vehicle types

There are a variety of vehicle types. It is important to be clear as to the precise definitions of each type because these definitions are used throughout the different areas of transport legislation. The main types are as described in this section.

The *motor vehicle* is a mechanically propelled vehicle intended for use on roads. Mechanical propulsion covers all those methods which exclude the use of human or animal power. Thus, a vehicle driven by petroleum spirit (the internal combustion engine), by gas turbine, by electric battery or by steam generation, is classified as a motor vehicle.

A *goods vehicle* is a motor vehicle or trailer which is constructed to carry freight. The term covers all such vehicles, but there are also distinct definitions that relate to the different weights of goods vehicles.

A *trailer* is a goods vehicle which is drawn by a motor vehicle. There are two main types of trailer:

1. A draw-bar trailer which has at least four wheels and actually supports its load of its own accord.
2. A semi-trailer which is the type of trailer that forms part of an articulated vehicle. This trailer does not support the load on its wheels, but only when it is standing, with the use of legs or jacks at one end.

As previously indicated, an *articulated vehicle* is a combination of power unit and trailer (ie motor vehicle plus semi-trailer) (see Figure 14.1). Thus, the trailer carries the load and the power unit pulls the trailer.

Courtesy of Renault

Figure 14.1 Articulated vehicle made up of a tractor and semi trailer

A *rigid vehicle* is a goods vehicle where the motor unit and the carrying unit are constructed as a single vehicle (see Figure 14.2).

Courtesy of Seddon Atkinson

Figure 14.2 Twenty-four-tonne rigid vehicle

A *small goods vehicle* is a goods vehicle where the permissible maximum weight does not exceed 3.5 tonnes. This weight includes the load and also any additional trailer that may be pulled.

A *medium goods vehicle* is one where the permissible maximum weight, including any trailer, exceeds 3.5 tonnes, but does not exceed 7.5 tonnes.

A *large goods vehicle* is a goods vehicle where the permissible maximum weight, again including any trailer, exceeds 7.5 tonnes.

The final definition, a *heavy goods vehicle* (HGV), is perhaps the most common. It is a more general definition as it includes all large goods vehicles as well as all articulated goods vehicles.

There are two main reasons why these definitions have been outlined so carefully. The first is to provide a clear definition of the main types of vehicle that are available. The second was mentioned earlier. It is to differentiate between vehicle types for the purpose of interpreting some of the legal requirements for transport. The two major vehicle classifications used for transport legislation are as follows:

1. A company must hold a special licence (an 'O' Licence) if it wants to use any vehicle that exceeds 3.5 tonnes gross weight. Thus, small goods vehicles are exempt from this requirement.
2. A driver must hold a special licence if he wants to drive a heavy goods vehicle (an 'HGV' Licence). This licence is required for the drivers of all vehicles exceeding 7.5 tonnes GVW.

Types of operation

Goods vehicles are required to undertake a wide variety of jobs. For each of these different jobs, it is important that the most appropriate type of vehicle is chosen. Some jobs or operations may require a vehicle with a powerful engine, others may necessitate a good clutch and gearbox because of high usage.

Consideration must thus be given to the type of work in which the vehicle will be engaged for the larger part of its working life, and also to the conditions under which it must operate. The most important classifications are described below.

Vehicles that are required to travel *long distances* tend to be involved in trunking operations. A trunking operation is one where the vehicles are delivering full loads from one supply point (ie a factory) to one delivery point (ie a warehouse or distribution depot). Such long-distance journeys tend to include a large amount of motorway travel, and the vehicle is involved in continuous high running, carrying heavy loads. Clearly, for this type of work, a very good 'work horse' is needed. As already indicated, it is likely that the load carried will be a heavy one, so a powerful engine will be essential. Articulated combinations are favoured for these operations.

Vehicles that are involved in *middle distance* runs (ie 100–200 miles per day) are probably delivery vehicles making one or two drops per day from a depot to large customers. Typical journeys might involve a mixture of motorway and A and B roads. The type of vehicle running on journeys such as these must, again, be a powerful one.

There are a number of different types of work that result in lorries travelling quite *short distances* in a day. The main example concerns local delivery work or what is often known as van deliveries.

A vehicle involved in this type of work will probably be making a large number of deliveries in the day, and so may only be driving from 40 to 100 miles. Indeed, in some city centre areas, the mileage may on occasion be even less. This type of operation tends to be concentrated in urban or city centres, although some of the delivery areas do involve rural settings.

One of the additional problems that this type of operation comes up against is the many constraints on vehicle sizes. Because of the problems of narrow streets, the banning of large lorries, and limitations on access at some delivery points, it is only possible to use vehicles up to a certain size.

The size constraints, the relatively short distances and the 'stop and start' conditions of town and city traffic are the main factors that go towards vehicle choice for this type of operation. As a consequence, the main vehicle type that is used is a rigid one with good gearbox and clutch mechanisms.

Combination running concerns operations that constitute a mixture of features. A typical example is that of the urban delivery vehicle which is working out of a regional depot. Such an operation involves a vehicle making medium distance runs to a given town or urban area, and then maybe six or seven drops or deliveries in that area.

There is a need to balance the requirements of distance running and local delivery, so a vehicle must have strong engine power, together with a chassis that does not violate any delivery size constraints. A small articulated vehicle, or 'urban artic', may be the most appropriate in this instance.

Multiple deliveries are made by vehicles where the distribution operations are concerned with the handling and delivery of many different types and sizes of commodities and packaging. They are sometimes known as composite delivery operations.

Typical examples are haulage contractors or 'third party' operators who run their businesses by handling and moving other companies' produce. Thus, they may get a wide variety of loads, and may have to run short and long distances and make single or multi-deliveries.

In this case, it is difficult to suggest any one type of vehicle that is the most appropriate. It is necessary to take account of all the different jobs that are undertaken, and then select a 'jack-of-all-trades' vehicle that can best cover them all, or provide for a mixed fleet of vehicles.

Site work is included as one of the main types of operation because there is a very high movement of sand, gravel, rubbish, etc to and from building sites and road works, etc. Vehicles that undertake this type of work are only travelling short distances, but the conditions in which they work are amongst the worst of all the different types of operation.

International operations also present some particular problems that need to be taken into account. It is likely that all types of terrain may be encountered – flat, hilly and mountainous. Distances will clearly be very long. In addition, it is important to minimise the likelihood of break-downs occurring in out of the way places where it may be very expensive to complete repairs.

Vehicles concerned in international operations thus need to be very powerful and very reliable. Such vehicles tend to represent the expensive end of the goods vehicle market. With the advent of 1992 and the elimination of European trading barriers, it is likely that this category of operation will become significantly more important.

Load types and characteristics

The particular load to be carried is another vital factor when choosing a vehicle. Once again, it is essential to consider the alternatives with the prime objective of selecting the best chassis and the best body that is suitable for the load. The principal load features are described below.

Light loads are those loads which consist of lightweight commodities which are extremely bulky. There are a large number of examples from the different industries. Some of these are:

- breakfast cereals;
- tissues; and
- polystyrene products.

The important point is that light loads such as these are high space users of vehicles in relation to the weight of the goods that are being carried. This is known as having a high cube factor. The consequence is that although a vehicle may have a high cube (or space) utilisation, it will have a very low weight utilisation (ie it is not carrying as much weight as it could).

Where a light load is carried, the consequent low weight means that the motive unit of the vehicle does not have to be a particularly powerful one. It is important not to over-specify vehicle requirements as the use of high quality, powerful equipment is very expensive.

One additional point concerning vehicle selection for light loads is that it is often possible to operate by using a large rigid vehicle together with a draw-bar trailer. This increases the volume capability.

Very *heavy loads* pose problems for vehicle choice due to the gross vehicle weight restrictions on roads and also due to axle weight restrictions. Some loads are even likely to require special vehicle construction, although special low loader vehicles are available.

Not all heavy loads are necessarily abnormal loads. For example, machinery that has a total weight within the legal limit can be carried on a standard trailer providing the weight is adequately spread over the axles.

The problem of *mixed loads* – where quite heavy products are mixed on the same vehicle as quite light ones – would not appear to indicate the likelihood of any constraining factors. The indication is that the mixture of light and heavy products would result in a balanced load where the total weight and the total cubic capacity are both about right for the vehicle, and this is indeed often true.

The problem that can occur, however, arises when a vehicle has to make a number of deliveries on a journey. What can happen is that the removal of parts of the load can change the spread of weight over the vehicle, and thus over the individual axle weights. These changes can mean that the vehicle suddenly has an illegally high weight on one of its axles.

This effect can occur for any delivery vehicle. When there is a mixed load of light and heavy goods, it can be much worse because of the variable spread of the load within the vehicle. Where this effect is likely to be a problem, it is important to select the most appropriate vehicle chassis and body from the outset, so that the problem can be overcome.

All *valuable loads* represent some sort of security risk. Vehicle selection must, therefore, take this into account. There may be a need for a special chassis or body construction. It should be appreciated that valuable loads are not just the more obvious ones such as money or jewellery. Many consumer products, when made up into a large vehicle consignment, represent a very high value. Examples include wine and spirits, electrical goods, clothing, etc. Thus, it is very often important to select vehicles which can be easily but securely locked during the course of daily delivery work.

Liquids and powders in bulk have to be carried by road tank wagons that are specially constructed. They are subject to the construction and use regulations. These regulations are related to the type of commodity that is to be carried. It is also important in vehicle selection to ensure that the correct input and output mechanisms are provided. For example, some products can be manoeuvred by gravity alone, while others require a variety of loading and discharging mechanisms for pumping products on to and off the vehicle.

The bulk movement of *hazardous goods* by road is carried out by road tanker, so the particular considerations for liquids and powders mentioned above apply automatically. In addition, the fact that hazardous substances are of a high risk means that care must be taken to select the correct material or lining for the tanker so as to avoid any potential chemical reaction. Another point to note is that special fitments may be necessary to stop electrical flashes from the vehicle's engine igniting inflammable goods.

Main types of vehicle body

The decision on the most suitable type of body to select for a vehicle should be based on both the operating and the load requirements. The various body types have particular advantages and disadvantages according to the work that is to be undertaken and the products that are to be carried.

Nearly all of the different vehicle bodies that are considered below can be fitted either to a rigid vehicle or to an articulated trailer.

A *box* is an enclosed body which normally has a sliding door at the rear, often known as a box-van (see Figure 14.3). As an alternative, some box vans may be fitted with side doors instead of or as well as doors at the rear. One common feature is the hydraulic tail-gate lift. This enables the load to be moved from the bed height to the ground automatically by lowering the tail-gate.

Box vans are by far the most common body type for urban delivery vehicles, especially for those delivering consumer products, food and packaged items. Their advantage lies in the protection to be gained from all types of weather, and also from the reduced risk of pilferage, because they are enclosed and so can be made secure.

Large box vans are also now in very common use for trunking

Courtesy of Seddon Atkinson

Figure 14.3 Articulated combination with 38-tonne tractor and enclosed box van body on the trailer. Access is from the rear

operations. The reasons are similar to those given for urban delivery vehicles. This additional popular usage has come about due to the great increase in the use of the wooden pallet as a unit load, and the fact that box vans with reinforced floors can be readily loaded by fork trucks.

The *platform* or flat bed is the traditional body type (see Figure 14.4). It merely consists of a wooden base above the skeletal trailer, with a range of heights of wooden sides and rear. It is, of course, uncovered. It is still in common use for many raw materials and products which are unaffected by inclement weather. The majority of loads need to be roped and sheeted; a skilled but time-consuming occupation.

Courtesy of Renault

Figure 14.4 Platform or flat bed rigid vehicle with wooden sides and rear

The *road tanker* is another very common vehicle. The tank body can be used to carry a variety of liquids and powders. The different requirements for loading and discharging tankers, and the problems of harzardous goods in terms of selecting the correct material or lining, were indicated previously in this chapter.

The *tilt* body is quite a recent innovation. The tilt is a curtain-sided vehicle which broadly consists of a fabric cover over a framework which is secured to the platform of a lorry (see Figure 14.5). This fabric cover can be drawn together to cover the load completely and then fixed by lacing or strapping down the length of each side of the vehicle.

Courtesy of Ferrymasters

Figure 14.5 Articulated vehicle with tilt soft top on trailer which provides all-round flexibility for loading and unloading

In appearance, a tilt body is very much like a box van, although the sides of the tilt van are, of course, made of flexible curtain fabric. The initial introduction of the tilt body was to eliminate the need for loads to be roped and sheeted, and thus to save considerably on loading and unloading times. The tilt is often called a 'tautliner' which is the trade name of the first curtain-sided body to be developed.

In addition, *curtain-sided* bodies are also used and have become very popular in recent years. They are different from tilt bodies in that they have a rigid roof, and one movable curtain each side of the body (see Figure 14.6).

Tipper is the description that applies to vehicles that have the capacity to tip loads directly. They are normally worked hydraulically, and are used to discharge a variety of bulk materials. Typical examples are grain, gravel, sand, etc. They may be covered, dependent on the particular characteristics of the product that is carried.

Courtesy of Seddon Atkinson

Figure 14.6 Curtain-sided trailer giving easy access to the load

As previously indicated, the *low loader* is used for the carriage of specifically large or heavy loads.

There are several other vehicle bodies that are used to carry certain types of product. These are basically self explanatory, but in their construction they do reflect the special needs and requirements of the products concerned (see Figures 14.7 and 14.8). Typical examples are those bodies used for livestock, furniture, hanging garments and refrigerated products.

Courtesy of Seddon Atkinson

Figure 14.7 Seventeen-tonne rigid vehicle with maximum cube body for high volume/low density goods

The final vehicle body to be considered is also a fairly recent alternative. This is the *demountable* box-van or 'swap' body which is used in a similar way to a standard container. The demountable body can be carried directly on the platform or flatbed of the vehicle or can be mounted on the

Courtesy of Seddon Atkinson

Figure 14.8 Rigid vehicle with specially produced dropframe body to facilitate loading and unloading the vehicle

skeletal chassis. In direct contrast to the container, however, the body is removed by the use of jacks which are positioned at each corner of the demountable, and are then raised, allowing the vehicle to drive away.

There are a number of ways of removing the body. These may include screw-type jacks, power or hand operated hydraulic jacks, electrically operated portable jacks, or power operated lifting equipment fitted to the chassis of the vehicle.

Demountable systems provide an increased flexibility to distribution operations by improving vehicle utilisation and fleet economy.

The wider implications of vehicle selection

There are several additional points that should be considered when choosing a vehicle. Some of these are clearly associated with those factors and features that have already been discussed; some reflect quite clearly the wider implications of vehicle selection; and others show how it is possible to use knowledge and experience to help in decision making.

These associated factors can be summarised as follows.

Is there a proven model or make of vehicle which is known from experience will be good at the job in question? This knowledge may be obtained from looking at other depots and their fleets from within the same company, it may be available from studying similar types of operation that are undertaken by other companies, or by reference to the trade press.

Similarly, it may be possible to assess the reliability of certain models and types of engine, etc by analysing the past history of similar vehicles. Thus various measures of performance can be produced and studied to give useful data on fuel economy, breakdowns, cost of maintenance, etc. Where information is not available from own company records, it is still possible to use a variety of published data that is available from the commercial press and other sources. Some companies now use fleet management computer packages to provide this type of historical information.

In selecting a vehicle, it is important to be aware of the need to undertake maintenance and repairs. If a depot has its own maintenance facilities or garage available then this is not a great problem. The likely problems can and do arise for companies which do not have their own facilities, and discover that the nearest dealer or garage with appropriately trained mechanics for their make of lorry is situated at a great distance from the depot itself.

One area which is difficult to cater for, but must nevertheless be borne in mind, is that of likely future transport legislation that might affect the choice of vehicle. There are a number of factors that may be of importance such as the construction and use regulations, drivers' hours, maximum vehicle weights, etc.

Another point concerns the driver himself. It should be remembered that it is the driver who has to work with the vehicle every day of his working life. He will understand many of the particular operational problems involved with the work that he has to do, and he will undoubtedly have an opinion on the 'best' type of vehicle from his point of view. It makes good sense to listen to his viewpoint. At least, it is important to consider the safety and comfort of the driver in this work.

The final factor for which allowance must be made is, in many ways, one of the most important ones. It has been emphasised that there is a need to balance a variety of operational and economic aspects to ensure that the lorry is efficiently run. Another vital factor to take into account is that, as well as loading at the depot or warehouse, and travelling legally on the roads, the vehicle also has to be able to get into the delivery points. Thus the accessibility at the delivery interface is a very important consideration. It is essential to be able to provide a vehicle that is capable of doing its job.

Vehicle acquisition

It has been shown that the process of vehicle selection is one that requires a good deal of thought and analysis to ensure that the most suitable vehicle is used for the job that is to be undertaken. Having determined the vehicle requirements, the next task is to ascertain the most appropriate means of acquiring the vehicle. There are several options available — purchase, rent, lease or contract hire.

The traditional means of vehicle acquisition is that of *outright purchase*. This gives the operator unqualified use and possession, together with the choice of when and how to dispose of the vehicle. Discounts for cash may well be available, and there are tax allowances for capital purchases. The major problem is likely to be the lack of capital availability for purchases of this nature. Other ways of obtaining finance include bank overdrafts, bank loans, hire purchase and lease purchase. These have a clear cost associated with them, and, although allowances can be set against tax, the recent reduction in capital allowances has made other methods of acquisition more attractive.

The *leasing* of vehicles is currently a popular alternative. Here, the operator does not actually own the vehicle. With fixed term leasing, the operator makes regular payments over an agreed period when he has full use of the vehicle. The payment covers all the usual financial costs, and may cover maintenance if required. Finance leasing means that the operator covers the full cost of the vehicle over the leasing period, and so may be given the option of extending the period of use at a significantly lower lease cost. The main advantage of leasing is that the standing (fixed) cost of the vehicle is known, the disadvantage is that the operator must keep the vehicle for a prescribed period in which time, for example, operational requirements may have altered. In addition, recent changes in accounting practice (SSAP 21) mean that vehicles acquired on finance leases have to be shown on the balance sheet, so the rate of return on capital employed is reduced.

Due to the changes in accounting practice previously mentioned, the *contract hire* of vehicles has become a much more attractive option. Contract hire arrangements can vary from the supply of the vehicle alone, through maintenance, insurance, drivers, etc to the provision of a complete distribution service. Thus, there has been a rapid growth in third party distribution companies offering a variety of services. The financial advantages of contract hire include the release of capital and the easier, more predictable costing of operations.

Vehicles can also be acquired via *rental* agreements. The vehicle does not become the user's property, but can be operated as required. Agreements may include maintenance and driver. Costs are generally higher than for the other alternatives, but rental periods are often very short term, allowing the user greater flexibility, particularly providing the means to accommodate temporary peaks of demand. Costs are predictable and can be treated as variable for specific jobs.

Summary

It can be seen from the various sections in this chapter that there are a multitude of factors that need to be considered when selecting road freight vehicles. The alternative options have been briefly discussed under the main headings, as follows:

- main vehicle types;
- types of operation;
- load types and characteristics;
- main types of vehicle body;
- wider implications of vehicle selection; and
- lease, hire or buy option.

A more detailed discussion on these aspects concerning vehicle costing and road transport legislation can be found in the following two chapters.

It is sensible not to treat the answers to the vehicle selection question as being hard and fast rules. They should be accepted as guidelines to be followed but not as strict rules. It must be remembered that companies, applications, operations and environments are all different in their own special ways, and all guidelines must be adapted to suit them accordingly.

CHAPTER 15

Road Transport: Vehicle Costing

Introduction

At the end of every company's financial year, the company has to produce a financial statement which shows how well or how badly it has performed during that year. This is known as a profit and loss statement.

This statement is useful because it can show whether or not the company's fleet of vehicles has performed satisfactorily. There is a drawback with this type of financial statement, however. Although it provides a good picture of the overall performance of the company's transport operation for that year, it does not provide a detailed account of exactly where any profit or loss is made within the operation itself.

In short, it fails to give sufficient details of each vehicle and its operation to enable good control of the transport fleet.

There is another problem. The final profit and loss statement is produced after the financial year has ended. Because of this, it is too late for management to make any effective changes to the transport operation if the results show that its performance is not acceptable.

The statement, therefore, fails to provide its information in sufficient time for any useful changes to be made.

In summary, there are two main reasons why a special form of cost reporting would be beneficial to a manager who is running a transport operation. These are:

1. The need to know the details of the vehicle and fleet performance in order to control the operations.
2. The need to know in sufficient time to make any necessary changes.

An example of how such a system might be used for monitoring and control is given below:

A weekly system of reports for every vehicle in a fleet will show, amongst other things, how many miles the vehicle has travelled and how much money has been paid out for fuel for this vehicle.

For several weeks, the fuel costs for this vehicle may be very similar week on week. All of a sudden, the fuel cost increases considerably. Is this important? What can be done about it?

There are a number of reasons why this might have happened.

- The cost of fuel per gallon might have increased.
- The vehicle might have travelled more miles in this week, and so used more fuel.
- The vehicle might not be performing properly, so its fuel consumption per mile has increased.

It is important to know the true reason and a number of checks can be made.

- The cost of fuel – this may not have changed.
- The vehicle mileage – the vehicle may not have run significantly more miles than usual.
- The amount of fuel used measured against the mileage travelled will give the vehicle miles per gallon. This may show that the vehicle is travelling fewer miles per gallon than in previous weeks.

It can be concluded that the reason for the increase in the money paid out for fuel is not a rise in the cost of fuel, not an increase in miles travelled by the vehicle, but it is because there is a fault in the vehicle. With this knowledge, the necessary steps can be put in motion to remedy the problem.

This example shows how useful an efficient costing system can be. In particular, it illustrates three important aspects of a good costing system.

1. To know, very quickly, that something is wrong.
2. To be able to identify where the problem lies.
3. To be able to take some form of remedial action and to solve the problem.

The main types of costing system

It has already been indicated that a good costing system can provide the means to make effective use of and keep adequate control over transport resources. Another important use for costing systems concerns the need to ensure that customers are being charged a sufficient price to cover the cost of the transport operation.

This type of costing system concerns the budgeting of costs in order to be able to determine an adequate rate at which to charge for the use of vehicles. For own account fleets this will enable a company to determine an appropriate cost to add to the price of the product or order to ensure that all own transport costs are covered.

Two types or aspects of a costing system have been identified as follows:

1. The recording of actual costs and performance in order to monitor and control the transport operation.
2. The budgeting for a job, or the amount to allow to cover costs.

Both of these types of costing system require the same detailed collection of cost information. This information concerns the resources that are used in a transport operation.

The types of transport resources that need to be considered are:

- men;
- machinery;
- materials; and
- money.

In order to be able to understand how costing systems can be used, it is helpful to be aware of common costing terminology in transport. These are described as follows.

A '*cost unit*' which is a unit of quantity in which costs may be derived or expressed.
Examples include:

- miles run;
- tonne-miles;
- packages.

A '*cost centre*' which is a piece of equipment, a location or a person against which costs are charged.
Examples include:

- a lorry;
- a fleet of lorries;
- a driver.

A '*direct cost*' which is a cost that is directly attributable to a cost centre. Example: if a lorry were a cost centre, then direct costs would include

- fuel;
- road licence;
- insurance.

'*Indirect costs*' which are the general costs that result from running a business. They are also referred to as overhead costs, administrative costs or establishment costs. These costs have to be absorbed or covered in the rates charged to the customer. Thus, they need to be spread equally amongst the vehicles in the fleet.
Examples include:

- office staff wages;
- telephone charges;
- advertising.

'*Fixed costs*' refer to the cost centre itself (ie the vehicle). These costs will not vary over a fairly long period of time (say, a year) and they are not affected by the activity or the mileage that the vehicle runs over this period. They are very often, in transport, referred to as *standing costs*.
Examples include:

- operator's licence;
- insurance

A '*variable cost*' is the opposite of a fixed cost in that it varies in relation to the activity or mileage of the vehicle. Thus, it varies according to the amount that the vehicle is used. It is sometimes known as a *running cost*.
Examples include:

- fuel;
- oil.

It should be noted that some cost factors can be defined as direct costs, and then classified once again either as a fixed or as a variable cost. In the examples above, fuel is both a direct cost (it is directly attributable to the lorry as its cost centre) and a variable cost (the amount used varies according to the mileage that the vehicle runs).

Vehicle standing costs

In this section consideration is given to the different resources that are included as vehicle standing costs. Each of these resources is necessary, regardless of the extent to which the vehicle is used. Thus, these resources are a cost that must be borne whether the vehicle is run for 5 or for 500 miles in any working week.

1. The vehicle is an expensive piece of equipment that in most companies is expected to last from about five to eight years. The working life of a lorry is dependent on the type of job that it has to do. A local delivery vehicle may carry relatively light loads and travel only 15,000 miles in a year. A long-distance trunking vehicle may be pulling heavy loads, and may be running for 50,000 miles a year.

   Whatever the working life of the vehicle, it is necessary to take account of its cost over the period of its expected life. One reason for this is so that appropriate costs can be recovered for the service that the vehicle performs. Failure to do this might affect the ability to run a profitable organisation.

   The method of taking account of the cost of a vehicle is known as *depreciation*. This is a means of writing down the annual cost of a vehicle over its expected lifetime.

   There are a number of different methods that are used for calculating depreciation, and their use depends on the particular policy of each individual company. The two main types are:

   - the straight line method; and
   - the reducing balance method.

   The *straight line* method of depreciation is the most simple method of assessing the annual cost of a vehicle. It requires three figures:
   - the initial cost of the vehicle (less tyres, which are treated as a running cost);
   - the anticipated resale or residual value of the vehicle (ie the amount for which the vehicle might be sold at the end of its life); and
   - the expected life of the vehicle in years.

   The annual depreciation of the vehicle is then calculated by subtracting the resale value of the vehicle from its initial purchase price, and then dividing the result by the expected life of the vehicle.

Example

	(£)
Purchase price of vehicle	16,000
less cost of tyres	2,000
	14,000
less anticipated resale value	1,500
	£12,500

Expected vehicle life = 5 years

Annual depreciation
(£12,500 divided by 5 years = £2,500)   £ 2,500

The *reducing balance* method is a slightly more complicated method, but possibly a fairer one. The method assumes that depreciation is greater in the early years of a vehicle's life, and becomes less severe in later years. This approach mirrors the fact that repairs associated with a vehicle's early life tend to be few and inexpensive, and tend to increase as the vehicle gets older.

The principle for the reducing balance method is to write down the vehicle to its expected resale value at the end of its life. The same data requirements are needed as for the straight line method.

Example
£14,000 to be written down at 36 per cent per annum.

	(£)
Initial value	14,000
Year 1 @ 36%	5,040
	8,960
Year 2 @ 36%	3,226
	5,734
Year 3 @ 36%	2,064
	3,670
Year 4 @ 36%	1,321
	2,349
Year 5 @ 36%	846
Resale Value	£ 1,503

2. There are two main licences that need to be costed against a vehicle. These are:

   Vehicle Excise Duty, which is based on the maximum gross vehicle weight of HGVs and the number of axles. The amount varies according to a series of weight bands.

   The Operator's Licence, which is a legal requirement for the transport operator to run his business.
   The Excise Licence is by far the most costly of the two. The sums required can be obtained from the Vehicle Registration/Log Book and from the Licensing Authority.

3. The cost of *insurance* is also a fixed or standing cost. The actual amounts can vary for a number of reasons, such as:

   - the area or region of operation,
   - the number of vehicles in the fleet (ie discount);
   - the type of loads carried; and
   - the value of the products carried.

   The sources for these costs are from company records or directly from the insurance broker.

4. Most companies treat *drivers' basic wages* as a fixed cost because wages are payable regardless of whether or not a driver is actually 'on the road'. Basic wages are treated as a fixed cost, and any additions, such as incentive bonuses and overtime, are classified as a running (or variable) cost, because they vary in relation to the amount of work that is done.
   Wages and other related costs can be found from payroll records.

5. An allowance for *interest on capital* is frequently omitted from cost calculations, being included, in the main, when assessing the overall performance of the company. It is an allowance which is made for one of two reasons:

   - the cost of borrowing money (that is, the interest repayable on a loan); or
   - the cost of forgoing interest on a company's own capital (that is, the interest that is lost because the money cannot be invested elsewhere).

   Because each individual vehicle is treated as a cost centre, the 'interest' can be included as a standing cost. This cost will be related to the current official interest rate or the rate at which company policy states that the company can borrow money.

Vehicle running costs

This section concentrates on the second major category of transport costs – vehicle running or variable costs. A variable cost is said to vary in relation to the activity of the particular object with which it is concerned. The cost centre that concerns us in this instance is the vehicle or lorry. The activity of the vehicle is the amount that it is used, which is the same as saying the mileage over which the vehicle is run.

Thus we can see that the running cost is directly related to, and can be measured by, the mileage run by the vehicle.

Vehicle standing costs were defined as the fixed costs that had to be accounted for before a vehicle could be used 'on the road'. Vehicle running costs are the virtual opposite, being the costs that are incurred as a result of the vehicle being used. The major classifications of vehicle running costs are discussed below.

1. The cost of *fuel* is normally the largest of all the variable or running costs. There are two reasons why fuel is a particularly significant cost. First, because of the high fuel consumption of commercial vehicles (ie low miles per gallon), and second, because of the steep rise in energy costs since the early 1970s, although in recent years this rise has not been as marked.

   Because the cost of fuel is such a significant portion of running costs, it is important that its usage is regularly monitored. Excess use of fuel can be the result of a number of factors, such as:

   - fuel leaks;
   - a worn engine; and
   - bad driving.

   Because running costs are related to an activity (ie the mileage that a vehicle travels) they are measured in pence per mile or pence per kilometre.

   Example
   Price of diesel = 160 pence per gallon

   Vehicle's average number of miles per gallon = 8 mpg

   Cost of fuel, in pence per mile:

   $$\frac{160}{8} = 20 \text{ pence per mile}$$

2. The use of engine *oil and lubricants* is a very small variable cost. It is

important to be able to measure usage, however, because high consumption may be a pointer to some mechanical problem. The costs of oil should also be measured in pence per mile (eg 0.5 pence per mile).

3. *Tyres* are classified as a running cost because tyre usage is directly linked to the mileage that the vehicle travels. Tyre usage is recorded as a variable cost in pence per mile as follows:

Example
6 wheeled vehicle

Cost of tyres	£200 each
Estimated tyre life	30,000 miles each
Total cost of tyres (6 × £200)	£1,200

Tyre cost per mile

$$\frac{1,200 \times 100}{30,000 \text{ miles}} = 4.0 \text{ pence per mile}$$

4. *Repairs and maintenance* costs (including spare parts) tend to be the second highest of the variable costs, and are again related to mileage because vehicles are (or should be) regularly maintained after a given number of miles (ie every 6,000 miles).

There are three principal factors that make up these costs. They are:

- labour (fitters, mechanics, supervisors, etc);
- spare parts; and
- workshop or garage.

Records should be kept for each vehicle in respect of the work that is done. Other information sources include mechanics' time sheets, suppliers' invoices, parts requisitions, etc. Costs are again in pence per mile.

Overhead costs

The two cost elements considered in the previous sections, vehicle standing costs and vehicle running costs could both be classified as *direct costs* that relate directly to an individual vehicle.

Vehicle overhead costs are *indirect costs* because they do not relate directly to an individual vehicle, but are costs that are borne by the whole fleet of vehicles. There are fleet overheads and business overheads.

1. Fleet overhead costs consist of the costs of all the 'back up' or 'reserve' equipment and labour that is required to run an efficient fleet of vehicles. As such, they cannot be costed directly to a particular vehicle. The main resources are spare tractors, spare trailers and spare drivers.

    These are over and above what are called the 'on-the-road' requirements. The spare equipment is necessary to cover for the other vehicles as they are repaired or maintained, or if there is a breakdown. The spare drivers are necessary to cover for holidays and sickness during the year. These 'spares' are apportioned by taking the total cost over a period (eg a year) and then dividing by the number of vehicles in the fleet.

2. Business overheads can be subdivided into transport department and company administrative overheads.

    Transport department overheads consist of the charges and costs that are clearly concerned with the transport department, but which cannot be directly related to any one vehicle (ie salaries and wages, cars and expenses, telephone, telex, rent and rates, and training).

    Company administrative overheads are those costs that are central to the running of a business, and which have to be apportioned between all the different company departments. They include, for example, directors' fees, legal fees, bad debts and bank charges.

Costing the total transport operation

This final section draws all the previous information together, so that it is possible to determine how to cost the total transport operation. The first step that must be taken is to estimate the likely vehicle utilisation. This is essential so that vehicle costs can be divided according to the activity of the vehicle. The estimate should be based on the past history of vehicle usage and on any likely increase or decrease in this usage that might be foreseen.

There are two areas of utilisation that need to be determined. These are for days worked in the year and mileage driven per year. Past history will indicate what the figures might be. Typical examples are:

- Number of working days per year, ie
  48 weeks × 5 days   = 240 days/year
- Estimated annual mileage   = 30,000 miles

It is possible to determine the costs for the three main cost elements, as illustrated in the following example:

1. *Standing cost*

   Annual standing cost $\quad= £9,000$

   Therefore, $\dfrac{£9,000}{240 \text{ days}} = £37.50$ per day

   or, $\quad\dfrac{9,000}{30,000 \text{ miles}} = 30$ pence per mile

so the standing cost can be expressed on a daily basis or on an average mileage basis.

2. *Running cost*

	Pence per mile
Fuel	20.0
Oil and lubricants	0.5
Tyres	4.0
Repairs and maintenance	6.0
Total	30.5

Running costs should be calculated on a mileage basis.

3. *Overhead cost*

   Apportioned vehicle overhead $= £1,200$

   Therefore, $\dfrac{£1,200}{240 \text{ days}} = £5.00$ per day

   or, $\quad\dfrac{1,200}{30,000 \text{ miles}} = 4.0$ pence per mile

Similar to the standing cost, the vehicle overhead cost can be expressed on a daily basis or an average mileage basis.

With this breakdown of costs, it is possible to derive in detail the costs of different elements of the delivery operation that is being undertaken. If this is achieved, accurate and realistic charges can then be made to customers to ensure that transport costs are adequately covered.

If vehicles are allocated as a whole to a particular operation, it is easy to identify the appropriate standing, running and overhead costs, and to make the necessary charges or allowances.

Where vehicles are multi-user for a number of customers, a further breakdown is required to reflect the extent of usage by the different customers. This is likely to be related to the number of cartons that are moved (or kgs, cubic metres – dependent on the measurement in use) and to the number of drops that are undertaken.

Summary

This chapter has been concerned with the fundamental aspects of road transport costing – how these costs can be broken down, and what use can be made of this type of information.

The major costs have been categorised as standing costs, running costs and overhead costs and examples have indicated how these costs are made up.

Emphasis has been placed on the need to know the details of vehicle and fleet performances and the importance of gaining this information in good time. The two main uses of these types of costing systems have been identified as the monitoring and control of operations and the formulation of budgets.

A more detailed discussion on the monitoring and control of operations is given in Chapter 18. This shows how key indices for both costs (ie cost per mile, etc) and performance (ie miles per drop, drops per journey, etc) can be determined and used to help management ensure that the transport operation is run cost effectively, and that any changes in both cost and performance can be readily identified.

Finally, the advent of a number of specific fleet management and costing computer programs and packages has enabled costing to be undertaken much more easily and with much greater accuracy. These packages are outlined in Chapter 20 which considers information technology and logistics.

CHAPTER 16

Road Transport: Legislation

Introduction

The transport function welds together the production, processing, storage and warehousing functions of a company to form a logistics chain that bridges the gap between raw materials, supply and final customer.

There was a time when the transport manager's knowledge of his products, his company, his customers, his fleet and drivers, and the road system was sufficient for him to operate effectively, adapting from year to year to the changing demands on the transport function. Those days are past. The modern transport manager must now be aware of the rapidly changing and increasingly complex legal framework within which he must operate. Since the Transport Act 1968, there has scarcely been a year without a major change in transport legislation, as the list of principal Acts outlined below shows. The transport manager must ensure that he is one stop ahead of this legislation, so that when changes in the law come into force, he can adapt the transport operation smoothly to the new requirements. He must also be able to accommodate any future cost implications and, most important of all, anticipate the impact that changes in the transport operation will have on the rest of the company's logistics system. This might, for example, concern packaging, warehousing and customer service – or even the overall company distribution strategy.

This chapter is thus concerned with road freight transport regulations. As already indicated, a large number of Parliamentary Acts and Statutes have been passed over the years in order to control the operations of road freight transport. It is only possible here to look very briefly at the major legislative landmarks. The main emphasis concerns how the different elements of a transport operation are affected by the law – operating a fleet of vehicles, the driver, and the vehicle itself.

Three points need to be borne in mind concerning the content of this chapter:

1. The complexity of the law is such that it is impossible to cover every detail in just a few pages of text.
2. Although the text is as accurate as possible, it cannot be regarded as a legal work of reference.
3. The progress of law is such that although up-to-date at the time of writing, there will almost certainly be some factors that have changed in the meantime.

The main legislative landmarks

There are several major Transport Acts and some minor ones which together contribute to road traffic law and make provision for the control of the industry. The content of each Act is often wide and very varied. Many of these Acts are what are known as 'enabling' Acts. They allow for (enable) certain elements of the Acts to be implemented at a subsequent stage. This is generally undertaken by a Statute.

Since the UK became a member of the European Common Market, there have also been a number of EC Directives that have applied to this country.

The Principal Acts applicable to the operation of road freight transport are:

- Special Roads Act 1949;
- Motor Vehicles (International Circulation) Act 1952;
- Road Traffic Acts 1960, 1972, 1974;
- Road Traffic and Roads Improvement Act 1960;
- London Government Act 1963;
- Carriage of Goods by Road Act 1965;
- Road Traffic Regulations Act 1967 and 1984;
- Road Traffic (Amendment) Act 1967;
- Transport Acts 1968, 1978, 1980, 1981 and 1982;
- Vehicles (Excise) Act 1971;
- Road Traffic (Foreign Vehicles) Act 1972;
- Heavy Commercial Vehicles (Controls and Regulations) Act 1973;
- International Road Haulage Permits Act 1975;
- Road Traffic (Drivers' Ages and Hours of Work) Act 1976;
- International Carriage of Perishable Foodstuffs Act 1976;
- Criminal Law Act 1977;

- Refuse Disposal (Amenity) Act 1978;
- The Carriage by Air and Road Act 1979;
- Road Traffic (Driving Licences) Act 1983; and
- Road Traffic (Production of Documents) Act 1985.

There have been numerous Orders made under these various Acts. In 1986 there were, for example, 50 transport related Orders; in 1987, there were 34.

Legislation arising from these various Acts and Statutes has affected all types of transport in the UK. Outlined below are some of the major implications for road freight transport.

There are two parts of the *Transport Act 1968* which are applicable to road freight operations. These are from Parts I and V of the Act, and the main points are as follows.

The National Freight Corporation was constituted, and certain assets were transferred from British Rail to the corporation. Freightliners Ltd and National Carriers Ltd became full subsidiary companies of the National Freight Corporation.

Operators' licences were established such that every vehicle with a gross plated weight of more than 3.5 tonnes was to be authorised by means of an operator's licence. This was to apply regardless of whether the vehicle was run solely for the purposes of moving a company's own products (own account) or for hire and reward purposes.

Provision was also made for the introduction of some sort of control and special authorisation for large goods vehicles. A large goods vehicle was defined in the Act as one which carries over 11 tonnes of goods on a journey and exceeds 16 tonnes plated weight. A controlled journey was to be over 100 miles between places in Great Britain, where the goods stayed on the vehicle. This portion of the Act was never brought into being.

Another important element was that authorised officials were empowered to enter premises in order to inspect large goods vehicles and their associated documents.

Several parts of the *Road Traffic Act 1972* were particularly relevant to the movement of freight by road transport. The most important aspects were as follows.

The importance of the construction and use of vehicle and equipment was emphasised. Regulations were allowed which covered the construction of vehicles and trailers. They could cover such aspects as width, length, height and loads carried. Vehicles were also to have satisfactory test certificates and goods vehicle inspections should be recorded and kept by the operator of the vehicle.

A number of lighting provisions were made, including the details of obligatory lights and reflectors as well as certain other provisions. The regulations also covered the marking of overhanging and projecting loads and the imposition of additional requirements for long vehicles and trailers.

Special driving licences became necessary according to the class of vehicle being driven, and a number of factors related to these licences were included in this part of the Act. The driving of a heavy goods vehicle on a road without the appropriate heavy goods vehicle licence became an offence. A test of competency was introduced and, for certain offences, these licences could be suspended or revoked. An appeals procedure was established.

An authorised person or police officer was empowered to check a vehicle's weight by requesting that the laden or unladen vehicle be driven to a weighbridge and weighed.

An authorised person could require a driver of a goods vehicle to produce documents and licences which the regulations deemed should be in his possession. A vehicle owner must provide information to identify a driver when requested to do so.

The appropriate Part of the Transport Act 1968 was strengthened by Schedule 4 of the *Road Traffic Act 1974*. This schedule permitted a Licensing Authority to issue an 'O' licence for periods of less than five years, and to terminate a licence if it so wished.

An operator is required to inform the Licensing Authority of any relevant conviction. This should include irregularities concerning lorry routes and test certificates.

Lighting equipment and reflectors were included in the Regulations for the Construction and Use of Vehicles.

With the *Road Traffic (Drivers' Ages and Hours of Work) Act 1976* a table of minimum ages was introduced below which a person could not hold or obtain a licence to drive certain vehicle classes. In addition, the definition of heavy goods vehicles was redefined with respect to HGV drivers' licences.

A provision was included for the amendment of the 1968 Transport Act to allow for the EC Rules on drivers' hours to be extended to UK domestic journeys.

The *Transport Act 1978* makes certain provisions about the regulations of goods vehicles. It also incorporates a number of amendments concerning

British Rail, Freightliners Ltd, the National Freight Corporation and other public sector transport bodies.

The Act extended the powers of goods vehicles inspection by means of spot checks for mechanical defects and overloading.

The transfer of the National Freight Corporation to the private sector was covered in the *Transport Act 1980*. The Act also repealed the relevant sections of the Transport Act 1968 which related to the control and special authorisations required by large goods vehicles to operate over 100 miles distance in Great Britain. These sections were never, in the event, brought into being.

The *Transport Act 1981* covers a wide range of subjects relating to private, public and freight transport. On the private side, it deals with driving disqualification and introduces a new system of penalty points rather than the totting up procedure. There are also provisions concerning offences relating to drinking and driving, restrictions on the carrying of children in the front seat of motor vehicles, and a provision for the compulsory wearing of seat belts.

For road freight transport, a new basis for vehicle excise duty for goods vehicles was put forward. This would apply to vehicles over 1525 kg unladen weight. The duty would be assessed on a vehicle's gross weight and, for vehicles over 12 tonnes gross vehicle weight, also on the number of axles.

The *Transport Act 1982* includes a limited number of aspects concerning freight transport. The main ones are the transfer to the private sector of the annual testing of goods vehicles and the allowing of environmental considerations to be taken into account when considering applications for goods vehicle operators' licences.

This brief description of the relevant road freight transport factors outlined in the Acts gives an indication of how extensive and involved transport legislation and regulation has become. For this reason, in the remainder of this chapter, emphasis is placed on the way that legislation impinges in three main areas – the operator, the driver and the vehicle.

It can be appreciated that the operation of a road transport fleet has, in recent years, become an area in which successive governments have taken a particular interest. It is important that anyone responsible for road transport operations has a good working knowledge of relevant regulatory factors.

Operating a fleet of vehicles

Those aspects of government legislation which are relevant to the operation of a fleet of goods vehicles are outlined in this section. In particular the Operator's Licence and the Certificate of Professional Competence are considered.

Governments in the UK have, for many years, sought to control the road freight transport industry through the use of licences. In order to operate a fleet of vehicles, therefore, it has long been necessary to hold the appropriate licence.

One area of debate has been the basis on which these licences should be granted. The arguments have been between the 'Quantity' or 'Quality' licensing alternatives:

- Quantity licensing emphasises the need to restrict the number of vehicles and fleets that can operate.
- Quality licensing is concerned with ensuring that every operator maintains his fleet and vehicles to specific operating standards.

Quantity licensing ('ABC' licensing) existed in the UK from before the Second World War until the 1968 Transport Act, when the change to quality 'operators' licences' was initiated. The original ideal of quantity licensing was to protect the established haulier and the railways from undue competition. Licences were difficult to obtain.

Prior to the 1968 Act, the licensing system also distinguished between the 'hire and reward' or contract haulier, which carried other companies' products, and the 'own account' company which only carried its own products. The former type of company had to 'prove need' before it was granted a licence, whilst the latter had few problems.

The 1968 Act introduced the *Operator's Licence* or 'O' Licence which dispensed with the quantity requirements and with the differentiation between hire and reward and own account fleets. The sole criterion for obtaining a licence was the ability of the operator to maintain and operate his vehicles in a fit and safe condition in accordance with regulations and road safety provisions. A single element of quantity restriction exists in that the operator must state the maximum number of vehicles that he wishes to operate in the licence.

An additional change occurred from 1 January 1978 when, as a result of an EC Directive, a distinction was again made between the operator carrying other companies' goods and the own account operator. The former type of operator would require a 'Standard' licence and the latter a 'Restricted' one. The requirements for these licences were broadly similar – that the applicant should be of 'good repute', have sufficient financial resources, a suitable operating centre and adequate maintenance facilities. An applicant for a 'Standard' licence also has to employ someone who is 'professionally competent'.

The current position can be summarised by highlighting certain aspects:

- A goods vehicle cannot be used for hire and reward or in connection with trade or business unless it is authorised by an 'O' Licence (Transport Act 1968).
- Vehicles requiring 'O' Licence authorisation are basically those with a plated weight of more than 3.5 tonnes or exceeding 1,525 kg unladen which belong to the applicant or are in his possession under an agreement for hire purchase or are on hire or on loan to him. The applicant may be termed the vehicle user (Transport Act 1968).
- Applications for 'O' Licences must be made to the Licensing Authority (LA) in whose area the vehicle or trailer is to be based. The vehicle or trailer may be based at another operating centre for a limited period. It may only be authorised on one 'O' Licence at any one time (Transport Act 1968).
- An 'O' Licence is issued normally for a period of five years, but the LA may direct that a licence should expire before that time (Transport Act 1968).

From 1 January 1978 'O' Licences were divided into two categories, the 'Standard' and the 'Restricted' (Goods Vehicle Operators (Qualifications) Regulations 1977 implementing EC Directive 74/561/EC). The main points are:

- The *Standard 'O' Licence* authorises hire and reward and own account operations either nationally or both nationally and internationally.
- The *Restricted 'O' Licence* authorises own account only, nationally or internationally.

The criteria for authorisation for a Standard 'O' Licence are that the applicant:

- is of good repute;
- has appropriate financial standing;
- is professionally competent, or will employ one or more full time Transport Managers that are of good repute and are professionally competent.

There are thus three main criteria for obtaining a standard 'O' Licence from the Licensing Authority. Their definitions can be summarised as follows:

- *Good repute* – here, due regard is taken of any recent relevant convictions that have occurred concerning the applicant. A significant number may well affect the LA's decision to grant the 'O' Licence
- *Appropriate financial standing* – this is to ensure that the applicant either has, or can obtain, sufficient financial resources to operate his business in a satisfactory manner. The proper provision of maintenance facilities is relevant.
- *Professional competence* – only an individual can be professionally competent. A person can obtain a Certificate of Professional Competence if:
  (a) He/she was engaged in road transport operations before 1 January 1975 and claims 'Grandfather Rights'. This claim had to be made before the end of 1979. In this context, 'engaged in road transport' means that the person held a 'O' Licence or was employed as a Manager with responsibility for the operation of vehicles used under an 'O' Licence.
  (b) He/she holds an appropriate approved certificate which indicates that he/she has the skills in the subjects listed in the EC syllabus.
  (c) He/she holds an appropriate alternative qualification, such as Fellow or Member of the Chartered Institute of Transport, Member or Associate Member of the Institute of Road Transport Engineers, etc.

The driver

There are a number of regulations which apply specifically to the driver of a goods vehicle. These mainly concern *drivers' hours, records* and the *tachograph*.

Drivers' hours

The Transport Act of 1968, together with a number of supporting regulations, addressed the problem of drivers' hours. This particularly concerns the observance of proper working and driving hours by drivers. This legislation also made the drivers' employer responsible for ensuring that these regulations were adhered to.

EC regulations laid down that the UK should adopt the same rules as the other EC countries as far as drivers' hours were concerned. The Drivers' Hours (Harmonisation and Community Rules) Regulations 1978 were made to allow for the gradual change-over during the two years after December 1978. This was accomplished, and as from 1 January 1981 the rules became the same for the UK as for the rest of the EC. Drivers' hours of work are now governed by the EC Council Regulations 3820/85 which covers working hours, and 3821/85 which covers the fitting and use of recording equipment.

The Drivers' Hours regulations apply to the drivers of vehicles which have a permissible maximum weight over 3.5 tonnes, and they take into account any journey or part of a journey made within the EC. The driver is any person who drives the vehicle or who is carried in the vehicle in order to be available for driving if necessary.

Prior to the completion of the change-over from UK to EC rules there were three 'types' of journeys.

1. EC National Rules – which allowed the UK to make its gradual change.
2. EC International Rules – the full EC Regulations that now apply.
3. British Domestic Rules – which apply to a few exemptions (ie local authority vehicles, etc) and to vehicles of less than the 3.5 tonnes plated weight.

The most important category is now for National/International Operations and is covered by EC Regulations 3820/85. This applies to drivers of vehicles exceeding 3.5 tonnes permissible maximum weight. The major requirements are as follows:

- *Daily driving*: a maximum of nine hours which may be extended to ten hours maximum not more than twice a week. (The 'daily driving period' is the period between any two daily rest periods or between a daily and a weekly rest period.)
- *Weekly driving*: the driver must, after no more than six daily driving periods, take a weekly rest period.
- *Total fortnightly driving*: 90 hours maximum (thus, a driver can drive up to 56 hours one week but only 34 hours in another).
- *Driving time*: a total of 4.5 hours after which a break must be taken.
- *Breaks from driving*: after not more than 4.5 hours a break of at least 45 minutes must be taken. The break can be split into three breaks of fifteen minutes spread over the driving period or immediately following it.
- *Daily rest period*: in every 24 hours, the driver must have a daily rest of at least 11 consecutive hours. (Reducible to nine consecutive hours three days a week, to be made up before the end of the following week.)
- *Weekly rest period*: each week a daily rest period must be extended into a weekly rest period totalling 45 consecutive hours. (Reductions to 36 and 24 hours are allowable under certain circumstances.) (A week is the period between 00.00 hours Monday and 24.00 hours Sunday.)

Note that there are a number of specific exemptions to the rules outlined above.

Tachographs
EC Regulation 3821/85 covers the law related to the fitting and use of tachographs to record drivers' hours of work. All vehicles of 3.5 tonnes GVW must be fitted with an approved instrument to record the drivers' hours. There are a few categories of exempted vehicles.

The tachograph is a recording speedometer combined with a self-contained clock. It records information in graph form on a circular chart. The tachograph automatically records a number of factors including:

- the distance travelled by the vehicle;
- the vehicle speed;
- driving time;
- periods of work;
- breaks from work; and
- daily rest periods.

The tachograph is capable of recording four modes of driver activity, although only three of these are currently used within the UK. The modes of activity are: daily rest period and breaks, driving period, periods of attendance at work, and other working time (not normally used in the UK).

The relevant symbols are shown in Figure 16.1, and an example of a completed tachograph is shown in Figure 16.2.

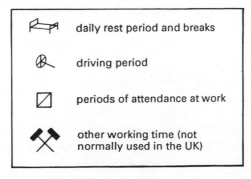

Figure 16.1   Tachograph symbols

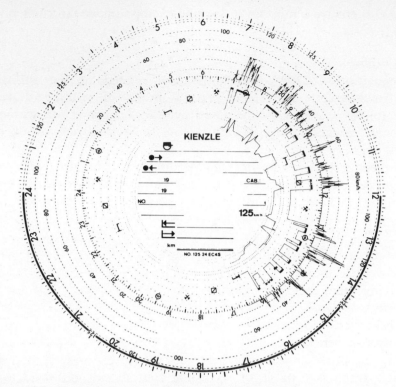

Figure 16.2 Example of a completed tachograph chart

The use of the so-called 'spy in the cab' was compulsory from the beginning of 1982 in the UK. The tachograph has been seen to be beneficial for a number of reasons. These include:

- better driving giving lower fuel consumption, engine wear, etc;
- improved planning and routeing;
- more effective vehicle maintenance;
- fewer accidents;
- more efficient administration and record keeping;
- guaranteed breaks and rest periods; and
- reduction in paper work for drivers, etc.

Drivers' records

Drivers of goods vehicles which are over 3.5 tonnes gross weight and are held on an 'O' Licence must all keep official drivers' records of the hours that they have worked, the driving time, and the rest and break periods. There is a major exception, and that applies to drivers of vehicles which are fitted with an officially calibrated tachograph. The tachograph records the relevant information so that handwritten records are not necessary.

Each driver must complete a separate record book according to the Drivers' Hours (Keeping of Records) Regulations 1987. The record book must be regularly countersigned by the employer, and when all the weekly record sheets have been used the driver must keep the book for 14 days. The employer must then retain the book for a minimum of one year.

A Department of Transport Officer or a uniformed Police Officer can inspect drivers' records or tachograph charts and detain a vehicle as long as is necessary for this purpose. Premises may be entered for inspection purposes.

The vehicle

Vehicle legislation is primarily aimed at restricting the maximum dimensions of vehicles, and the maximum weights of laden vehicles and axle loadings. Legislation is also increasingly geared towards restricting noise, reducing pollution and improving vehicle safety.

The main purpose of the legislation affecting goods vehicles has, therefore, been for environmental and safety reasons – a not necessarily bad thing in itself. It has, however, by its very nature, tended to be restrictive in terms of its effect on transport and distribution operations.

The agreement to raise the UK limit to 38 tonnes Gross Vehicle Weight (GVW) was thus a step in a new direction. It has been criticised by environmentalists as a retrograde step, but must be viewed against the prevailing European climate which allows for even heavier vehicles.

It is certainly true that this type of legislation which allows for an increase in gross vehicle weights is rare because it enables a potential improvement in transport performance for some types of operation. The majority of legislation has had the opposite effect of increasing costs and reducing operational flexibility. The addition of under-run bars, for example, is a very useful safety feature but has the impact of not only increasing vehicle capital costs but can also reduce the potential payload and thus increase operating costs.

Legislation affecting vehicles impacts, therefore, not only upon vehicle design and selection but also on operating costs and performance. Ultimately, this will affect the costs and service levels that are provided for customers.

There are a large number of regulations that affect the vehicle and they go into great detail. It will only be possible here to summarise the main points, to give a general understanding of what is covered. The rules related to the vehicle are generally known as the *Construction and Use Regulations*.

The construction of goods vehicles is controlled by a number of regulations whereby manufacturers and body builders concerned with the construction of commercial vehicles and trailers must observe, amongst other things, limitations relating to:

- the length and width of chassis and bodies;
- maximum weights in relation to vehicle wheelbase;
- lighting equipment;
- brakes;
- tyres;
- power unit capacity; and
- steering mechanism.

Owners and operators are also bound by these regulations whenever they use a vehicle on the road. Unless an operator alters a vehicle, however, it is unlikely that he will be concerned with the construction regulations. As he is responsible for maintaining the vehicle in a roadworthy state, the operator is very much concerned with the use regulations.

A Type Approval Certificate is required for a vehicle. It is in line with EC Regulations, and it counts as proof of conformity to the construction regulations.

The use regulations cover the use on the road of motor vehicles and trailers. Every operator has a responsibility for ensuring that all vehicles conform to the standards laid down. The regulations state that a 'motor vehicle, trailer and all parts and accessories, shall at all times be in such a condition that no danger is caused or likely to be caused to any person in or on the vehicle or on the road'.

The use regulations are very comprehensive and very detailed. They cover a wide variety of items of which the major ones are:

- brakes (ie a requirement for one system with two means of operation, or, two systems with a separate means of operation);
- braking efficiency;
- speedometers;
- mirrors;
- safety glass;
- windscreen wipers and washers;
- audible warning device;
- fuel tanks;
- silencer;
- excessive noise;
- emission of smoke;

- steering gear;
- tyres (types, condition, load rating, speed rating);
- spray suppression;
- power to weight ratio;
- under-run protection and sideguards;
- vehicle marking; and
- lighting.

Regulations and associated regulations are continually amended, so operators must take care to be aware of any changes.

Weights and dimensions of vehicles

There are various restrictions related to the weights and dimensions of vehicles. When a goods vehicle is 'on the road', the operator has the responsibility and the liability to ensure that the vehicle is operating legally and is complying with the statutory regulations.

There are four main areas to consider. These are as follows:

1. The maximum permitted gross weight for different types of vehicles which are:
   - Two axle rigid: 17,000 kg at an axle spread of at least 3 m.
   - Three axle rigid: 24,390 kg (24 tons) at an axle spread of at least 5.1 m.
   - Four axle rigid: 30,490 kg (30 tons) at an axle spread of at least 6.5 m.
   - Articulated Combination

     – with total of three axles: 24,390 kg (24 tons);

     – with total of four axles: 32,520 kg (32 tons);

     – with total of five axles: 38,000 kg (38 tons).

   - Draw-bar Trailer Combination: 32,520 kgs (32 tons) with power assisted brakes.
2. The maximum permitted gross axle weights are determined by axle spacing and tyre equipment. The 'imposed' axle weight is the total weight which is transmitted to the road by all of the wheels on any given axle.

   Axle weight limits are the permitted individual axle weights as shown on the vehicle plates.
3. The plating and testing of vehicles was introduced to ensure that any goods vehicle which was subject to the regulations was not operated above its maximum axle weights and gross vehicle weight, and that it conformed to the appropriate construction standards.

Motor vehicles must all be fitted with a manufacturer's plate which contains the relevant particulars demanded by the Construction and Use Regulations.

4. In addition to maximum gross and axle weight restrictions, there are also limits to the dimensions of vehicles. These are for maximum lengths and widths for vehicles and trailers and are outlined in the Construction and Use Regulations.

Maximum lengths for the main types are as follows:

- rigid vehicles: 11 m;
- articulated vehicles: 15.5 m;
- vehicles with draw-bar trailers: 18 m;
- draw-bar trailers: 12 m.

The maximum width allowed for most goods vehicles is 2.5 m (8 ft 2 ins).

The load

There is a jungle of legislation affecting the carriage of hazardous goods, with consequences for packaging and labelling requirements, the size of primary containers and gross allowance weights per load, the mixing of hazardous goods on the same vehicle and procedures for loading and unloading. There has been legislation to regulate the handling of a limited number of substances since 1881, and just over one hundred years later the myriad of laws, proposals and voluntary codes of practice testify to the vastly increasing complexity of the problem.

For all types of goods, there is an obvious impact of weight restrictions on vehicle loading in terms of gross weight limitations and axle weight limitations as indicated in the previous section. These factors impinge directly on load planning, itself an area that interacts very significantly with both warehousing operations and customer service.

Summary

In this chapter, the major legislative and regulatory factors affecting road freight transport have been outlined. As already emphasised, the complexity of the law is such that it has not been possible to include all the detailed aspects that may be relevant to the daily operation of a fleet of vehicles. There are already many texts available that provide this information and they are given in the bibliography at the end of this book.

This chapter has covered the main legislative landmarks and has also described how legislation affects the major aspects of a transport operation – the operator, the driver, the vehicle, and the load.

CHAPTER 17

Road Transport: Routeing and Scheduling

Introduction

This chapter concentrates on the need to provide an efficient delivery operation from a distribution depot. The reasons why the efficient routeing and scheduling of vehicles is so important are outlined, the main uses of vehicle routeing and scheduling are considered, and the major factors of road transport delivery are discussed. Finally, a simple method of daily scheduling is described, and manual and computer techniques which can be used for planning longer term requirements are outlined.

From the point of view of distribution and logistics as a whole, vehicle routeing and scheduling is concerned with the efficient organisation of road transport delivery to the final customer or retail outlet. Many large manufacturing, retailing and distribution companies have systems with many depots spread nationwide. Each depot will be responsible for supplying customers within a given region, that is, within the depot boundary.

This supply of products from a depot is often undertaken by a fleet of delivery vehicles which vary in size and capacity. Equally importantly, the particular demand for products from the depot may vary day by day and week by week. The main problem is, therefore, to try to deliver this variable amount of goods and products as efficiently as possible. 'Efficiency' in this instance can be many things, but it is mainly a balance between supplying an adequate service to customers, on the one hand, at an acceptable cost on the other hand.

Vehicle routeing and scheduling is a means of obtaining this balance between service and cost. In addition a great many other problems or constraints must also be taken into account.

The main objectives of vehicle routeing and scheduling

It has been indicated that the main aim of routeing and scheduling is to provide a balance between supplying an acceptable service at a reasonable cost. From the viewpoint of a depot manager or transport operator this can be stated more simply as follows:

> To plan journeys for vehicles operating from a single depot, delivering known loads to specific customers and returning to the depot after completing the journey.

Although this sounds relatively straightforward, it should be noted that there are a number of additional constraints which must be considered. Some examples are:

- weight or volume capacity of the vehicles;
- total time available in a day;
- loading and unloading times;
- vehicle speeds;
- traffic congestion; and
- access restrictions.

A fairly general definition of the aim of vehicle routeing and scheduling has already been outlined. This can be summarised as the 'best' use of vehicles when providing a particular delivery service (known as the 'optimisation' of vehicle usage). There are, however, a number of different ways in which this can be achieved, and any or all of these may be acceptable objectives for vehicle routeing and scheduling, depending on the particular transport operation concerned. Some examples of these different objectives are:

- to maximise the time that a vehicle is used (ie make sure that it is working for as long as possible);
- to maximise the capacity utilisation of a vehicle (ie ensure that all vehicles are as fully loaded as possible);
- to minimise mileage (ie complete the work by travelling as few miles as is possible); and
- to minimise the number of vehicles used (ie to keep the capital or fixed costs to a minimum).

Vehicle routeing and scheduling problems

Vehicle routeing and scheduling problems are relatively complicated. There are several reasons for this. First, the many detailed aspects which need to be taken into account (some of which were listed in the previous section); second, the various methods or algorithms that can be used to produce solutions; and finally the different types of problem which can arise, each of which needs to be understood and approached in a different way.

This latter point is an important one and the major differences are described below. There are, in fact, three main categories of routeing and scheduling problem:

- strategic problems;
- tactical or operational problems; and
- planning problems.

Strategic problems are concerned with the longer term aspects of vehicle routeing and scheduling, in particular where there is a regular delivery of similar products and quantities to fixed or regular customers. Typical examples are most retail delivery operations (such as grocery multiples), bread delivery and beer delivery to 'tied' houses.

The main characteristic is that of a fairly regular demand being delivered to virtually the same locations. Thus, it is possible to derive vehicle schedules which can be fixed for a certain period of time (ie three to six months). Some changes will be necessary as shops open or close, or as new products come on to the market, but, in general, the schedules can be maintained for a reasonable length of time. These schedules are drawn up on the basis of past or historical data. Strategic scheduling is now often undertaken by using modern computer techniques.

Tactical or operational problems are concerned with routes that have to be scheduled on a weekly or a daily basis. This type of scheduling is typically undertaken by parcels delivery companies, by companies supplying spare parts and by contract haulage companies who work for a number of different clients. The major factor of importance is that either the demand (quantity) of goods cannot be estimated (ie it is 'random' demand), or that the location of delivery points can vary – or that both of these occur.

Thus, for tactical or operational scheduling it is impossible (or very difficult) to plan delivery schedules based on historical information. It is necessary to look at each series of orders on a daily (or weekly) basis, and plan vehicle routes and schedules according to this ever-changing demand. This type of scheduling is normally undertaken manually by a load planner in a depot, but very recently due to technical innovations, some computer applications have become available.

The final type of routeing and scheduling problem concerns planning and the measurement of the effect of change. This use of routeing and scheduling has really come into its own as a result of the development of computer-based techniques. As indicated, models may be used to test or simulate the effect of changing demand, new products, vehicle development, etc.

One important planning aspect using computer routeing and scheduling is as part of much broader studies concerning total distribution and logistics systems. Associated with this type of use is that of determining the importance of the different cost elements that go to make up a delivery transport operation. Routeing and scheduling models can help to identify high cost areas, which can subsequently become specifically monitored and controlled.

The actual method used for routeing and scheduling vehicles varies according to the nature and difficulty of the problem, and whether a manual or computer-based approach is adopted. Each different method is known as an *algorithm*. The earliest, and most common algorithm is the savings method.

The samings method can be explained by a relatively simple example, as indicated in Figure 17.1. Depot O services two delivery points, A and B. The distances between these two delivery points OA, OB and AB are *a*, *b* and *c* respectively. If each delivery point is served by a single vehicle from the depot, then the total distance is $2a + 2b$. If only one vehicle is used in a single trip then the total distance covered is $a + b + c$. The savings achieved by linking together the two delivery points A and B are thus:

$$(2a + 2b) - (a + b + c) = a + b - c$$

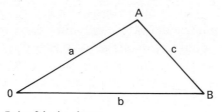

Point 0 is the depot
Points A and B are delivery points
a, b and c represent the distances between points

Figure 17.1 The savings method. In this example the savings effected by linking together A and B are a+b−c

In any problem with a significantly large number of delivery locations the advantage of using a computer is quite obvious. The distance between every delivery location is recorded. A 'savings matrix' is then generated, recording the savings made by linking together each of these pairs of locations. Taking the link with the highest potential saving first, and then adding successive links, a route is put together, measured against the vehicle capacity and driver time constraints. Eventually all delivery points will be allocated to a vehicle route, and the schedule will be complete.

As indicated previously, other algorithms have been developed and are used in the many different computer packages that are available.

Major characteristics of road transport delivery

It has already been noted that there are many different factors which need to be taken into account when planning the delivery operation of a road transport fleet. It is relevant here to consider these major characteristics. It is important to understand that the advent of new computer techniques has enabled many more detailed aspects to be analysed, which more simple manual methods are unable to include.

As well as the basic demand data, the different characteristics of road transport delivery can be split into five major sections, as follows:

- distance factors;
- customer constraints;
- vehicle restrictions;
- route factors; and
- product/unit load constraints.

The most important data requirement is for *demand data*. Where possible this should be for weekly or annual demand by customer at the point of delivery. This can often be the most difficult data item to collect, will certainly be the most time consuming, and will also require the most manipulation and clarification prior to use within the manual method or computer package. It may be necessary to undertake additional analyses (and collect additional data) to take account of peak demand periods because they are likely to require different schedules.

There are several ways in which demand data can be represented, some of which are far more appropriate for modelling distribution-related problems. Often, however, the most appropriate choice of data is not available, so second or even third choice has to be sufficient. Examples include:

- product item (generally too detailed);
- product group;
- weight (per product or as a tonnage figure);

- cube;
- carton/case/parcel (common in retail distribution);
- unit load (ie pallet, roll cage); and
- value in revenue or sales (rarely appropriate due to the problem of interpreting as a physical measure).

Demand data can also be organised or classified in a variety of ways. Certain computer packages are more amenable to some classifications than others. The best alternative is usually the one that is in general use within the company. Usually there is little (or no!) choice. The main alternatives are:

- postcodes;
- Plumbly management bricks (a marketing, sales-based system);
- Ordnance Survey codes;
- 10 kilometre grid squares;
- gazetteer (main town or city); or
- population based.

Distance factors

These are concerned with the distance from the depot to the many delivery locations, and with the distances between the different delivery locations. In the real world these are, of course, the mileages that are travelled by the vehicles as they go about the distribution operation.

For routeing and scheduling analysis, there are various methods for estimating or measuring distance travelled. The three main alternatives are:

1. *True-distance method* – where all the actual distances are physically measured on a road map. This is very time consuming and could not be undertaken for large applications.
2. *Co-ordinate method* – where the depot and customer delivery points are located (on a map) by grid reference, and the straight line distances are measured and factored up to an approximate road distance (sometimes called the 'crow-fly' or 'aircraft' methods). Some computer applications adopt this technique. This method uses 'barriers' to represent practical constraints such as rivers, railways, etc.
3. *Computerised road network* – many computer scheduling systems now have a special road network of the UK (and Europe) which usually consists of the major roads and junctions of the national road network. These provide a very accurate representation of travel distances. They also make allowances for different road types (eg motorway, trunk, etc) and for land use (eg city centre, town centre,

etc) which allows for variable speeds to be used when calculating the time taken to travel.

Customer constraints

There are a number of customer constraints relating to the ease or ability of delivery to certain destination points. They may be concerned with physical aspects, or be time-related. These often need to be taken into account when planning a delivery schedule. Some of the more detailed ones can only be applied if computer routeing is undertaken.

The most common customer constraints are:

- specified times for delivery (ie 0800 hours);
- early closing days;
- lunch breaks;
- access restrictions (eg only vehicles of a certain size can deliver);
- unloading restrictions (eg no fork lift truck available to unload pallets);
- drop size limitation (eg only a certain number of packages/pallets can be delivered);
- parking problems (eg cannot park or unload in the main road); and
- paperwork problems (eg all goods must be checked by the driver and signed for).

Vehicle restrictions

Typical vehicle restrictions which might need to be taken into account are:

- the type of vehicles available;
- the number of vehicles available;
- the need to pre-load trailers;
- mixed fleets (ie rigid and articulated);
- vehicle capacities (in weight or volume); and
- use of compartmentalised vehicles.

Route factors

These refer to the different constraints that apply to the make-up of individual routes. These include:

- maximum or minimum distances allowed;
- maximum or minimum time allowed;
- driving hours;
- maximum number of calls per route;
- multiple trips (ie more than one journey in a day by one vehicle);

- two-day trips (eg vehicle and driver do not return to the depot every night); and
- simultaneous delivery and collection.

Product or unit load

There are a variety of factors which may need to be considered with reference to the product or unit load that is being distributed. Typical examples are:

- variable unloading times (different products or unit loads may vary in the time it takes for their unloading);
- products may need to be separated within a vehicle due to potential contamination or fire hazard;
- dimensions and weights of the different products or unit loads must be known; and
- there may be a need to collect empty containers.

Manual methods of vehicle routeing and scheduling

In this section two examples of vehicle routeing and scheduling procedures are described. Because of the detailed nature of such exercises only a broad picture of what actually takes place will be painted. Bearing in mind the objectives and major characteristics that were described in the previous section, however, it should be possible to get a good general understanding of what is required.

The examples include a manual system for day-to-day scheduling and a manual system for long-term planning.

An example of a daily (manual) scheduling system

This example describes the daily routeing and scheduling system and procedure undertaken by a load planner for a depot situated in London. The company is a contract haulier with a few large and several small clients for whom it undertakes delivery. This particular depot covers London, East Anglia and the south east of England. Although some locations are visited quite often, there are no regular deliveries made and new locations occur quite frequently.

Procedures at the depot are relatively straightforward. The majority of orders are received from the head office by telex, although some may come directly to the depot. The orders give information relating to the delivery address, deliver by date, product, quantity, packaging, gross weight and any special delivery instructions.

The deadline for receipt of orders is midday. This leaves the afternoon for the load scheduling and preparation of order picking notes for the following day's work. It also provides for some time allowance for the adjustment of the existing planned loads to take account of urgent orders which are required for delivery the next day.

On the day following the receipt of order, the goods will be picked and marshalled by the warehouse staff and then loaded on to a vehicle by the driver when he returns in the late afternoon. Delivery takes place the next day.

A copy of every order is date stamped, and then order types are categorised according to delivery status. These different categories are as follows:

- Forward orders (ie delivery required at a later date). These are placed in a forward-order pigeon hole one week ahead, two weeks ahead, etc.
- Normal delivery – these are to be delivered according to the company's standard service level (within ten days).
- Delivery in the current week – these orders are used as the basis for making up loads.
- Urgent orders – these occasional orders are for delivery within 24 hours. They are also used as the basis for making up full vehicle loads, but outside contractors are used if this is not feasible.

		Beds	Cambs	Norfolk
Oxon		Bucks	Herts	Suffolk
Berks		N	NW	Essex
		W	E	
		SW	SE	
Hants		Surrey	W Kent	E Kent
Hants/ I of W		W Sussex	E Sussex	

Figure 17.2 Pigeon-hole racking. Orders are placed in pigeon-holes which are arranged on the basis of county areas in a formalised geographical layout. The depot is placed near to the centre of the system

The orders are accumulated in a system of *pigeon hole racking* which is arranged on the basis of county areas in a formalised geographical layout. The aim is to have a number of main delivery areas spread around the depot. The depot should be near the centre of the system. For the East London depot, the pigeon hole racking is arranged as shown in Figure 17.2.

After the orders are placed in the pigeon holes, the load scheduling and routeing exercise takes place. As already indicated, the loads are assembled with urgent orders as a priority when forming the basis of a load. The planner schedules such that the farthest drops in each area are chosen first. The full load is then made up from other drops within that pigeon hole which are relatively close, and from drops which can easily be made *en route* from or to the depot. These additional drops can be readily selected using the pigeon hole system because of its geographical format.

Using a system such as this, it is easy, on a daily basis, for a load planner to develop 'petal-shaped' routes which have the depot as their central point. This can give very efficient vehicle routeing.

Manual scheduling for strategic purposes
Manual vehicle scheduling can also be undertaken for strategic or long-term planning. The procedures that are used are somewhat similar to the scheduling system that has just been described, but they are in much greater detail. The results are used to plan fleet schedules which may be used as the basis of a delivery operation for up to about six months.

The main information and data requirements are the same as those characteristics of road transport delivery that were outlined in the previous section. The main categories of these different characteristics were as follows:

- distance factors;
- customer constraints;
- vehicle restrictions;
- route factors; and
- product/unit load constraints.

Within these different categories there are many detailed pieces of information that need to be collected and then used when the scheduling procedure takes place. The main data sources for this information may be as follows:

- historical records of a company (eg sales figures);
- special surveys that are undertaken specifically for the scheduling exercise (eg vehicle loading times); or

- from 'standards' of performance that are accepted within an industry, by law or by union agreement (eg driving hours, lunch breaks, etc).

The different data requirements for any one schedule can vary for several reasons. This may be due to the type of product, type of company, type of vehicles, etc. Examples of typical data are given below. These are from a manual scheduling exercise that was actually undertaken. They are listed according to the main categories that have previously been used.

Distance factors

- Journey mileage: measured from a map of the delivery area. For this manual scheduling exercise straight line distances were used. These were factored up to an estimated distance (straight line multiplied by factor of 1.2)
- Speeds: these should be related to road types and vehicle types. In the example average speeds were as follows:

City centres	10 mph
Town centres	12 mph
Built up areas	22 mph
Suburban areas and country roads	28 mph
Motorways	50 mph

Customer constraints

- In the example, customer constraints were rare, because the company in question was a retail one, undertaking its own delivery. It was thus in a position to ensure that most potential constraints at the different shops were not a problem (ie specified time for delivery, lunch breaks, unloading restrictions, etc).

Vehicle restrictions

- There was just one type of vehicle in the fleet, a 7 tonne rigid diesel box van with a tail lift.
- There were ten vehicles in the fleet.
- Vehicle capacity was based on the average number of cartons that a vehicle could load (rather than by weight or by volume). This figure was 960 cartons.

Route factors

- Maximum driving time was nine hours.
- Maximum daily attendance time was ten hours which included a one hour break time, leaving a work day of nine hours.
- Two day trips were allowed.
- More than one journey in a day by a driver and his vehicle was allowed. The turnaround time at the depot (ie to reload) was one and a half hours.

Product/unit load characteristics

- The fixed time allowed at every delivery drop was four minutes (ie an 'average' time taken to park the vehicle, locate the shop manager, open the rear doors, etc).
- The variable time allowed was based on the average time taken to unload one carton. For small drops (less than 50 cartons) this was 30 seconds per carton. For large drops (50 cartons or more) this was ten seconds per carton, because the cartons could be unitised on to a wooden pallet, and unloaded by hand pallet truck.
- The unit load was a wooden pallet for loads of 50 cartons or more.

Demand data

- For each demand location (shop) there was an 'average' drop size.
- Each shop had one delivery per week.

The scheduling procedure was very similar to that previously described for the daily scheduling system. In this instance, instead of a pigeon hole system being used, a large map of the delivery area was divided into grid squares (of about ten kilometres each side). The demand data within each grid square was calculated for the whole delivery area. An example of part of the delivery area is illustrated in Figure 17.3.

This represents the south-western tip of Cornwall. In each grid square there is the number of the grid square, the total number of cartons to be delivered, and the total number of drops to be made. At Land's End, for example, grid square number one, there are 24 cartons and just one drop.

The scheduling exercise then proceeds as did its daily counterpart, by starting from the perimeter of the delivery area, and making up loads based on the number of cartons which are a vehicle's capacity (ie 960 cartons).

In the small section of the map that is represented in our example, one

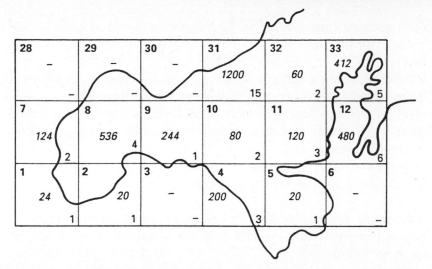

Figure 17.3 Demand data map. In each square on the grid, the grid number, total demand and number of drops are written

vehicle load might be in the grids numbered 1, 2, 6, 7, 8 and 9. This represents a total of 948 cartons (24 + 20 + 124 + 536 + 244) at nine different shops (1 + 1 + 2 + 4 + 1).

All the different routes are noted on a journey planning sheet, and total times calculated for each route based on distance, speeds, unloading times, etc. Thus the whole fleet schedule can be derived.

Computer routeing and scheduling

The computer provides the transport planner with the ability to go into even greater detail than is possible with a manual system because it can undertake many more calculations. Also many more alternatives can be investigated than when using a manual system.

There are a number of different routeing and scheduling computer packages available. New ones are brought on to the market quite regularly, and existing ones are continuously developed and updated. The three main types of routeing and scheduling problems which were outlined earlier are also represented by three types of computer packages:

1. *Strategic* models which are used for planning purposes and for determining the appropriate fleet size and mix.
2. *Tactical* models used to determine regular vehicle schedules over a given period (three to six months).
3. *Operational* models which are used for operational day-to-day scheduling. These 'interactive' packages allow for a load planner to input route changes based on his special local knowledge.

Data requirements are also very similar to those already discussed. Typical input data can include:

- customer or shop data – location, vehicle access constraints, drop sizes, restricted delivery days, delivery frequency (eg once a week);
- fleet or vehicle data – vehicle sizes, vehicle capacities, number of vehicles, total day and driving time restrictions, turnaround times for second deliveries; and
- other data – variable vehicle speeds, loading and unloading rates, product/unit load data, depot location.

The scheduling procedures used in computer packages vary according to the sophistication of the answers that are required. A relatively simple system is as follows:

A grid system can be used based on the geographic area in which deliveries are to be made. Information is recorded for each grid square according to the number of calls (drops) and the quantity of goods to be delivered. The computer program will calculate for each grid square (or individual shop location) the time it takes from the depot, using the speeds and distances applicable to the type of grid square (or type of road) that is used.

The amount of work in each grid square is calculated on the basis of the time for unloading and travel, according to the constraints that apply (ie unloading times, number of cartons, number of drops, etc).

Squares or individual locations are then linked together to form vehicle routes. These are, of course, constrained by vehicle capacity, time available, early closing days, vehicle access restrictions, etc, all of which are tested by the program as each practical route is found.

The principal advantage of using the computer is that it can take account of many more constraints, and measure many more alternatives than can ever be done manually. The basic methods or algorithms are, however, very similar to those used for manual scheduling.

There are many different computer routeing and scheduling models available in the market. Additional comments, including a list of some of the different packages are described in Chapter 20 entitled 'Information technology and logistics'.

Summary

In this chapter, the many aspects concerning the routeing and scheduling of road freight vehicles have been discussed, and the main objectives have been outlined.

Three different types of routeing and scheduling problems were noted: strategic, tactical and planning.

The major characteristics related to road transport delivery were categorised in terms of data requirements as follows:

- demand data;
- distance factors;
- customer constraints;
- vehicle restrictions;
- route factors; and
- product/unit load constraints.

Some examples of vehicle routeing and scheduling procedures were described and aspects concerning computer routeing and scheduling were considered.

PART 4

Information and Control Systems

CHAPTER
18

Information Systems for Planning and Control

Introduction

The recent rapid developments in information technology have focused attention on the importance of good information systems to support distribution activities. This requirement for information has always existed, but the computer has enabled the development of more sophisticated means of data storage, processing and presentation. Examples of relevant distribution packages and programs are discussed later in this book. This chapter is concerned with design strategies for distribution information systems and the detailed functions of these systems within the overall distribution environment.

Information can be seen as the 'lifeblood' of a distribution system. Without the smooth flow and transfer of information it is impossible for a distribution system to function adequately and effectively. To this end, it is important that a company should develop an appropriate corporate strategy for its information requirements. This plan will need to take account of a number of different objectives from strategic planning through to operational control.

The many different facets of strategic, operational and tactical distribution functions have been outlined in earlier chapters. It is easy to appreciate that the means for planning for these different functions requires an enormously varied and extensive supply of information. Thus, it is important to be aware of the different types and levels of information that are used.

One way of viewing these different levels is on the basis of the hierarchy within the company, as depicted in Figure 18.1. This shows how the extent and detail of information requirements changes according to the level of the individual within the company organisational structure. The

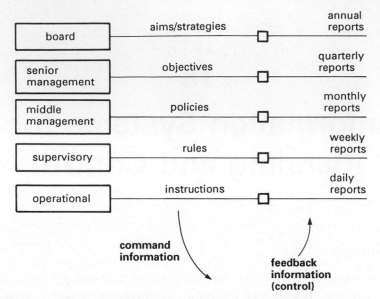

Figure 18.1 Information and control; a hierarchy in a typical company

higher the level, the more aggregate the information requirement; the lower the level, the more detailed and more frequent the requirement.

One essential factor, however, of a good information system is that the detailed information that is collected will form the basis of the information system itself. Thus, the operational data is collected and collated and is then aggregated as necessary to provide the information to support the control and planning procedures at the higher levels. This then is the distribution 'database'.

In the initial design of a distribution information system, there are a number of key questions that need to be considered in relation to the type and nature of the information system itself. The considerations include:

- what information is required;
- how much information is required;
- how quickly the information is required;
- how the information is to be stored;
- how the information is to be presented;
- what the cost implications of the alternatives are;
- etc.

Clearly a very detailed initial analysis must be undertaken to determine the appropriate managerial requirements based on the above. Some form of audit will need to be undertaken, together with an assessment of any potential trade-offs with other elements within the distribution system as a whole (ie better information may reduce overall costs through lower stock-holding costs, increased vehicle utilisation, better labour utilisation, etc).

Before considering these detailed information requirements, the distribution audit technique will be described.

The logistics or distribution audit

For many years, logistics and distribution costs received scant attention from management and accountants. This was because there was no clear means of allocating these costs, except as an arbitrary overhead charge on the rest of the business. For many companies, this attitude stemmed from a general ignorance of the significance of the costs of distribution, as well as an inability to comprehend a method of clearly identifying these costs.

In recent years, there has been a definite change in attitude, and a realisation that for many companies the cost of distribution is high. Thus, there is a genuine need to be aware of both the detailed as well as the total costs and performance of distribution systems.

One of the main ways of identifying costs and performance is a tool known as the Distribution Audit. This is, as the name suggests, an audit of distribution operations, where the main elements of cost are broken down and allocated to separate cost centres within the distribution process. Various activity measures are then used to identify appropriate cost and performance indices.

The distribution audit can be used for a variety of different purposes. Although generally a tool for determining costs, it can also be used to assess the performance of various operating methods. In general, it can be described as a tool for distribution planning and management. It is thus a technique for evaluating costs and performance in a distribution system.

The main uses for the distribution audit include, as follows:

- The identification of sub-system and total system costs – as previously indicated, this is the most common use of the audit.
- The evaluation of cost effectiveness – detailed and total unit costs can be derived, and these can be used to determine how cost effective are various parts of the distribution process. Comparison with similar operations might be made.
- The monitoring of costs and performance – regular auditing can provide a useful monitoring of the costs and performance of a system.
- The improvement of the existing system – the audit can be used to identify areas of poor performance.

- The establishment of performance/productivity indices to use as standard measurements.
- As a check on system deterioration over time – another useful result of regular auditing is to be able to assess the effectiveness of sub-systems or the system as whole.
- The identification of high cost areas – the audit can be used to identify the key areas for the concentration of management time and effort with a view to system cost reduction.
- Special problem solving – very often there is an awareness that a system is not working efficiently or cost effectively. An audit can be used to break down activities and costs, and so identify particular problems.
- The evaluation of system alternatives – particularly relevant where direct comparisons can be made between depots which use differing systems.
- The identification of main product and/or information flows – this may be a type of methods audit which identifies major flows and enables the identification of various areas for improvement.

This is by no means a definitive list of alternative uses, and many of these overlap to a certain extent. It is also worth emphasising two points. First, audits may be undertaken regularly, say annually, or on an intermittent or one-off basis. Second, audits may be qualitative as well as quantitative – having identified certain costs it is important to be able to understand or explain them, and a descriptive back-up is often essential.

For any distribution audit, there is a significant amount of data that must be collected and collated. The precise nature of these data requirements will vary according to company, industry, product and the main objective of the audit. The major areas of data coverage are set out below.

Distribution environment: this covers a wide range of elements that are likely to be important factors in relation to the system that is being audited. These might include:

- customer profile;
- sales characteristics;
- product characteristics; and
- source of goods.

Distribution resources: this will involve the drawing up of a total resource list, together with the resource costs.

Operating costs: these costs need to be determined in sufficient detail that they can be broken down across the main cost centres. The major costs might cover wages and salaries, space costs, equipment costs and service costs in relation to warehousing, transport and administration/overheads.

Activity levels: to gain a measure of cost and performance it is important to be aware of the amount of activity within the total system and the different sub-systems. The precise measure that is used will vary from one activity to another. In the warehouse, for example, consideration might be given to physical throughput measures of outers (for receipts), pallets (for storage), items (for picking) and cages (for despatch). To determine picking performance, it might be necessary to know the number of picking lists, the number of lines per list, the number of items per line, etc.

Service: the levels of service required and achieved need to be assessed. There are various means of measuring service and the relevant ones need to be considered. These might include lead time, stock availability, minimum drop/order size, order and delivery frequency, etc.

Systems audit: it may be appropriate to undertake a systems audit, although this is not essential to a 'physical' distribution audit. Such an audit would require data related to information flow, documentation, procedures, computer hardware, computer software, etc. Systems based audits are often linked to the entire company operation, so necessitate the crossing of intra-company boundaries to achieve satisfactory results.

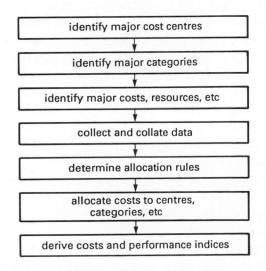

Figure 18.2 Distribution audit procedure

Before discussing the detailed steps for the completion of a distribution audit, it is useful to have an appreciation of a more general approach. This is outlined in Figure 18.2.

The steps can be further defined as follows:

- *Identify major cost centres* – these should reflect the main areas of activity within the distribution operation under consideration. In the context of a warehouse, for example, these are likely to be related to the material flow through the system (receipt, storage, picking, etc).

- *Identify major categorisations* – once again, this will depend on the type of operation. In a warehouse, these are likely to be the main product groups, especially where these product groups require different storage or handling facilities. For transport, one obvious categorisation is into different vehicle types.

- *Identify major costs, resources, etc* – as indicated in the previous section on data coverage – environment, resources, costs, activity levels, etc.

- *Collect and collate data* – it is important to be aware of several factors here. Perhaps the most important, especially where an audit is being used for comparative purposes, is that of consistency in data collection. Relevant time periods need to be determined (weekly, monthly, annually), and these may vary according to the data requirements. There will be a need to rely on sample data for some aspects of data collection. It is not feasible, for example, to try to analyse every tachograph for a complete year.

- *Determine allocation rules* – these should be according to the activity concerned. For example, the allocation of warehouse space to different cost centres may be completed on the basis of cubic capacity used; the allocation of space within the reserve storage area to different product groups might be on the basis of pallets stored.

- *Allocate costs* – this is the actual process of allocation, once the rules have been drawn up. It includes the most important element of cross-checking all totals once allocations are made to ensure that no double-counting takes place.

- *Derive cost and performance indices* – the precise nature of the indices that are used will depend on the use of the audit. Some examples are given in the next section.

Several different distribution audit methods have been developed over the past few years. In this section, a fairly straightforward audit technique is described which should help to provide a better understanding of the audit approach and the data required. A computer spreadsheet package can be an invaluable aid to audits of this nature.

For a typical distribution operation, the major warehouse cost centres are based on the flow of material through the system, and are as follows:

- goods receipt;
- main storage;
- order picking;
- marshalling;
- loading; and
- auxiliary services.

Several categorisations might be considered, especially if there are distinctive differences in the respective storage and handling procedures. These might, for example, be standard products, high value products (requiring additional security) and spare parts (requiring small parts storage facilities).

The main costs are split into buildings, building services, equipment and labour. The major elements of cost for each of these are as follows:

1. Buildings – rental or, if owned, depreciation plus interest on original capital cost.
2. Building services – to include such items as rates, heat, light, power, maintenance, cleaning, security, insurance, fire protection.
3. Equipment – to include leasing and rental charges, depreciation plus interest on capital, running costs, maintenance.
4. Labour – which can be categorised into managerial, supervisory, direct (ie order pickers) and indirect (ie cleaners). Costs will include basic wages and salaries, incentive and bonus payments, overtime, shift allowance, social security, holiday and sickness payments, etc.

The cost elements are then allocated to the main cost centres according to a framework such as that proposed in Figure 18.3.

The rules for cost allocation are based on the following principles:

1. Building and building services costs apportioned by volume.
2. Static and mobile equipment apportioned by direct usage (ie picking trucks to order picking) or by pallet throughput if shared.
3. Labour apportioned by direct usage (ie order pickers to order picking) or by throughput if shared.

Cost and performance indices can then be derived in a variety of ways:

cost elements \ cost centres	goods receipt	main storage	order picking	marshalling	loading	auxiliary services	total
buildings							
building services							
equipment – static – mobile							
labour – management – supervisory – direct – indirect							
total							

Figure 18.3 Warehouse cost framework. The various cost elements are allocated across the different cost centres

- Percentage comparisons can be made between the cost elements within the main cost centres. For example, order picking may represent 70 per cent of the total direct labour cost.
- Percentage comparisons can be made between the different product categories and cost centres. For example, high security products may represent 40 per cent of the main storage costs.
- The use of activity level measurements can produce unit cost and performance figures. These can be determined according to unit throughput (pallets, cartons, etc), volume throughput (cubic metres, etc), weight throughput (tonnes, kilos, etc) or value throughput. It is generally felt that the number of units throughput over a given period of time presents the most appropriate measure. Thus, suitable cost and performance measures can be derived to measure various activities within the warehouse. There are many examples – these include order picking cost per case, total labour cost per case, picks per hour, etc.

A similar type of cost framework can be derived for the allocation of transport costs. The major difference is that the cost centres are time-based according to the vehicle (or driver) activity and the cost elements relate directly to the transport operation. An example is shown in Figure 18.4.

cost centres / cost elements	loading time	driving time	unloading time	other work time	unallocated time	total
direct labour						
management						
vehicle costs – fixed – variable						
equipment						
buildings						
building services						
total						

Figure 18.4 Transport cost framework. The cost elements are allocated according to the time-based transport activities.

Cost allocation rules can be derived on a similar basis to those adopted for the warehouse example. Relevant cost and performance indices should also be determined. These should include an appropriate throughput measure which is related to the limiting factor of the vehicle (ie volume, weight, unit loads, etc) as well as indices based on mileage.

Functions of a distribution information system

It is possible to identify a number of specific functions or roles that a distribution or logistics information system should fulfil. They can be summarised as follows:

- planning;
- co-ordination;
- monitoring and control; and
- operational.

The planning function refers to the need for information to enable distribution and logistics systems and operations to be adequately and appropriately planned. As already indicated, distribution is a dynamic activity which is undergoing continual change. Because of this, there is a requirement for information to be used as input into strategic or operational planning activities. This information may not necessarily be required on a regular basis, but should certainly be available fairly readily from the existing company database.

One associated aspect is that of forecasting demand to enable a planned response to customers' orders. Such straightforward forecasting should be based on patterns of customer demand and then linked to information on replenishment lead times. In this way, more effective measures can be adopted with respect to stock levels and stock location.

The co-ordination function of distribution information systems refers to the facility of communication which such systems provide. This communication is important both internally within the company and externally to other interrelated systems – customers, carriers, etc.

The importance of effective internal co-ordination through an efficient information system cannot be over-emphasised. This importance reflects the nature of the physical distribution system itself which has been described as an integrated system crossing many boundaries within a company's structure. The information system must be set up to support this approach. Thus the physical material flow from raw materials through production to finished goods and then to delivery vehicle must have a suitably co-ordinated information system to support this flow of materials and products. The means of achieving this is to ensure that the information used to support these processes is of a common base which can be used by the different functions, as required.

This same approach needs to be adopted for communication with external systems. This will apply particularly to the company's customers, and be based on the order requirements. Additionally important are the communication links with suppliers, be they of raw materials, packaging materials, transport services, etc.

One of the major requirements of an effective information system is to provide adequate reporting facilities to enable the appropriate monitoring and control of distribution operations. The three main areas within distribution where this applies are costs, performance and profitability.

To establish an effective system for monitoring and control it is, once again, important to be aware of the overall role of physical distribution within the company – to identify the major objectives. Care is needed in the definition of any aims or objectives. Those such as 'the aim for physical distribution is to minimise costs' or, 'the level of service is "as soon as possible"' are meaningless. They do not reflect the integrated approach and cannot be expressed as appropriate measures for monitoring performance.

A generalised approach to establishing an appropriate system is described in the next section.

The other major area of importance related to distribution information systems is that of the operational requirements. These are concerned with the very detailed aspects of information and communication that are essential to the effective day-to-day operation of a distribution system. Although not a part of the planning process, it is vital that these information requirements are adequately planned to cater for the smooth and effective operation of the warehousing and transport functions. These aspects are described in the final section of this chapter.

Monitoring and control: a general approach

The monitoring and control of logistics and distribution operations is often approached in a relatively unsophisticated and unplanned way. Control measures are adopted as problems arise, almost as a form of crisis management.

It is important to adopt a more formal approach, although this should not necessitate a complicated format. A simple and straightforward approach might be as follows:

- Determine the scope of physical distribution activities;
- Identify the departmental objectives;
- Determine operating principles and methods;
- Set productivity/performance goals;
- Measure and monitor performance.

The scope of physical distribution activities will, of course, vary from one company to another. Because of this, it is impossible to identify a standard system that can be adopted generally. A company must first determine the scope of activities that need to be considered.

More detailed, departmental objectives should be defined. These will include such items as stock-holding policies by individual line or product group, customer service levels by product, by customer type or by geographical area, etc.

Operating principles and methods need to be determined with respect to trunking and delivery transport, warehousing resources and usage, implications for seasonality, etc.

Productivity and performance goals should then be set in relation to the detailed operational tasks which are performed. These should cover all the essential aspects of the physical distribution system. It is often easier to categorise these under the major sub-systems of warehousing (order picking performance, labour utilisation, cost per case, etc); transport (vehicle utilisation, cost per mile, fuel consumption, etc); and administration/stock-holding (customer orders received, stock-outs, percentage of orders fulfilled, etc).

Standards should be set based on the distribution budget and on engineered/work study measures. From the budget, an operating plan should be determined, in which costs are split by period (ie month) and by element (ie fuel, wages, etc). The operational control systems can then be devised to measure actual against budget costs so that any deviations from the plan are easily identified and can be investigated and action taken where necessary. This type of variance analysis can be used for all the operations within the physical distribution system.

In measuring these deviations it is important to be aware of three major causes of deviation. These are:

- changes in levels of activity (ie less work is available for a fixed capacity – labour, equipment);
- changes in efficiency (ie the resource, labour or equipment, is operating less effectively); and
- changes in price (ie the price of an item, say fuel, increases so costs will increase).

Key indices and ratios need to be developed to allow for appropriate monitoring and control to be undertaken (ie actual work against planned work, cost per case, cases per hour, tonnes per journey, etc). These need to be representative of the distribution operation, and they should be capable of clearly identifying why a deviation has occurred as well as if a deviation has occurred.

Operational requirements

The importance of information handling and processing within a distribution operation has been demonstrated in several studies. Figure 18.5

illustrates one example, where it was shown that for the part of the goods receiving cycle in which an operator was involved, over 60 per cent of the time was spent in information related activity (sorting, identifying, counting, recording) and less than 40 per cent with the actual moving of the goods.

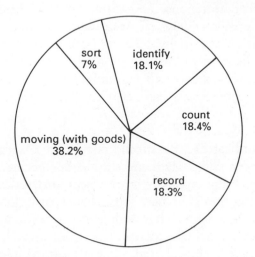

Figure 18.5 Operator's time breakdown; less than 40 per cent of the time is spent in actually moving goods

It is possible to identify five major elements within the data/information process:

- data input;
- data processing;
- data storage;
- data transmission; and
- data output.

These elements can take place at varying levels of technical sophistication, from the single human undertaking of a manual picking operation using a handwritten picking list, to a conveyorised system sorting and despatching parcels by bar code to a marshalling area. Both of these operations require properly planned information systems if they are to function effectively.

The order processing system provides the basis for the information requirement of most warehouse and transport operations. In simple terms, the inputs to the system are the customers' orders and the outputs are the various documents that are used (replenishment lists, picking lists, delivery schedules, delivery documents, invoices, etc). There are many different ways of accepting, processing and redistributing this information, ranging from manual through to varying degrees of computerisation. Recent developments in information technology such as the use of electronic point of sale (EPOS) systems in stores and direct computer links are continuing to increase the options that are available.

Within individual warehouse and transport operations there are many additional functions which require due consideration in terms of their detailed information requirements. It is important that appropriate systems to support these operations are set up and maintained. These need to be planned along with the overall distribution information system as they are likely at one time or another to be linked together. The main ones include:

- Product identification (this should consist of a written description as well as a stores code. The code should be specifically developed for use throughout the company stores, accounts, sales, etc).
- Other identification (this may vary – such as colour coding, symbol coding to denote danger, bar coding for sortation purposes).
- Location systems within warehouses (they may be designed to be fixed or random). They should include physical marking at locations as well as an appropriate system to support the storage and identification process – two ticket, three ticket, analogue, etc.
- Stock record systems (these may be manual or computer-based). They may be required to hold various items of information per product – stock levels, locations, order history, re-order level, etc.
- Issue documents (works orders, route cards, assembly notes, replenishment notes, picking lists, etc).
- Delivery documents.

Within the operational environment a number of detailed factors need to be taken into account when monitoring and controlling operational performance. In the remainder of this chapter, a number of these detailed points are described, using the warehouse as the basis for this description.

Service can be described as the quality of performance of a distribution system. More detailed aspects of customer service have been discussed in an earlier chapter. In warehousing, the measure of service depends on the type of operation being carried out, but can include:

- percentage of orders satisfied in full;
- percentage of items supplied at first demand;
- percentage of orders satisfied within specified time;
- numbers of stock-outs;

- amount of damage/loss;
- consistency of delivery performance; and
- orders overdue

Service depends on effective operating methods and systems with no unnecessary time delays in processing orders. Service also depends on the availability of stock. Note that a comparatively small increase in required service level can necessitate a disproportionate increase in average stock, with consequences for inventory and associated costs.

The effective use of resources is a vital element of good operational control. There are a number of important aspects.

Personnel costs are a high proportion of the total costs of running a warehouse, and the largest element, up to a half, of personnel costs is usually order picking. This is influenced very much by the way the stock is laid out, and the picking methods used.

The usual measure of order picking performance is the picking rate – the number of units picked per man hour. Other performance parameters include fork truck loads moved per hour, vehicle loading/unloading rates, packing rates, and of course, overtime and absence levels.

Some of the factors which adversely influence manning performance and levels are:

- double-handling;
- manual sortation;
- equipment downtime;
- inappropriate equipment;
- wrong type of unit load;
- waiting for documentation;
- poor scheduling of work; and
- poor layout – excessive movement.

Space costs are also very important. Building and building services costs can be as much as 40 per cent of the total cost of a warehouse operation, hence poor utilisation of space is expensive. Good space utilisation can be achieved by utilising the available headroom in the warehouse, providing adequate but not excessive aisles, and using the right types of handling and storage equipment. It also requires proper systems and discipline for locating stock, and the avoidance of obsolete stock-holding. Some measure of space utilisation is necessary to monitor the efficiency of space usage.

The decision to use random or fixed location storage also influences the amount of space required to hold a given stock range.

Good work planning within a properly designed system, the right equipment, and planned and effective maintenance, all improve equipment utilisation.

Utilisation is adversely affected by:

- inappropriate or non-standard unit load;
- excessive travel – poor layout;
- unbalanced work loads – poor scheduling;
- obstruction – poor housekeeping;
- back tracking;
- poor access; and
- waiting for instructions/paperwork.

Monitoring of utilisation can include checks on stock quantities held compared with stock capacity, and measures of quantities moved against truck capacities, eg using work measurement techniques.

Management responsibilities should include materials management, involving the maintenance of the integrity of the stock held, and preventing loss – missing or misplaced items and pallets (wrong location), deterioration, and damage. A well-planned layout with suitable unit load and handling and storage equipment will minimise handling, movement and the risk of damage, and provide a secure environment. Other factors are the adoption of appropriate measures to minimise fire risks, the training of personnel, and the establishment of responsible attitudes to security and the general care of stock.

Control and monitoring systems (the checking of receipts, despatches and stock balances; stock location and stock rotation systems; stock checks and audits) also provide the means of identifying when problems are starting to occur and where they are located.

Typical parameters and characteristics which indicate unsatisfactory performance or potential for improvement and which may need to be monitored can thus be summarised as follows:

- Poor utilisation
  - space,
  - handling equipment,
  - storage equipment;
- people
  - long movements,
  - waiting time,
  - high overtime,
  - sickness,
  - accidents,
  - imbalance of work between departments;

- output performance
  - daily pallet or case throughput,
  - low picking rates,
  - poor levels of service,
  - long lead time,
  - high errors,
  - stock-outs,
  - damaged goods,
  - complaints;
- stock loss or damage
  - in warehouse,
  - in transit;
- stock levels
  - excessive or too low,
  - obsolete;
- stock location
  - mislaid goods;
- speed of response to orders or changes;
- high frequency of 'panic' situations; and
- poor housekeeping.

Clearly any high cost area is a candidate for improvement. When monitoring costs, and any other parameters, it is particularly informative to monitor the trends, ie how a parameter varies over a period of time, since this can give early warning that performance is beginning to fall away.

Summary

The need for effective information systems in distribution cannot be overemphasised. In the first section of this chapter the importance of an adequate distribution database to support the logistics and distribution function was discussed. Following from this, the distribution audit was outlined. It was shown that the audit is a tool with a variety of uses. Not the least of these is to provide the basis on which a distribution information system can be formulated.

The major functions of a distribution information system were outlined. These included planning, co-ordination, monitoring and control, and operational aspects. A general approach to monitoring and control was described. Operational requirements were also considered in some detail, specifically the means of monitoring and controlling the major resources within the distribution environment.

A prerequisite for good control is an effective information handling system. In recent years there have been very significant developments in the use of computerised information systems. These are discussed in Chapter 20.

CHAPTER 19

Inventory Management and Stock Control

The need to hold stocks

There are a number of reasons why a company might choose or need to hold stocks of different products. In planning any distribution system it is essential to be aware of these reasons, and to be sure that the consequences are adequate but not excessively high stock levels. The main reasons for holding stock can be summarised as follows:

- To keep down productions costs – often it is costly to 'set up' machines, so production runs need to be as long as possible to achieve low unit costs. It is essential, however, to balance these costs with the costs of holding stock.
- To accommodate variations in demand – the demand for a product is never wholly regular so it will vary in the short term, by season, etc. To avoid stock-outs, therefore, some level of safety stock must be held.
- To take account of variable supply (lead) times – additional safety stock is held to cover any delivery delays from suppliers.
- Buying costs – there is an administrative cost associated with raising an order, and to minimise this cost, it is necessary to hold additional inventory. It is essential to balance these elements of administration and stock-holding, and for this the Economic Order Quantity (EOQ) is used.
- To take advantage of quantity discounts – some products are offered at a cheaper unit cost if they are bought in bulk.
- To account for seasonal fluctuations – these may be for demands reasons whereby products are popular at peak times only. To cater for this while maintaining an even level of production, stocks need to

be built up through the rest of the year. Supply variations may also occur because goods are produced only at a certain time of the year. This often applies to primary food production where, for example, large stocks result at harvest time.

- To allow for price fluctuations/speculation – the price of primary products can fluctuate for a variety of reasons, so some companies buy in large quantities to cater for this.
- To help the production and distribution operations run more smoothly – here, stock is held to 'decouple' the two different activities.
- To provide customers with immediate service – it is essential in some highly competitive markets for companies to provide goods as soon as they are required – 'ex-stock'.
- To minimise production delays caused by lack of spare parts – this is important not just for regular maintenance, but especially for breakdowns of expensive plant and machinery. Thus spares are held to minimise plant shutdowns.
- Work in progress – as already indicated, to facilitate the production process by providing semi-finished stocks between different processes.

Types of stock-holding

The main stock types can be categorised as follows:

- Raw materials – generally used to feed into a production or manufacturing process.
- In-process stocks – sometimes known as work-in-progress, these consist of part-finished stock that is built up between different manufacturing processes.
- Finished products – the most common type of stock-holding. Stocks are held at the end of the production process or further up the distribution chain for eventual transfer to the final customer.
- General stores – containing a mixture of products used to support a given operation.
- Spare parts – a special category because of the nature of the stock. These provide a crucial back-up to machinery or plant where any breakdown might be critical.

Within the above categories, stock can again be broken down into major classifications:

- Working stock – this is likely to be the major element of stock within a distribution depot's stock-holding, and it should reflect the actual demand for the product.

- Cycle stock – this refers to the major production stock within a production warehouse, and it reflects the batch sizes or production run lengths of the manufacturing process.
- Safety stock – this is the stock that is used to cover the unpredictable daily or weekly fluctuations in demand. Sometimes known as 'buffer' stock, it creates a buffer to take account of this unpredictability.
- Speculative stock – can be raw materials that are 'brought forward' for financial or supply reasons or finished stock that is pre-planned to prepare for expected future increases in demand.

The implications for other distribution functions

There are many ways in which the need to hold stocks affects the other distribution functions and vice versa. It is essential for effective distribution planning that the various costs associated with inventory are minimised in relation to other distribution costs. As already discussed in previous chapters, it requires a process of balance between these functions to avoid any sub-optimisation and to create a cost effective total system. With this in mind, it is useful to review those areas where this balance may be needed.

The number of depots in a distribution system significantly affects the overall cost of that system. The reasons given for having a large number of depots are generally the perceived need to have a 'local presence' within a market, and the need to provide a given level of service to customers. A distribution system that does have many depots will require high stock levels, specifically with respect to the amount of safety stocks that are held. In addition, a large number of depots is likely to mean fairly small delivery areas, reflecting poor stockturn and higher unit costs in the warehouse.

Many companies in the UK in recent years have undertaken depot rationalisation exercises whereby they have cut significantly the number of depots within their distribution network. This particularly applies to retail companies. Although this leads to an increase in local transport costs because delivery distances are greater, there are large savings to be made in inventory reduction – specifically in safety stock reduction.

A simple rule of thumb exists for estimating these savings, known as the 'square root law'. Basically, the law states that the total stock-holding in a distribution system is proportional to the square root of the number of depot locations. The law thus gives a broad indication of prospective inventory savings from any depot reduction. For example, a depot reduction from, say, ten to five can lead to inventory savings as indicated in the following calculation:

$$\text{Inventory reduction} = 1 - \left(\frac{\sqrt{5}}{\sqrt{10}} \right)$$

$$= 1 - \frac{2.24}{3.16} \times 100\%$$

$$= \quad 29\%$$

Another major factor to be considered is the effect that an excess of inventory can have on the size and operation of a depot. This might be caused by obsolete stock, dead stock, unnecessary storage of slow-moving lines, etc. This may mean that depots are larger than necessary, that extra outside storage is required, or that the depot operation is hindered through a shortage of working space.

One means of tackling these problems is to be more aware of the range of products that are held. This can be achieved by using Pareto Analysis (or ABC Analysis). Pareto's Law provides the '80/20 rule' whereby there is an 80/20 relationship for products in many conditions. For example, it is often found that approximately 20 per cent of storage lines represent 80 per cent of the throughput in a warehouse.

Using Pareto Analysis, it is possible to categorise product lines on the basis of:

'A' lines = fast movers
'B' lines = medium movers
'C' lines = slow movers
'D' lines = obsolete/dead stock

Policy decisions can then be made. For example, 'A' lines should be held at all depots and have a 95 per cent availability; 'B' lines held at all depots but only at an 85 per cent availability; 'C' lines held only at a limited number of depots and at 75 per cent availability; 'D' lines should be scrapped.

Clearly this policy will differ according to product type, industry type, service level requirements, etc. The essential point is to be aware of the appropriate stock-holding costs and recover the costs accordingly.

There are several ways in which stock-holding policy and practice can affect the transport operation. One that has already been indicated concerns the number of depots in a distribution system. Whereas inventory savings can be made by reducing depot numbers, this will be associated with an increase in local delivery costs because mileage will increase as depot areas become larger. It is generally true, however, that any increase in transport cost will be more than offset by inventory and warehouse cost savings.

One other area where inventory policy can influence transport is in the provision of back loads for return journeys by trunking vehicles and sometimes by delivery vehicles. Empty return journeys are a recognised cost that transport managers are always keen to minimise. It may be possible to arrange for raw materials or bought-in goods to be collected by own vehicles rather than delivered by supplier's vehicles.

A company's stock-holding policy may also affect the distribution structure that the company adopts. There are three main patterns:

1. direct systems;
2. echelon systems; and
3. mixed or flexible systems.

1. Direct systems have a centralised inventory from which customers are supplied directly. These direct systems are of two main types — either supplying full vehicle loads, or specialist services such as mail order.
2. Echelon systems involve the flow of products through a series of locations from the point of origin to the final destination. The essential point is that inventory is stored at several points in the distribution chain. There may be several links or levels within these structures, perhaps from production warehouses through a central stock-holding point to regional and/or local depots. Typical examples include some of the multiple grocery retailers.
3. Mixed systems are the most common, linking together the direct and echelon systems for different products, and being dependent on the demand characteristics of these products (order size, fast/slow moving, substitutability, etc).

Inventory replenishment systems

The aim of an effective inventory replenishment system is to maintain a suitable balance between the cost of holding stock and the particular service requirement for customers. The need for this balance can be illustrated by considering the disadvantages of low stock levels (which should provide very low costs) and high stock levels (which should provide a very high service).

The disadvantages of low stock levels are that customers' orders cannot be fulfilled, which may lead to the loss of both existing and future business, and that goods have to be ordered very frequently, which may lead to heavy ordering costs and heavy handling and delivery costs. High stock levels have the major disadvantage of capital being tied up which might be better invested elsewhere. Also, there is the risk of product deterioration (eg food, drink) and of products becoming outdated or superseded (eg computers, fashion goods) if they are stored for long periods. A final disadvantage, previously discussed, is the expense of providing additional storage space.

Inventory replenishment systems are designed to minimise the effects of these high/low stock level disadvantages. There are a variety of systems, but the two major ones are the periodic review (or fixed interval) system and the fixed point (or continuous) re-order system.

The periodic review system works on the premise that the stock level of the product is examined at regular intervals and, depending on the quantity in stock, a replenishment order is placed. The size of the order is selected to bring the stock to a predetermined level. The system is illustrated in Figure 19.1.

For the fixed point re-order system, a specific stock level is determined and a given quantity is re-ordered when that stock level is reached. The time when the order is placed varies. This is illustrated in Figure 19.2.

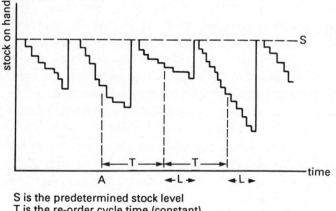

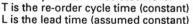

S is the predetermined stock level
T is the re-order cycle time (constant)
L is the lead time (assumed constant)

Figure 19.1 Periodic review system. Replenishment orders are made on the basis of a regular review of stock levels

These systems, and variations of them, have been used for many years. Apart from the vagaries of lead time reliability they generally work quite well. They do have one significant drawback, however, which is that they can create unnecessarily high or low stock levels, especially when demand occurs in discrete chunks. This applies, in particular, to multi-echelon distribution systems where the demand at each level is aggregated at the

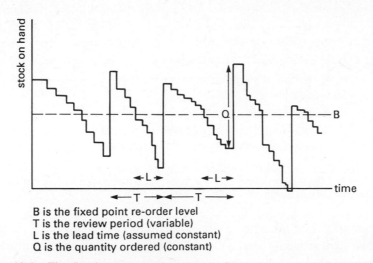

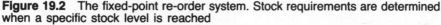

B is the fixed point re-order level
T is the review period (variable)
L is the lead time (assumed constant)
Q is the quantity ordered (constant)

Figure 19.2 The fixed-point re-order system. Stock requirements are determined when a specific stock level is reached

next level. Thus it can be very difficult to forecast demand based only on the immediate lower level. Accurate forecasts need to reflect the requirements at all of the lower levels.

Re-order quantities

The two systems described in the previous section require either fixed or variable quantities of different products to be ordered. The next question is how much product should be re-ordered?

To answer this question is not easy, and there are many different views as to the best means of arriving at an answer. One particular method of calculating the appropriate quantity, is known as the *economic order quantity (EOQ) method.*

The EOQ method is an attempt to estimate the best order quantity by balancing the conflicting costs of holding stock and of placing replenishment orders. The effect of order quantity on stock-holding costs is that the larger the order quantity for a given item, the longer will be the average time in the store, and the greater will be the storage costs. On the other hand, the placing of a large number of small quantity orders produces a low average stock, but a much higher cost in terms of the number of orders that need to be placed, and the associated administration and delivery costs. This different effect is illustrated in the diagram of Figure 19.3.

The large order quantity gives a much higher average stock level (Q1)

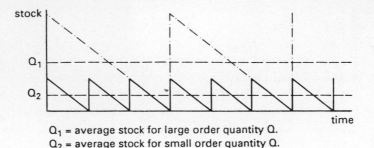

Q_1 = average stock for large order quantity Q.
Q_2 = average stock for small order quantity Q.

Figure 19.3 Re-order quantities. Small, frequent re-orders result in low average stocks (Q2) but high re-ordering costs. Larger, less frequent re-ordering results in higher average stock levels at lower re-ordering cost

than the small order quantity (Q2). The small order quantity necessitates many more orders being placed than with the large order quantity.

The best answer is, once again, one of balance, and it is this which the EOQ method aims to provide. The diagram of Figure 19.4 helps to illustrate how this balance is achieved between the cost of holding an item and the cost of its ordering. There is a specific quantity (or range of quantities) which gives the lowest total cost (Q_0 in the diagram), and this is the economic order quantity for the product.

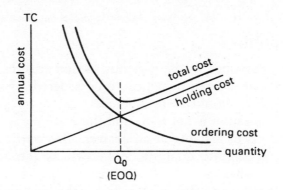

Figure 19.4 Economic order quantity (EOQ) principle. Total cost comprises holding cost and ordering cost. EOQ is a minimum of the total cost curve

There are a number of additional factors that need to be considered before the final order quantity is confirmed.

These factors are of two types. The first applies specifically to an individual company operation, or to a particular industry. The second relates to factors of a more general nature, which tend to be relevant to most stock control or stock re-order systems.

The main point to appreciate is that factors such as these may need to be considered together with any suggested order quantity that derives from a stock control system. Some of these factors may be included within the system itself, but this is often not the case.

The first series of special factors relates to specific companies or industries. The order quantity requirement for each product must be assessed and readjusted accordingly. The factors include the following:

- *New product lines* – these may be 'one-off' items, or items that are expected to show a sharp increase in demand. There will be no historic data on which to base demand forecasts, so care must be taken to ensure that adequate stock levels are maintained.
- *Promotional lines* – national or local promotion (via TV, newspapers, 'special' offers, etc) may suddenly create additional demand on a product, so stock levels must cater for this.
- *Test marketing* – this may apply to certain products, and may be for a given period of time, or in a given area only.
- *Basic lines* – some companies feel that a certain number of their basic stock lines should always be available to the customer as a matter of marketing policy. To provide this service, higher stock levels must be maintained.
- *Range reviews* – a company may adopt a policy to rationalise, or slim-down, its range of products – particularly if new lines are being introduced. To do this it may be necessary to reduce the re-order quantities for some products.
- *Centralised buying* – sometimes, where centralised buying occurs, it is necessary to hold excess stock, or run out of stock, because the buying department is negotiating large bulk discounts.

The more general factors which may need to be taken into account are:

- *Outstanding orders* – ie orders already placed but not delivered. It is important to include these, otherwise overstocking may occur.
- *Minimum order quantities* – for some products there may be a minimum order quantity, below which it is uneconomic (or even impossible) to place an order.
- *Pallet quantities* – similar to minimum order quantity it is often more economic to order in unit load quantities – which are often a pallet or number of pallets. A good economic unit load order is often a full lorry load.
- *Seasonality* – many products have a peak demand at certain times of the year. The most common peak occurs just prior to Christmas (toys, games, wines and spirits, etc). When estimating stock levels, and when forecasting trends in demand, it is essential to take these into account.

Demand forecasting

There are many different forecasting methods that are available and it is important to select the most appropriate alternative for whatever demand is to be measured. Two of the most common methods of forecasting are described here. One of the most simple is the *moving average*, which takes an average of demand for a certain number of previous periods and uses this average as the forecast of demand for the next period.

Another, more complicated, alternative is known as *exponential smoothing*. This gives recent weeks far more weighting in the forecast. Forecasting methods such as exponential smoothing give a much quicker response to any change in demand trends than methods such as the moving average. The diagram of Figure 19.5 illustrates this.

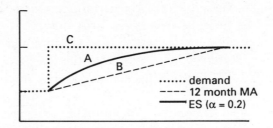

Figure 19.5 Exponential smoothing of demand curve (A) gives recent demand heavier weighting than moving average curve (B), in response to stepped demand (C)

The dotted line represents actual demand and it can be seen that the single line (exponential smoothing) responds more quickly to the demand change than does the dashed line (moving average).

There are a number of ways in which the demand for a product can vary, these can be accounted for in different ways. The different elements of a demand pattern are illustrated in Figure 19.6.

It can be seen from the graphs that the overall demand pattern can be divided into the following patterns:

- A *trend line* over several months or years. In the diagram, the trend is upwards until the end of year 4, and then downwards.
- A *seasonal fluctuation* which is roughly the same year in, year out. In the diagram there is high demand in mid-year and low demand in the early part of the year.
- *Random fluctuations* which can occur at any time.

Each of these elements should be allowed for by a good stock control system:

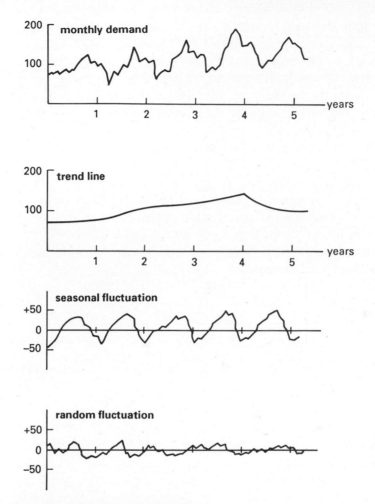

Figure 19.6 Elements of a demand pattern

- trend, by a good forecasting system;
- seasonality, by making seasonal allowances; and
- random, by providing sufficient buffer stock.

Developments in inventory planning

Very recent developments in inventory planning are aimed at solving some of the problems encountered by the use of the more traditional approaches to stock replenishment. They are based on the concept of Materials Requirements Planning (MRP), which is a computerised system for forecasting materials requirements based on a company's master production schedule and bill of material for each product.

Broadly, the system is used to calculate the time-phased requirements for components and materials with respect to production schedules, taking into account replenishment lead times, etc. This approach enables inventory levels to be significantly reduced, and service levels, in terms of shorter production lead times, to be improved.

MRP systems are now quite well established, as are other related techniques such as 'just-in-time' or Kanban systems. The obvious advantages of these systems to manufacturing have led to the development of associated techniques for distribution – distribution requirements planning (DRP).

DRP systems are designed to take forecast demand and to reflect this through the distribution system on a time-phased requirements basis. DRP thus acts by pulling the product through the distribution system once demand has been identified. It is particularly useful for multi-echelon distribution structures to counter the problems of requirements occurring as large chunks of demand.

Summary

In this chapter on inventory management and stock control a number of important factors have been outlined. In the first section, the reasons for holding stock were summarised. Following on from that, the main stock types were categorised as:

- raw materials;
- in-process stocks;
- finished products;
- general stores; and
- spare parts.

A further breakdown of stock includes four major classifications:

- working stock;
- cycle stock;
- safety stock; and
- speculative stock.

The implications of inventory management and stock control on other distribution functions were highlighted, with particular emphasis on providing a suitable balance and so avoiding any sub-optimisation of resources.

The two main inventory replenishment systems were explained –

periodic review and fixed point re-order. The question of re-order quantity was then discussed, including the EOQ method and the other important factors which need to be taken into account.

Two methods of demand forecasting were outlined, the moving average and exponential smoothing. It was shown that demand could be broken down into trend, seasonal and random factors. Finally, some of the most recent developments in inventory planning were described.

CHAPTER 20

Information Technology and Logistics

Introduction

Developments in information technology (IT) have continued to progress at a fast pace in recent years, and there is no reason to suppose that this pace will slacken in the near future. Indeed, it seems certain that the number of innovations and enhancements will increase significantly in the next decade. This speed of change has now begun to affect distribution to the same extent that other areas of business, such as financial management, have been affected. The major advances have been directly concerned with the computer, although other areas of development are important.

In the past few decades, computer power has increased dramatically as far as large mainframe computers are concerned. In addition, there has been the introduction of mini- and microcomputer hardware which has brought the computer facility to the office desk. All this at vastly reduced hardware costs. Linked to this has been the development of improved communications enabling distributed networks to be used, fourth generation languages and a new variety of software programs and packages.

A number of associated developments in IT have also impacted on distribution and started to impose on the ways in which distribution systems are planned and operated. On the production interface, the use of CAD/CAM (computer aided design/computer aided manufacturing) and CIM (computer integrated manufacturing) has enabled the materials management concept to be effectively realised. The introduction of EPOS (electronic point of sale) systems linked to bar coding and article numbering using laser scanners has also added to the pressure on distribution systems in terms of the improved information that is now available and the speed of response that is required.

The next major development of significant importance is likely to be that of expert systems or artificial intelligence. These 'fifth generation' computer languages should enable the user to describe his or her problem directly to a computer until it is sufficiently defined that the computer can complete relevant analyses and produce appropriate solutions.

There are a multitude of words and definitions that are applicable to computers and information technology. It is impossible here to include all of them, but the two most common ones are worth mentioning:

- *hardware* – which refers to the equipment that is used (computer, screen, keyboard, printer, etc); and
- *software* – the programs or packages that are used. These are broadly the sets of statements and rules that the computer system follows.

The current computer software available for use by the distribution specialist can be roughly categorised as follows:

- General purpose computer packages which are easily adapted for use in the context of distribution (ie spreadsheets, databases).
- Simulation and modelling languages and packages. These are used for the more sophisticated planning and distribution facilities and systems.
- Specially designed distribution software which may be used for planning or operational purposes.

Selecting computer hardware and software

There are a very large number of potential uses for the computer in distribution, ranging from fairly minor applications to major strategic planning tools. Systems can be bespoke – designed specifically for a company, or can be bought 'off the shelf' and then adapted as necessary. It is vital when considering the introduction of a computer system to undertake a careful selection procedure to ensure that the correct approach is adopted with regard to hardware and software. Aspects that need to be considered include flexibility, user friendliness, security, cost, etc. A typical five-stage requirements evaluation process might be as follows:

Stage one is the recognition of the need for a system and the definition of requirements. This might include the following aspects:

- determination of need or problem;
- a review of the scope of the required system and the interfaces with the rest of the business;

- an evaluation of the existing systems and procedures;
- definition of precise system requirements; and
- determination of benefits required.

For the identification of available alternatives, all possible software packages need to be identified and a preliminary evaluation should indicate the major alternatives. Other points to consider include the following:

- The availability of suitable packages. A custom built system may be the only alternative.
- If custom built, are in-house data processing skills sufficient or should a software house be used?
- If a software option is chosen, it may be necessary to compromise on precise original requirements.
- If there are time constraints, this may mean that a package is the only alternative because original systems development takes time.
- If there are cost constraints, a custom built system may be too expensive an option.

System requirements need to be carefully formalised and evaluated. It is likely that a software package will be the most attractive alternative for many distribution applications. Care is required in formalising requirements and should be based around the following:

- Functional requirements – develop a checklist of the features that are required, including their priority. This checklist should be a detailed requirements summary, covering all aspects of the particular application.
- Technical requirements – these should cover hardware implications, peripheral device requirements (terminals, etc), documentation, technical skill required, etc.

With software selection potential suppliers should be chosen with care. After the initial selection phase, the alternatives should be narrowed down to three or four and then detailed comparisons should be made. Points to consider include:

- getting an 'objective' view of alternatives where possible;
- using a functions and features checklist to compare alternatives;
- completing 'benchmark' tests on the different systems, where possible, and comparing results;

- taking into account the experience and the location of the supplier;
- ensuring that suppliers are willing, and able, to undertake any special changes to the software that may be required;
- asking for and talking to existing users of the system, and seeing the system demonstrated;
- ensuring that there are agreed deadlines for any additional programming work; and
- being sure the total system costs are included when making comparisons.

Installation and implementation will take time, particularly with respect to the loading of the initial master data, system testing, the development of user procedures and the training and familiarisation of staff.

Logistics and distribution strategy

A limited number of computer software packages have been developed to represent or simulate the overall logistics and distribution structure. These are designed as an aid to planning.

These packages aim to answer overall system-related questions such as:

- How many depots?
- Where should the depots be located?
- How much stock should be stored at the different depots?
- What are the factory to depot product movements?

The models are generally simulation-based rather than optimising. They evaluate the flow and stock-holding of goods within a distribution system. According to the physical requirements of the different alternatives that are tested, a model will produce a total cost solution based on the assessment of a number of cost variables, ie:

- primary transport costs;
- local delivery costs;
- warehousing costs; and
- inventory holding cost.

Typical features of such a system will include:

- the specification of demand according to major product groups, within given areas and for certain delivery sizes;
- the fact that most facility-types can be accounted for – factories, source points for 'bought-in' materials, main depot/warehouses, regional and local depots, transhipment points etc;

- the accommodation of different modes of transport, together with variable delivery sizes;
- the incorporation of detailed local delivery routeing and scheduling models; and
- the allocation of costs to provide customer and product costs.

Strategic computer packages tend to be very complex and large scale and are thus expensive to buy and run, both from the hardware and software point of view.

General applications software

The recent development of inexpensive but powerful microcomputers and personal computers (PCs) has helped to widen the accessibility of computing facilities quite significantly. Alongside this has been the increase in the availability of high quality spreadsheet and database programs. These types of programs and packages allow for the evaluation of quite complex problems with relative ease.

There are many potential applications for these general packages in distribution – they are particularly useful for planning purposes.

A *Spreadsheet* package is basically an electronic worksheet, together with graphics facilities and simple data management facilities. The spreadsheet is, in fact, analogous to a very large sheet of paper divided into columns and rows. Data is entered into discrete cells within the worksheet related to these columns and rows. The spreadsheet module has a large and comprehensive set of commands that allow the user to manipulate data in the worksheet very easily. This can include the use of mathematic and statistical functions, the storage, retrieval and copying of files and the production of various types of graphs.

As already indicated, there are many potential applications for spreadsheet packages. These include:

- preparation of budgets;
- development of business plans;
- data files for vehicles, employees, etc;
- management of inventories;
- forecasting;
- project planning; and
- simple 'what if' simulation models.

Database packages are data management programs developed for use with personal computers. The program consists of a set of tools with which data can be organised and manipulated in a simple and effective manner. A customer address list is a typical database. Such an address list, keyed into and recorded on a database package, can be used and organised as required. Dependent on the data included, the package could provide an immediate response to questions such as:

- Which customers are in a given geographic area?
- Which customers are in a given postcode?
- How many delivery locations for a certain national account customer?
- What is the address of a certain customer?
- What new customers have been included this year?

Database packages are structured to provide a very fast response, and to enable relatively complicated 'search' type questions to be asked and answered. Data can be sorted and resorted according to user requirements.

Potential applications in distribution include:

- customer records;
- inventory management;
- equipment records;
- planned maintenance schedules; and
- repair and maintenance records.

Storage and warehousing

There have been a number of developments in the use of computers in storage and warehousing systems. The warehouse is an area where a very large amount of data and information is required in order for operations to be planned and run effectively. Computers have provided management with a tool to help manipulate data, and this has been of considerable benefit in many instances.

Better customer service and operational control continue to follow from the improvement in information handling, perhaps more so than from equipment developments. Mini- and microcomputers have given the ability for fast and accurate control and the availability of the correct up-to-date information which should enable further major improvements to be made.

A prerequisite for control is the facility for collating, transmitting and analysing information accurately and quickly. The objectives and benefits of good information systems in the warehouse include:

- greater speed of response;
- reduction of clerical effort;

- stock item selection procedures to minimise movement and clerical effort;
- greater accuracy; and
- improved management control.

There are systems which go some way towards achieving many of these objectives. The ultimate will be an integrated information system which collects, analyses and disseminates information in the required format to the required operating centres, at the right time, and at high speed, to drive the different parts of the stores system. This is further outlined in the final section of this chapter.

Benefits also come from the better use of resources:

- reduced inventory resulting from more accurate and immediate stock data, and hence a lower storage capacity requirement; and
- reduced clerical and operating costs by reducing duplication, errors, stock-outs and handling and movement.

Other benefits come from the accuracy and immediacy of information handling and the ability to respond quickly to changing or unexpected situations so maintaining and improving customer service.

The major areas of application for computers in storage and warehousing are outlined below.

An effective *order processing/sales accounting* system is vital to a successful distribution operation. There are a number of features which should be included in a good order processing system. These are:

- a range of order entry techniques (telesales, telex, hand-held terminals, written forms, Prestel, POS equipment, etc);
- stock allocation at order entry;
- scheduled delivery time, assigned at order entry;
- generation of picking lists, loading schedules and delivery notes;
- interface to sales ledger or credit control and invoicing; and
- analyses and reports.

Demand forecasting is vital to support any stock control system. Statistically based techniques can be quite readily used with computer-based models. As indicated in Chapter 19, account must be taken of availability, seasonality, promotions, etc.

Stock control systems provide the basis for cost effective stock management. Computerised systems have been available for several years. A good package should include:

- records of total stock-holding, all issues, receipts, purchase orders and allocations;
- records of supplier performance, lead-time information and purchase price;
- re-order level, re-order quantity and buying units;
- units of issue;
- reports on stock levels, back orders and service levels;
- interfaces with order processing and sales ledger;
- action reports covering information such as zero stock, excessive high stock, stock variance, etc;
- an allowance for in-transit stock; and
- multi-site stock information (where necessary).

A much more recent development in computerised systems in the warehouse environment is that of *warehouse management* computer packages. As the name suggests, these systems are concerned with the provision of effective operational management and control of the warehousing and storage functions. These systems might include:

- order, load, or bulk picking;
- picking route selection;
- picking checks and verification;
- stock rotation;
- replenishment management;
- location selection for incoming goods;
- reports on space utilisation, picker productivity, etc; and
- stock-taking.

The development of high technology equipment and handling systems such as *automated storage and retrieval systems* (AS/RS) has only been feasible because of the associated development of the related information technology. AS/RS systems require extremely sophisticated and rigorous computer software to direct, monitor and control the cranes and other automated equipment.

New applications for information technology in storage and warehousing are continuously being tested. It is still not uncommon, however, to see order picking from non-computerised paper requisitions in warehouses.

Amongst the more recent developments have been the use of 'paperless' systems for order picking, including truck mounted terminals (on-line) and portable data entry terminals.

Truck mounted terminals communicate with a supervisory computer via a radio link, on-line anywhere within the signal range. The driver is in continuous contact with the control computer via a simple terminal and visual display mounted on the truck.

Portable data entry terminals are not always on-line but hold data in memory which is periodically changed using remote data exchange ports. During down loading, stock-outs or damaged stock can be reported back to the host computer and the memory cleared and recharged with the next requisition list. Check digits can also be used to ensure that the storeman has correctly located stock items.

It is common for goods received data to be batched and passed to a VDU operator, possibly at the end of each day, to be keyed into the system. In terms of accuracy and speed, this is not wholly satisfactory, because of the following factors:

- Delay – there is delay between receiving goods and entering them on the computer.
- Mismatch – using advice notes for data entry assumes they are accurate, which may not always be the case.
- VDU entry – apart from being a fairly slow process, this is also a source of error.

More accurate and fast data entry is achieved by systems which transfer information without human interpretation, eg bar coding. Instead of checking off goods against an advice note, the receiving clerk reads bar codes attached to either pallets or cases, using a hand-held laser scanner or light pen. This requires that incoming stock is suitably marked.

Bar code labels are inexpensive to produce, especially if printed with other information by the case manufacturer, and improved printing and reading equipment is continuously being developed.

Transport

There are a large number of IT applications concerning road freight transport. They can be broadly categorised into three main system types:

- fleet management;
- fleet planning and operations; and
- vehicle-based.

Fleet management systems are aimed at assisting the transport manager to monitor, control and administer the transport operation. There are a number of typical packages.

Maintenance scheduling

This includes the monitoring of the service life of vehicles in a fleet and the scheduling of routine and non-routine maintenance and repairs. Package features include:

- service history;
- maintenance schedule reports; and
- workshop costs analysis.

Vehicle parts control

This is the stock control function of spare parts requirements. Features may include:

- stock enquiry;
- maintenance of supplier information;
- stock location;
- stock reports; and
- the generation of purchase orders.

Fleet administration

Fleet administration packages are used to ensure that vehicles are legal and roadworthy. Package features may include:

- vehicle licence;
- DTp due reports; and
- insurance lapse reports, etc.

Fleet costing

These packages provide detailed information relating to vehicle and fleet costs. They assist the manager by providing analyses and information concerning individual vehicle and overall fleet profitability. Features include:

- vehicle cost analysis;
- driver cost analysis; and
- overall fleet costs.

Systems for fleet planning and operations include a number of packages that have been developed to help determine basic transport resource requirements as well as packages that aim to maximise the utilisation and effectiveness of these resources.

Tachograph analysis

Information from tachograph recordings provides the input data for the analysis of driver/vehicle performance. Typical package features are:

- infringement reports;
- driver and vehicle utilisation reports; and
- fleet reports.

Tachograph analysis packages/modules are usually stand alone, but can be integrated with other transport management modules.

Routeing and scheduling

As discussed in Chapter 17, there are three main uses to which computer vehicle routeing and scheduling packages may be put – strategic, tactical and day-to-day operational. Computer packages are generally designed to address one of these specific aspects. A few packages can be used to cover more than one of these areas and road database programs are often used to support all of these types of package.

The general aim of these packages is to 'optimise' vehicle usage whilst providing a given service level for a given level of work. This may be achieved in a variety of ways – maximise vehicle time utilisation, maximise capacity utilisation, minimise mileage, etc, and will be constrained by a number of factors – vehicle capacities (weight, volume), time restrictions, etc. Note that the majority of packages do not, in fact, provide an optimum solution to a problem. They provide the best answer within a given set of constraints and demands.

The four major types of package can be summarised as follows:

1. *Strategic* – part of the overall distribution system/structure. Models how the transport element is positioned within the total system. A significant use is to determine the appropriate fleet size and mix for an operation.
2. *Tactical* – a three-month to one-year timescale. Ideal to set up regular vehicle schedules for fixed location/delivery points. Based on historical data and can be easily adapted to the manual 'pigeon hole' scheduling systems. May set up different schedules for significant seasonal variations in demand.
3. *Day-to-day/operational* – routes scheduled on a daily basis using actual (not historic) demand (see Figure 20.1). A dynamic system taking account of daily alterations in constraints, etc. Used for random demand operations (ie variable order sizes and delivery points). Can result in varied routes day by day.

Courtesy of Istel

Figure 20.1 PC with a graphic display of a daily vehicle route plan

4. *Single vehicle routeing* – these computer packages are based around very detailed computerised road databases. By indicating origin and destination points, and any intervening points to be visited on the route, the program will construct routes based on the real road network. Routes can be determined on the basis of shortest, quickest, cheapest, etc. Very detailed parameters can be user-input, such as road speeds, costs, etc. Output is provided by a detailed description of the route, giving instructions on when to change from one road to another, together with the times and distances between these road links. Some packages provide coloured screen maps of the chosen routes, enabling visual comparisons to be made.

Typical data requirements were described in Chapter 17.

Some of the main packages available for the different routeing and scheduling requirements are as shown in Table 20.1. Additional information on these and other packages can be found in several annual guides to distribution software.

Table 20.1: Routeing and scheduling packages

Tactical	Operational	Single routeing
Pathfinder	Carp	Autoroute
DIPS	Dayload	A to B
Mover	Paragon	JAP
Paragon	DIPS	Whichway
Routemaster	Routemaster	Micropath
Transit	Loadstar	Pathway
Vanplan	Pigeonhole	Routefinder
	Visit	

The absolute accuracy of any package can by no means be guaranteed. The bulk of the packages named above are in quite common use, but advances, particularly in operational packages are very recent, and there are still only a limited number of packages successfully in operation. A number of other packages are on the market, but they are generally unproven.

It should also be noted that the scope of computer packages is very varied. Some are very simplistic, others quite sophisticated. In general, the more sophisticated package is significantly more expensive than the simpler one.

Some of the advantages claimed for computerised vehicle routeing and scheduling systems are as follows:

- decreased standing costs as the vehicle establishment can be minimised;
- decreased running costs as efficient routeing reduces mileage;
- less need to hire-in vehicles;
- increased customer service through consistent and reliable schedules;
- less chance of breaking transport regulations through the ability to program in legislative constraints;
- savings in management time as schedules can be calculated quickly; and
- increase in level of control because more accurate management reporting is possible.

Vehicle-based systems are a recent development in the application of information technology to transport. These systems are generally aimed at monitoring the driver and his vehicle. Included are:

- data loggers, for monitoring fuel, etc;
- local monitors, for monitoring security, weight, etc;
- diagnostics, for measuring vehicle conditions such as stress factors on engines, suspension, etc;
- in-cab display, for providing driver information on preferred routes, road conditions, etc.

Integrated systems

The demands on logistics and distribution have now reached a stage whereby very advanced and sophisticated information systems are essential to provide a sound basis for the physical systems to flourish and operate effectively. To achieve this, software packages are being developed to provide a fully integrated information system which is aimed to reflect the distribution organisational structure.

The major features of an integrated distribution information system are twofold:

1. To unify the many and varied functions and components within the distribution organisation.
2. To provide access to data and information at all levels so that any task can be undertaken without the necessity to re-input data or use parallel systems.

For such a system to operate it is vital that all information from each of the various sub-systems (sales, finance, warehousing, etc) is made available to any other sub-system. Information concerning product purchases, for example, may need to be available to primary transport, warehouse goods receipt, inventory control, etc.

In practical terms, the means of achieving this is in the form of 'networking' which provides the opportunity for the linking of computer terminals at various locations and the use of a common database. Thus, virtually instantaneous electronic information sharing is possible. Some of the feasible opportunities include the following:

- *Electronic mail* – where considerable time and paperwork reduction can be achieved as communication is undertaken via the computer.
- *Vertical network* – where, for example, continuous links are available from head office to all depots.

- *Horizontal network* – here, depot to depot communication allows information sharing between the different distribution points.
- *Channel networks* – these allow for electronic links across company boundaries. Here, for example, continuous communication is possible direct from the customer through retail outlets, retail head office, distribution company, supplier or to whoever is a part of the distribution channel or supply chain.

There are very significant developments already taking place regarding *Electronic Data Interchange* (EDI). The definition of EDI is 'the transfer of structured data by agreed message standards from computer to computer by electronic means'. A common language or translation standard is essential, and currently there are two standards in use: TRADACOMS developed by the Article Numbering Association and used widely in the UK retail distribution; and EDIFACT, a message standard developed for international trade.

Various services have been set up to facilitate data interchange. These *Value Added Data Services* (VADS) are used for the storage and transfer of data and they include:

- TRADANET – used very widely by the food, white goods, DIY and clothing industries;
- CEFIC – used by the chemical industry;
- EDIFICE – used by the electronics industry;
- MOTORNET – used by the automobile industry; and
- CHIEF – developed by the UK Customs and Excise for customs clearance purposes.

The potential benefits of integrated distribution systems can be summarised as:

- productivity improvements resulting from automatic data transfer;
- reduced errors due to elimination of transcribing and keying;
- vast reduction in paperwork handling;
- improved information systems in terms of speed of response and accuracy; and
- drawing together of previously unlinked units.

For the future, the progress towards integrated information systems seems likely to follow the same path that the previously disparate elements of physical distribution have taken – towards the concept of a total system. The first steps along this path that have already been taken are:

- the pressures to minimise stock levels and reduce order lead times;
- the introduction of distribution requirements planning (DRP) computer systems;
- improvements in electronic data capture – office automation, paperless systems, voice data entry, etc;
- developments in computer hardware; and
- the greater involvement and understanding of distribution users in what they want from a computer information system.

Summary

In this chapter, recent developments in information technology have been discussed, in particular those aspects directly concerned with logistics and distribution. The main factors considered were:

- the development of IT and logistics;
- computer hardware and software selection;
- software packages for logistics and distribution strategy;
- the use of general applications software;
- storage and warehousing packages;
- transport packages; and
- integrated systems.

PART 5

Associated Factors

CHAPTER 21

The Organisation of Logistics and Distribution in the Company

Introduction

This chapter is concerned with the way in which logistics and distribution is organised within the company. The importance of the integration of the distribution function into the business as a whole has been emphasised at various times throughout the contents of this book. In addition to this need for integration in the business sense, is the need for the organisational structure to reflect a similar form of integration. Thus, the organisational structure and the human resource or 'people' aspects are considered here.

There are four main factors that are covered, the first being a brief summary of those aspects, discussed in Chapter 2, related to the relationship of logistics and distribution with other corporate functions. The second factor is concerned with the main distribution organisational structures that are found. Next, the role of the distribution manager is considered – particularly with respect to his or her position within the company. Finally, an attempt is made to take a more 'grass roots' view of distribution using the results of a recent survey of payment schemes within the distribution environment.

Relationships with other corporate functions

In the first two chapters, logistics and distribution were considered in the context of business and the economy as a whole. In particular, the interfaces with other corporate functions were discussed, the major ones being with production, marketing and finance. In many subsequent chapters, the importance of these corporate relationships has been emphasised. This importance is particularly valid where the planning of corporate strategy is concerned.

There are two main points that bear emphasis at this stage. First, the fact that logistics is, for many companies, such an integral part of the corporate being. Because of this, the second major point becomes apparent – the need for logistics planning and strategy to be recognised and used as a vital ingredient in the corporate plan.

The first point – that logistics is such an important element within many companies' total business structure – has been illustrated using the interrelationships of logistics to other functions:

With production Production scheduling
Production control
Plant warehouse design
etc

With marketing Customer service
Packaging
Depot location
Order processing
etc

With finance Stock holding
Stock control
Equipment financing
Distribution cost control
etc

The need to include the planning of logistics and distribution into the overall corporate plan is thus self evident. The business planning process is summarised very broadly in Figure 21.1.

Even within this broad framework it can be seen that distribution factors are a vital input. Within the process of market analysis and the

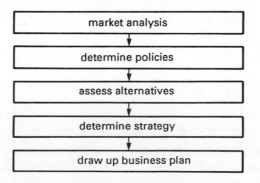

Figure 21.1 Business planning procedure summary

determination of policies, the elements of customer service requirements and channel choice are, for example, very relevant. With any assessment of alternative policies and in any subsequent determination of competitive strategies, the different costs and performance factors of the various distribution systems are vital. Any factors related to the procurement, storage and movement of goods must, of necessity, be relevant to the determination of a company's business plan.

The reason that companies fail to take sufficient account of the distribution/logistics input to corporate planning is probably due to the dynamic nature of the distribution environment and operation. Distribution is seen to be very much about doing and providing. As such, it is often treated as a short-term factor, with little relevance to long-term planning.

Distribution is both a long- as well as a short-term function. Its very dynamism tends to mould the one into the other, making it difficult at the operational level to distinguish between the two. The size and extent of financial and physical investment makes it imperative that this differentiation is made, where necessary, and that elements of distribution and logistics are included in the overall business plan.

Distribution organisational structures

Associated with the failure to include relevant distribution factors within the corporate business plan is the need to recognise that the distribution function may also require a specific organisational structure.

For many years, the concept of distribution has been unrecognised within the organisational structure of a company. Although recently the importance of distribution and logistics has become much more apparent to a broad range of companies, a number have still failed to adapt their basic organisational structures to reflect this changing view.

Such companies have traditionally allocated the various physical distribution functions among several associated company functions. This failure to represent distribution positively within the organisational structure is thus often a result of historical arrangement rather than a specific desire to ignore the requirement for a positive physical distribution management structure. Clearly, some positive organisational structure is essential, if the distribution function is to be planned and operated effectively.

A typical structure, showing physical distribution functions based on traditional lines is illustrated in Figure 21.2.

The problem with this type of organisation is that the lines of communication are unclear. Thus, it is often impossible to optimise the

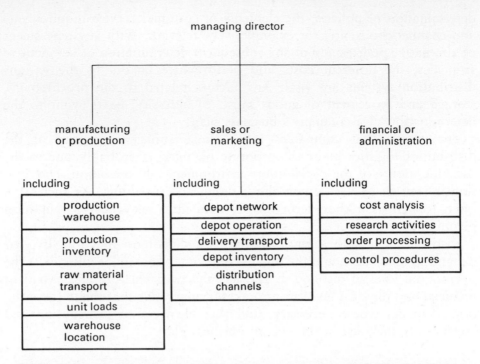

Figure 21.2 Traditional organisation structure of physical distribution functions

efficiency of the different distribution sub-functions, let alone create an overall physical distribution system which is both effective and efficient.

Several of the more forward looking distribution-orientated companies have seen the need for some formal organisational change to represent the recognition now being given to the distribution and logistics activity.

This new functional approach emphasises the need for physical distribution to be planned; operated and controlled as one overall activity. The precise structure will obviously differ from one company to another. A typical structure might be, as illustrated in Figure 21.3.

This type of structure allows distribution to be managed as a function in its own right although the need for close liaison with other company functions remains vital.

Other organisational structures may also be relevant. One such is called mission management (Figure 21.4) and is based on the concept of the management of computer systems or flows. This is undoubtedly relevant to logistics and distribution which are concerned with material flow and the associated information flow often from raw material through various processes, storage and movement to the final customer. Some of the larger chemical companies, for example, adopt this type of management

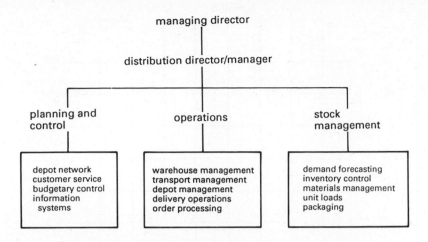

Figure 21.3 Functional structure of physical distribution activities

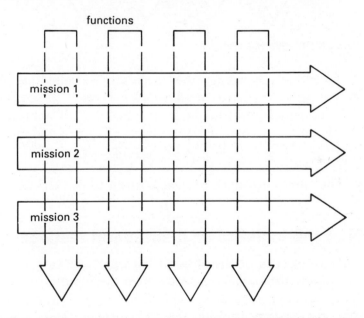

Figure 21.4 Mission management which acts across traditional functional boundaries

structure to provide co-ordination and control throughout the process of particular products.

Mission management is cross-functional, and as such can pose problems in a traditionally functional organisation. Because of this, a further development, matrix management, has evolved (Figure 21.5). Here the product or flow is managed by a 'flow' or logistics manager,

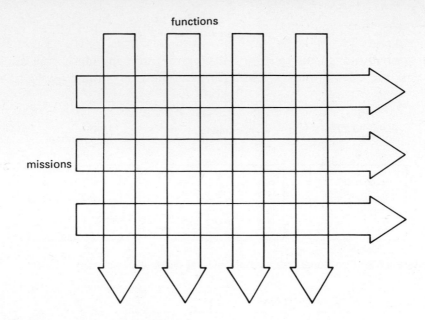

Figure 21.5 Matrix management

with the functions providing the necessary inputs as they are required.

Clearly the potential problems lie in the inability to manage and co-ordinate across functional boundaries. However, where good management practices have been followed, and in the appropriate operational context, organisational structures such as these have been made to work very effectively. They are particularly relevant for customer service orientated businesses.

The role of the logistics or distribution manager

The role of the logistics or distribution manager can vary considerably from one company to another, dependent on the internal organisational structure, the channel type (own account, third party, etc), the industry or product, and the customer profile. Factors such as these will certainly effect the extent of the operational role and to a lesser extent the nature of the planning role.

In an earlier section of this chapter, the need for companies to include the planning of logistics and distribution in the overall corporate strategy was emphasised. It is useful here to consider the part that the logistics/distribution manager can play in the planning process.

In a recent article, M A McGinnis and B J Lalonde discussed this question. A summary of the main points provide an interesting framework.

They take three main themes: the contribution that the logistics/distribution manager can make to corporate strategic planning; the advantages of this contribution; and the preparation that the manager can make to increase the effectiveness of his/her input. The main points are as follows:

- Contribution to corporate strategic planning
    - an understanding of the functional interfaces;
    - an understanding of distribution's activities;
    - familiarity with the external environment as it relates to distribution;
    - insights regarding competitor distribution strategies;
    - familiarity with customer distribution needs;
    - familiarity with channels of distribution; and
    - distribution data.
- Advantages of contributing to corporate plan
    - understanding of impact of corporate strategy on distribution activities;
    - increased physical distribution responsiveness;
    - increased sensitivity to the distribution environment;
    - identifying distribution opportunities; and
    - improving communications.
- Preparation for strategic planning
    - know the company;
    - develop a broader perspective of distribution;
    - know the distribution environment;
    - develop rapport/liaison with others;
    - know customer needs; and
    - improve communication skills.

Distribution related planning activities are thus a vital input in the overall business strategy. The more specific activities were outlined in the early chapters of this book. They involve a medium- to long-term planning horizon and will include aspects such as the number of facilities, their size and location, transport networks, fleet size and mix of vehicles, stock levels, information systems, etc.

As already indicated, the operational role for managers can vary significantly according to the size and nature of the business, the product, the channel type and the customer profile, among other factors. Also, there are a number of different job titles and job functions that exist. These range from the distribution or logistics manager who might have overall responsibility for an entire distribution network, including central depots, regional depots, trunking and delivery vehicles, stock location and control, computer systems, etc to a shift manager or supervisor who might, for example, be concerned with the detailed performance and control of an order picking operation on a night shift.

In general, the three main operational areas of responsibility are related to:

- transport – trunking, delivery operations, vehicle routeing and scheduling, vehicle procurement, etc;
- warehousing – goods inward, bulk storage, order picking, marshalling, equipment, etc; and
- information – stock location, stock control, order processing, budgeting, monitoring and control, etc.

In addition to these broad functional areas, there is a staff role concerning the management of human resources and the linkage to other distribution interfaces such as production/supply, marketing/sales and finance.

Over and above all of these aspects of the operational role, and probably common to all types of distribution organisations, is the responsibility for, and the need to control, the balance between the service to the customer and the cost of providing this service.

Payment schemes

One relatively neglected area in the literature on logistics and distribution concerns the payment mechanisms and incentive schemes that are used within the industry. Having looked at the broad role of the manager within distribution, it is interesting to gain a better understanding of the 'grass roots' position related to the type of payment systems that are commonly used.

There are a number of different types of payment mechanism. These can be broadly divided into the three main systems of daywork, piecework and payment by results. These three systems are illustrated in Figure 21.6. Here it can be seen that daywork is a method of payment based entirely on the hours attended at work; piecework is payment entirely related to the amount of work undertaken; and payment by results is a mixture of these, providing a basic wage plus a bonus based on work undertaken.

The main payment systems can be summarised as follows:

- *Daywork* (also known as graded hours, fixed day, etc) – based entirely on hours worked.
- *Measured daywork* – basic attendance wage plus bonus for achieving a given level of work performance.

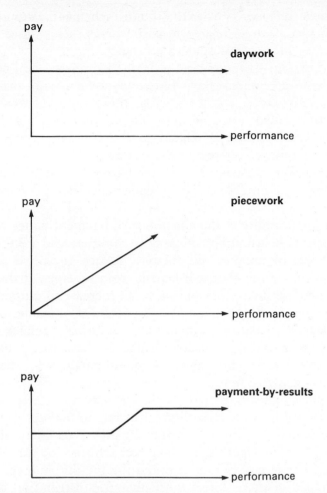

Figure 21.6 Three different pay-performance schemes showing varying sensitivities to performance between each

- *Stepped measured daywork* (stabilised incentive scheme, premium payment plan) – introduces 'steps' in the measured daywork scheme, so providing additional incentive.
- *Merit-rated bonus scheme* (incentive bonus scheme) – a bonus scheme on top of a basic wage, but not productivity related.
- *Piecework* – payment related entirely to the amount of work completed.
- *Payment by results* – in its purest form this is piecework, usually it is a results-based payment on top of a basic wage.
- *Commission* – a piecework or payment by results scheme, but based on effort and achievement (ie sales, cost savings). A common type of management bonus scheme.

- *Plant-wide schemes* – collective bonus schemes based on collective performance. Can be related to costs versus sales, added to value of operations, increased output or efficiency.
- *Fringe benefits* – various non-performance related add-ons covering such items as holiday pay, Christmas bonus, subsidised canteen, clothing allowance, etc. Eventually, these types of benefit become taken for granted.
- *Profit sharing scheme* – related to the company profit. Aimed at fostering employee interest in the company.
- *Share schemes* – usually limited to managers and directors, though there are some notable company-wide schemes.

Clearly, the applicability of these methods of payment varies considerably from one type of distribution company to another, and from one type of distribution job to another. Productivity-related incentive schemes are only valid in operations that will benefit from schemes of this nature, ie where increased worker effort will mean an increase in output. For many distribution operations, for example, the need for accurate, timely order picking may far outweigh the number of picks made per picker per hour. Additionally, it is likely to be both dangerous and illegal to propose a driver incentive scheme which gives additional payment for the speed with which the work is completed.

It is worth emphasising two particular aspects related to payment schemes, and to show how these vary according to the type of scheme that is operated. The first is the significance or power of financial incentives. This is illustrated in Figure 21.7. In direct contrast to this, Figure 21.8 shows the extent of supervision required for the different schemes.

The relevance of these different schemes for distribution is best summarised according to the main breakdown of distribution personnel – drivers and warehouse staff.

Drivers are most likely to be paid on hours worked or hours guaranteed – some form of daywork. There may also be a special rate for the job, based on work experience or driving qualifications. In terms of incentive, a form of 'job and finish' might be operated, giving extra leisure rather than extra cash as the incentive. Financial bonuses might be offered as a form of payment by results based on such things as miles run, cases delivered, etc. Once again it must be emphasised that any bonus payments are prohibited if they endanger road safety.

Warehouse staff are also likely to receive remuneration based on hours worked or guaranteed. In the more controlled environment of a warehouse, daywork is likely to be measured. Additionally, there are likely to be different rates according to different job functions (fork life truck

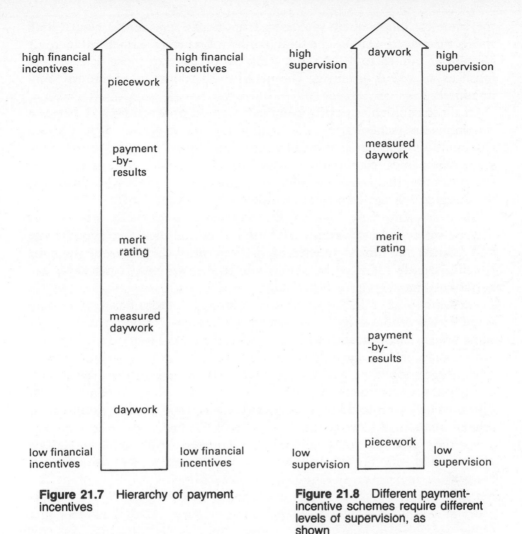

Figure 21.7 Hierarchy of payment incentives

Figure 21.8 Different payment-incentive schemes require different levels of supervision, as shown

drivers, pickers, etc). Merit-rated bonuses based, perhaps, on attendance might be offered, and certainly productivity-related bonuses are likely to be very common, based on cases picked, pallets moved, etc. Measured performance schemes are operated based on work study standards for specific tasks.

A recent survey undertaken by the Distribution Studies Unit at Cranfield provides some interesting pointers to the use of payment and incentive schemes in distribution in the UK. The main results are described below.

For drivers, the most commonly used payment structure was the basic guaranteed wage plus a productivity bonus (38 per cent of companies in the sample), followed by guaranteed hours (28 per cent). Figure 21.9 shows the overall results. The total number of schemes with a productivity element amounted to 46 per cent while 56 per cent of those had job and finish as an added incentive. The majority of transport operations were unionised.

Of those companies paying bonuses based on productivity, 62 per cent ran individual schemes, 34 per cent group schemes and 4 per cent a combination. The basis of performance assessment is quite varied, with some companies combining several different measures. Figure 21.10 illustrates that the most common is miles driven (54 per cent) followed by drops made (46 per cent) and cases dropped (38 per cent).

An assessment of the benefits of productivity-based bonus schemes for drivers was determined. Figure 21.11 indicates that increased productivity and reduced idle time were cited by 77 per cent of the survey as the main benefits, closely followed by better industrial relations (73 per cent) and better customer service (70 per cent).

For warehouse staff, 32 per cent of companies used a basic guaranteed wage with a productivity bonus, with an additional 12 per cent using the same system incorporated with a rate for the job. Twenty-four per cent have a guaranteed wage only with a further 8 per cent a guaranteed wage plus a rate for the job. Figure 21.12 shows the overall results. A comparison with drivers indicated that there are a few more warehouse operators on guaranteed hours (daywork) and slightly fewer on productivity-related bonuses (43 per cent compared with 46 per cent).

For the warehouse productivity-based schemes, 76 per cent were group schemes and only 24 per cent individual schemes, an almost complete reversal of the driver situation. The most common measure of performance was cases picked (53 per cent), followed by orders picked (43 per cent) and vehicles handled (28 per cent). Figure 21.13 illustrates this. Other measures included pallets picked, lines picked, distance travelled (fork lift trucks) and volume handled. Sixty-two per cent of companies allocated standard times to these measures.

As with the driver results, increased productivity heads the list of benefits at 66 per cent following in this instance by reduced overtime (62 per cent) and better industrial relations (52 per cent). Figure 21.14 illustrates these results.

Summary

This chapter has considered various aspects of the organisation of logistics and distribution in the company. The first section concentrated on the

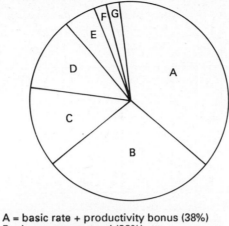

A = basic rate + productivity bonus (38%)
B = hours guaranteed (28%)
C = hours worked + rate for the job (13%)
D = hours worked (12%)
E = basic rate + productivity bonus + rate for the job (5%)
F = basic rate + productivity bonus + rate for the job
  + miles driven (2%)
G = basic rate + guaranteed bonus (2%)

Figure 21.9 Driver payment schemes; the result of a Cranfield survey

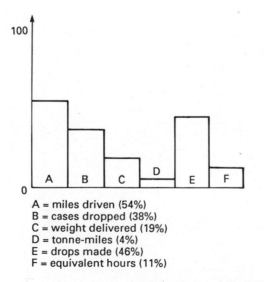

A = miles driven (54%)
B = cases dropped (38%)
C = weight delivered (19%)
D = tonne-miles (4%)
E = drops made (46%)
F = equivalent hours (11%)

Figure 21.10 The basis of driver performance assessment; the result of a
Cranfield survey

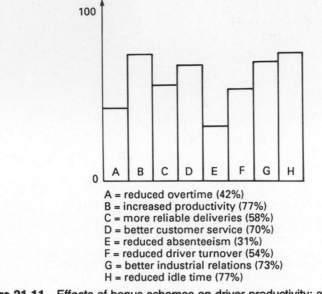

A = reduced overtime (42%)
B = increased productivity (77%)
C = more reliable deliveries (58%)
D = better customer service (70%)
E = reduced absenteeism (31%)
F = reduced driver turnover (54%)
G = better industrial relations (73%)
H = reduced idle time (77%)

Figure 21.11 Effects of bonus schemes on driver productivity; a Cranfield survey

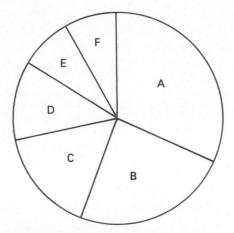

A = basic rate + productivity bonus (32%)
B = hours guaranteed (24%)
C = hours worked (16%)
D = basic rate + productivity bonus + rate for the job (12%)
E = hours guaranteed + rate for the job (8%)
F = basic rate + guaranteed bonus (8%)

Figure 21.12 Warehouse payment schemes; the result of a Cranfield survey

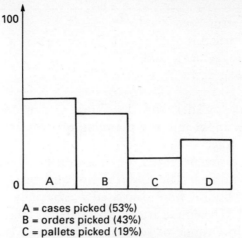

A = cases picked (53%)
B = orders picked (43%)
C = pallets picked (19%)
D = vehicles loaded/unloaded (28%)

Figure 21.13 The basis for warehouse productivity schemes; the result of a Cranfield survey

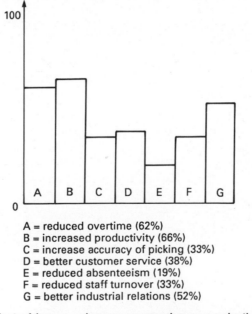

A = reduced overtime (62%)
B = increased productivity (66%)
C = increase accuracy of picking (33%)
D = better customer service (38%)
E = reduced absenteeism (19%)
F = reduced staff turnover (33%)
G = better industrial relations (52%)

Figure 21.14 Effect of bonus schemes on warehouse productivity; a Cranfield survey

relationship with other corporate functions and concluded that there is a need to include the planning of logistics and distribution within the overall corporate/business plan.

The next section discussed the basic organisational structures that are used in distribution. These included:

- traditional structure;
- functional structure;
- mission management; and
- matrix management.

The role of the logistics and distribution manager was assessed with regard to his/her input into the planning process and with respect to his/her operational role.

Finally, the different types of distribution payment and incentive schemes were outlined. The applicability and relevance of these various schemes to distribution were discussed – especially regarding drivers and warehouse staff. The implications on financial incentives and degrees of supervision for the range of schemes was noted. The results of a recent survey indicated the extent of the use of the different payment and incentive schemes in UK distribution operations.

CHAPTER 22

The Product, Packaging, and Unitisation

Introduction

One of the major factors to be considered when planning for distribution is, perhaps not surprisingly, the product itself. The product is, in fact, perceived as an amalgam of its physical nature, its price, its package and the way in which it is supplied (ie the service).

The implications regarding customer service were considered in Chapter 3. In this chapter, the importance of the physical nature of the product and its package are discussed with respect to the planning and operation of distribution systems.

For the distribution planner, the physical characteristics of the product and package are seen to be of great significance. This is because, in distribution, we are directly concerned with physical flow – movement and storage.

The physical characteristics of a product, any specific packaging requirements and the type of unit load, are all-important factors in the trade-off with other elements of distribution when trying to seek least cost systems at given service levels. In the consideration of the product and its package, the trade-off potential should continually be borne in mind.

Product characteristics

There are a variety of product characteristics that have a direct, and often important, impact on the development and operation of a distribution system. This impact can affect both the structure of the system and also the cost of the system. The major characteristics are:

- volume;
- weight;
- value;
- perishability;
- fragility;
- hazard/danger; and
- substitutability.

It is possible to classify these into four main categories:

- volume to weight ratio;
- value to weight ratio;
- substitutability; and
- special characteristics.

Volume to weight ratio

Volume and weight characteristics are commonly associated, and their influence on distribution costs can be a significant one.

A low ratio of volume to weight in a product (such as sheet steel, books, etc) generally means an efficient utilisation of the elements of distribution. Thus, a low volume/high weight product will fully utilise the weight-carrying capacity of a road transport vehicle. Similarly, the handling cost component of storage costs decreases with full equipment utilisation (most other storage costs are not significantly affected by low volume/weight ratios).

The converse, a high volume to weight ratio, tends to be very inefficient for distribution. Typical products include paper tissues, crisps, disposable nappies, etc. The products have a very high space utilisation, and are costly for both transportation and storage. In the UK, for example, there has recently been a noticeable increase in the use of draw-bar trailer outfits in an attempt to increase vehicle capacity and so decrease the transportation costs of high volume products.

Thus overall distribution costs tend to be greater for high volume as against high weight products. This effect is shown in Figure 22.1. It can be seen that the total costs of movement and storage tend to increase as volume to weight ratio increases.

Value to weight ratio

Product value is also important to the planning of a distribution strategy. This is because high value products are more able to absorb the associated distribution costs. It is often essential for low value products to have an inexpensive distribution system because the effect on the total cost of the

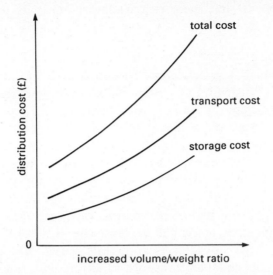

Figure 22.1 Effect of product volume to weight ratio on distribution costs

product might then make it non-viable in terms of its price in the market place.

Once again, it is useful to assess the value effect in terms of a weight ratio, the value to weight ratio. Low value to weight ratio products (ie ore, sand, etc) incur relatively high transport unit costs compared with high value to weight products (ie photographic equipment, computer equipment, etc). Storage unit costs of low value to weight ratio products tend to be low in comparison with high value products because the capital tied up in inventory is lower.

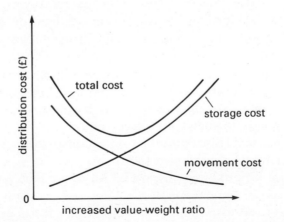

Figure 22.2 Effect of product value/weight ratios on logistic systems costs

Figure 22.2 shows that there is a trade-off effect as value to weight ratios increase.

Substitutability

The degree to which a product can be substituted by another will also affect the choice of distribution system. When customers readily substitute a product with a different brand or type of goods, then it is important that the distribution system is designed to avoid stock-outs or to react to replenish stocks in a timely fashion. Typical examples are many food products, where the customer is likely to choose an alternative brand if the need is immediate and the first choice name is not available.

In a distribution system, this can be catered for either through high stock levels or through a high performance transport mode. Both options are high cost. High stock levels will decrease the likelihood of a stock-out, but will raise average stock levels and, thus, costs. The provision of a faster and more dependable transport function will reduce acquisition time and length of stock-out, but this increase in service will be at a higher transport cost.

Special characteristics

In many ways, the various special characteristics of products (perishability, fragility, hazard/danger, contamination potential, extreme value) represent a degree of risk associated with distributing the product. The need to minimise this risk (sometimes a legal obligation) means that a special distribution system design must be used. As with any form of specialisation, there will be a cost incurred. Examples of this effect include the following items:

- Hazardous goods which may require special packaging, a limited unit load size, special labelling, isolation from other products. Regulations for the movement of hazardous goods differ between the different modes of transport.
- Fragile products which require special packaging to take account of handling and transport shocks. In the UK, specialist distribution companies now exist for some types of fragile goods.
- Perishable goods in many instances require special conditions and equipment for their distribution (ie refrigerated storage and transport facilities for frozen and chilled food).
- Time-constrained products – almost all foods are now time-constrained in the UK now that 'best before' dates are so common. This has implications for distribution information and control systems (ie first-in, first-out). Some products have fixed time or seasonal deadlines.

Daily newspapers have a very limited lifespan which allows for no delivery delays; fashion goods often have a fixed season; agro-chemicals such as fertilisers and insecticides have fixed periods for usage; there are the classic seasonal examples of Easter eggs and Christmas crackers which are time-constrained. There are significant implications for the choice of distribution system for many products such as these.

- Very high value products – cigarettes, videos, etc are attractive high value products which demand especially secure means of distribution.

There are many and varied product characteristics which can impose important requirements and constraints on all of the main distribution functions. They also affect the interrelationships between the functions, providing quite complex alternatives which need to be measured according to the implications on service and on cost.

The product life-cycle

One marketing concept which concerns the product and is also very relevant to distribution is that of the product life-cycle (PLC). The principle behind PCL is that of the staged development of a product. This begins with the introduction of the product into the market, follows (for successful products) with the steady growth of the product as it becomes established, continues with the accelerated growth of the product as competitors introduce similar products which stimulate total demand, and ends as the product life runs into decline. The PLC concept is illustrated in Figure 22.3

It is important that physical distribution performance is able to reflect the life-cycle of a product. This can be differentiated as follows:

- Introductory stage – need for a high response to demand with a distribution system that gives stock availability and quick replenishment, and can react to sudden demand increases. Initial retail stock-holdings are likely to be low so there is a need for speedy information and physical systems.
- Growth stage – here, sales are more predictable. The requirements for distribution are now for a better balanced, more cost effective system. The trade-off between service and cost can be realised.
- Maturity stage – where the introduction of competitive products and substitutes will increase price and service competition. An effective distribution service becomes vital, especially for key customers.
- Decline stage – the product is becoming obsolescent. Here, the

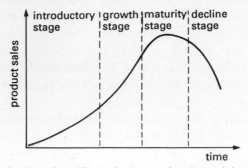

Figure 22.3 Standard product life cycle curve showing original growth, maturation and decline

physical distribution system needs to support the existing business but at minimum risk and cost.

There is a clear requirement to take into account the PLC concept when planning the distribution function. A different emphasis needs to be placed on certain aspects of the distribution system according to the stage of a product's life. For systems where there are many products at varying stages of their PLC, this will not be crucial. In some instances, however, there will be a need to plan for a distribution system which is suitably dynamic and flexible.

Packaging

In discussion of the product, it is important to be aware of other relevant physical characteristics that influence any decisions regarding the choice of distribution systems. In terms of the physical nature of a product, it is not generally presented to the distribution system in its primary form, but in the form of a package or unit load. These two elements are thus relevant to any discussion concerned with the relationship of product and distribution.

The packaging of a product is broadly determined for product promotion and product protection, the latter being the function which is particularly pertinent to distribution. There are also some other factors that need to be considered when designing packaging for distribution purposes. In addition to product protection, packages should be easy to handle, convenient to store, readily identifiable and be secure.

Once again, there are trade-offs that exist between these factors. These trade-offs will concern the product and the distribution system itself. It is important to appreciate that for distributors the package is the product and so, where possible, should be given the characteristics that help rather than hinder the distribution process.

Packaging can be defined as 'the art, science, and technology of preparing goods for transport and sale' (BSI) or alternatively as a means of ensuring the safe delivery of a product to the ultimate consumer in sound condition at minimum overall cost.

Packaging is very much a part of the total distribution system and the design and use of packaging has implications for other functions such as production, marketing, and quality control, as well as for overall system costs. The different departments within an organisation will probably have different requirements for packaging. For example:

- marketing – concerned with presentation;
- technical – concerned with protection;
- distribution – concerned with identification and ease of handling; and
- accounts – concerned with cost.

Packaging therefore, fulfils various functions, depending on particular applications.

- Protect and preserve from physical, chemical and mechanical damage, deterioration, or contamination.
- Contain.
- Communicate
  - instructions and hazard warnings;
  - identification of contents; and
  - sales appeal/presentation.
- Be convenient
  - act as a dispenser and as a measure;
  - ease of handling;
  - ease of unitising; and
  - be disposable.
- Be compatible with packaging machinery – the faster the filling machine, the better quality the pack must be.

To these should be added a requirement that packaging should ideally be readily disposable or reusable. Note, too, that the functions of a package can vary according to the category of package, categories being:

- primary package – ie in direct contact with the product, eg sachet, bottle, tube, sack;

- secondary package – contains one or more primary packages; and
- temporary package – eg tote bin, box pallet for work-in-progress, etc.

The package in the distribution system

A package will be subject to significant handling and movement both before it is filled or applied to the material/goods it is designed to protect and contain, and afterwards.

The potential damage and deterioration which can happen to a product, and which the packaging is designed to prevent or minimise can arise from a number of different causes. These can be categorised under three headings, ie mechanical, environmental, and other causes.

Causes of mechanical damage include drops, other impacts, compression, vibration and abrasion or erosion. Environmental factors include water (condensation, rain, sea), extremes of dryness or of temperature, pressure changes (eg in aircraft), corrosion, light and solar radiation, odours or contamination from other products, and exposure to air. Other possible causes of damage include infestation (insects, vermin), fungi, bacteria, radio activity, and pilferage.

Packaging materials

There are a wide variety of packaging materials available and recent developments in plastic and other technologies have given rise to significant expansion in the range of materials available to the package designer. Each material, or combination, will have its own properties and characteristics, and it is these attributes which determine the suitability or otherwise of a material for a particular application.

Packaging materials commonly encountered include paperboard and wood, various metals such as tinplate and aluminium, glass, and a wide range of plastics such as nylon, polystyrene, and PVC. Various composite materials are also used and bonded laminates.

Properties of material which determine suitability for use in packaging include strength, flexibility, tear resistance, imperviousness to light and to moisture, heat and electrical insulation, and resistance to grease, solvents, chemicals, and bacteria.

Types of package

Retail packages, in many shapes and sizes, and familiar to us in the supermarket, the chemist's shop and the hardware store include, cans, jars and bottles, bags various, sachets, blister packs and thermo-formed containers. Their shape and material are all chosen to best contain, protect and display their contents.

Other primary packages found in industrial applications include sacks, kegs and drums.

Secondary packages which contain or enclose primary packages include fibreboard kegs, lined drums, boxes and crates, and shrink and stretch wrapping.

Other forms of protection
For product protection, often against moisture, there are special techniques which involve providing a barrier film, or moisture removal, eg:

- corrosion inhibitors, often in vapour form, which inhibit rusting of ferrous metal components;
- barrier films applied by spraying or dipping; and
- desiccant materials, such as silica gel, which absorb and retain moisture and are enclosed with the item to be protected, in an enclosed and sealed space.

Package marking
The Health and Safety at Work Act requires that adequate information about the nature of materials and substances for use at work should be available and this is now partly achieved by labelling and printing on to the package.

Package marking is used to communicate information, such as product description, grade, code, quantity, instructions for handling, storage, use, hazards, and manufacturer or supplier and destination information.

Unit loads

One important development in recent years has been the concept of the unit load. This came about due to the realisation of the high costs involved in the storage and movement of products – particularly in the inefficient manual handling of many small packages. The consequence of this realisation has been the unit load concept, where the use of a unit load enables packages to be grouped together and then handled and moved more effectively using mechanical equipment.

The two familiar examples are the wooden pallet and the large shipping containers both of which, in their different ways, have revolutionalised physical distribution. From the product point of view, it has, and is, possible to introduce unit load systems to alter the characteristics of a product and thus use more effective means of distribution. One classic example in recent years has been the development of the roll-cage pallet which is in common use in the grocery industry. Although the cages are expensive units, the trade-off, in terms of time saving and security, is such that overall distribution costs decrease significantly.

A unit load is defined as: 'The assembly of individual items or packages usually of a like kind, to enable convenient composite movement.'

Much of distribution is structured round the concept of load unitisation, and the choice of unit load – type and size – is fundamental to the effectiveness and economics of a distribution system.

Choosing the most appropriate type and size of unit load minimises the frequency of material movement, enables standard storage and handling equipment to be used with optimum equipment utilisation, minimises vehicle load/unload times, and improves product protection, security and stock-taking.

Examples of unit loads are small tote bins, stillages and pallets, intermediate bulk containers (IBCs), ISO freight containers, and garment hanging rails.

Small containers

This category includes tote bins made in polypropylene, galvanised steel, fibreboard or wire mesh, and uses include motor spares, hospital supplies, engineering small parts, and electronic and electrical components.

Depending on the individual design, unitised small containers will be modular, capable of either stacking or nesting, and have provision for label holders, internal sub-dividers and the facility for fitting to louvre panels. Bins made in polypropylene tend to be lighter weight, don't rust, and come in a range of colours for ease of identification, but there is some element of fire risk and plastic is temperature sensitive.

Stillages

The BSI definition of a stillage is:

> A load board comprising a single deck supported on bearers or legs, with an uninterrupted space between the bearers or legs for the entry of a stillage truck. If required the deck may be fitted with a superstructure.

Stillages can be used for horizontal movement, and for racked storage but cannot safely be block stacked. They can be made of timber, steel, or timber with steel legs and can be moved by stillage truck or fork lift truck.

Pallets

The BSI definition is:

> A load board with two decks separated by bearers, or a single deck supported by bearers, constructed with a view to transport and stacking and with the overall height reduced to a minimum compatible with handling by fork lift trucks and pallet trucks.

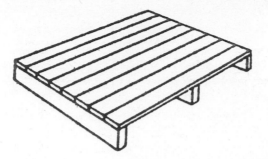

Figure 22.4 Two-way entry, non-reversible pallet — close boarded.

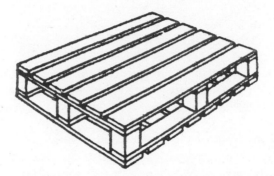

Figure 22.5 Four-way entry, non-reversible pallet – open boarded

The most common type of pallet is the flat timber pallet. There are numerous designs and sizes, although the BSI and the ISO have produced standards. Pallets can be lifted and block stacked (if the load is stable and strong enough) using fork lift trucks.

A significant parameter in choice of pallet is whether to use two-way fork entry or four-way fork entry design.

Generally, two-way entry pallets are cheaper but more robust, where four-way entry give more flexibility for storage and for vehicle loading patterns.

Some pallets are reversible, ie decked on both sides, and pallet decks may be open boarded (gaps between individual boards) or close boarded. Note that pallet trucks can only pick up non-reversible pallets which have space in the base for the truck front rollers to contact the ground.

Probably the most common sizes of pallet are the 1,000 × 1,200 mm and the 800 mm × 1,200 mm (Europal).

A pallet load is not always sufficiently level, or strong, to take the weight of another pallet load on top of it. In this circumstance a pallet converter – a detachable metal framework – can be fitted to the lower pallets to enable block stacking.

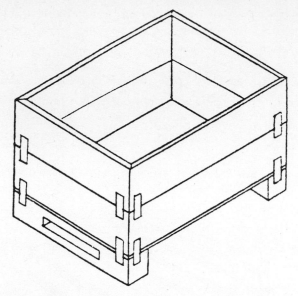

Figure 22.6 Pallet collar

Protection and restraint of the payload on a pallet can also be achieved by the use of pallet collars, which can be built up, one on top of another, to the required load height. When not in use the collars fold flat.

There is a variety of post, cage and box pallets, mainly used in engineering manufacture, which allow pallets to be stacked vertically, transmitting the superimposed load via the corner posts, and which provide side retention.

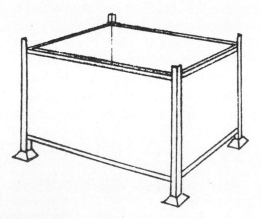

Figure 22.7 Box pallet

The 'bell' feet give a self-locating action when being stacked, but do lose some lateral space. Some designs of cage pallet have collapsible sides for space saving when not in use.

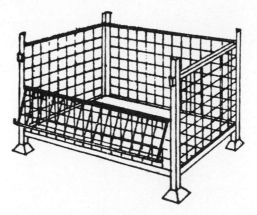

Figure 22.8 Cage pallet with half drop side

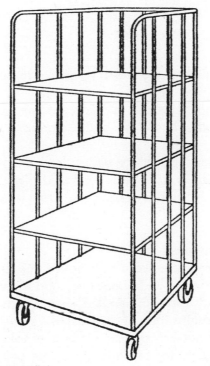

Figure 22.9 Roll cage pallet

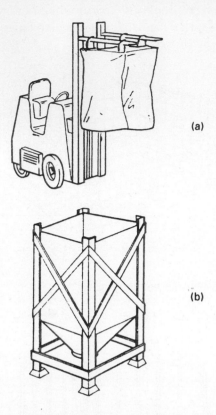

(a)

(b)

Figure 22.10 Intermediate bulk container (a) flexible, (b) rigid

Roll cage pallets find wide use in large grocery warehouse operations supplying supermarkets. The trays and sides are removable for space saving when empty.

There can be problems of getting pallets back for re-use after delivery. Low cost 'one trip' pallets have been produced using various materials — fibre-board, plyboard, polystyrene, etc; to try to alleviate this problem.

Intermediate bulk containers (IBCs)

The IBC is at the interface between bulk solids and unit load handling. It is designed for containing 1 to 2 tonnes of solid material (some IBCs are used for liquids) and can be handled using conventional unit load handling methods, usually fork lift trucks. IBCs can be rigid (metal or plastic), or collapsible (canvas, plastic) for ease of folding up when empty. They are usually designed for top filling, bottom emptying.

IBCs are used for in-plant storage, and for transportation, and they cut

Courtesy of Boss Warehouse Systems

Figure 22.11 International Standard Organisation (ISO) containers in stack

out the need for conventional sized sacks (25/50 kg) and associated filling, bag flattening and handling equipment.

Non-returnable, one trip, IBCs are also in use. They consist of a square or octagonal section corrugated cardboard outer box with a plastic bag liner, the whole sitting on a non-returnable wooden pallet with the deck boards spaced to permit bottom discharge.

International Standard Organisation (ISO) freight containers

The basic ISO freight container is a steel framed box, in a range of standard external sizes that can fit and stack together to make up modular loads.

The standard sizes and defined weight limits, enable standard handling, loading, and unloading systems to be used, irrespective of the materials in transit, and compatible with whatever transport mode – road, rail, ship – is being used. Containers, therefore, help to reduce transport turn round times, they provide a secure transport medium in terms of pilferage and potential damage to goods, and they enable the use of TIR carriers. Different designs of container enable their use for general cargo, bulk solids, bulk liquids, and refrigerated goods.

Summary

In this chapter on the product, packaging and unitisation, consideration has been given concerning how these factors can influence the effectiveness of a distribution operation. The following aspects have been covered:

- product characteristics
  - volume to weight ratio,
  - value to weight ratio,
  - substitutability,
  - special characteristics;
- the product life cycle (PLC) concept;
- packaging; and
- unit loads.

CHAPTER 23

Security and Safety in Distribution

Introduction

Security and safety are important areas of responsibility for distribution management.

Security is concerned with maintaining the condition, status and integrity of stock and other assets.

Safety, is for the well-being of people and it should be noted that the Health and Safety at Work Act imposes a duty on employers not only for the safety of their employees, but also for the safety of people other than their employees who may be on their premises. Safe practices also affect the security of stock since accidents can damage stock and equipment, as well as people.

Security

The security and integrity of goods in a distribution system can be affected by loss or theft, by being mislaid, or by damage or deterioration.

A well-planned workplace, the use of appropriate unit loads and handling and storage equipment, proper transport and monitoring systems, will minimise handling, movement and the risk of damage, and will provide a secure environment.

Training of personnel, and encouraging a responsible attitude to security and the care of stock are also vital.

Control and monitoring systems, checking of receipts, despatches and stock balances, stock location and stock rotation systems, stock checks and audits, all help to show when trouble is beginning to develop.

Measures to monitor these factors, and to minimise loss or deterioration include:

- perpetual inventory stock checks;
- security staff and systems
  - stop and search,
  - vehicle seals,
  - in/out documentation;
- stock records;
- suitable environment – heating, ventilation, lighting;
- fire precautions;
- housekeeping; and
- effective supervision.

Loss or theft

When considering security risks and possible preventive measures, it is always sensible to consult the local police crime prevention officer.

Measures to reduce the risks in a warehouse can include a whole range of systems and devices.

Observation and access

Supervisory offices should be located to have a clear view of areas where goods are at risk, such as receipt and despatch areas, and other building access points. Closed circuit television systems can be appropriate in some circumstances.

The number of building access doors should be kept to a minimum, consistent with safty. Other measures include lockable doors or lockable isolating switches for powered roll shutter doors, appropriate locks (eg glass bolts) on fire doors, a minimum number of keyholders and restricting access to warehouse stock areas for drivers or other unauthorised persons.

High value goods may need special facilities such as a separate compound, secure lockable cabinets or drawers, or using high level parts of the storage racking to reduce accessibility.

A chain link boundary fence may be erected, with manned or controlled access on to the site.

Employee car parking ought to be in view of the offices and ideally outside the security fence.

External security lighting to illuminate the building at night may be appropriate.

Detection

There are various available security devices for detecting intruders, including closed circuit television, sound sensing devices, infra-red sensors, pressure mats and microwave beams. These tend to be sophisticated and should be installed by, and after consultation with, appropriate experts.

It is sometimes feasible to have a direct link to the local police station, but care should be taken that malfunction, or over-sensitivity of the equipment does not lead to false alarms.

Personnel

Some organisations search a sample of individuals at random on leaving the premises. This clearly has to be discussed with and made clear to the employees, ideally as part of the conditions of employment.

Security outside normal working hours must also be considered. The options include round the clock manning by security staff, either own staff or a security company, or having a security company make random visits and checks.

Information systems

Proper documentation or computer records of stock levels, transactions in and out, and stock location, all help to identify quickly, incidences of theft or of stock becoming mislaid. Stock location systems which incorporate the use of check digits are effective in reducing the frequency of mis-locating stock.

Systems for control and location

Computer packages are now widely available for stock management and control. These record receipts and despatches to maintain a stock balance, and also record, or in some cases make the decision on where stock is to be located. In some applications it is also important to issue goods in age sequence to maintain First-In, First-Out and to check shelf lives.

Computer packages are also available which combine stock management with order processing and charging out. Computers handle data fast and accurately giving lower lead times compared to manual systems, better control over stock levels, early warnings of low stocks, replenishment requirements and abnormal demands. It is also possible to identify patterns and trends in the throughput of goods.

Damage and deterioration

Product damage and deterioration can result from mechanical, environmental, fire and other causes.

Mechanical damage can occur through drops or other impacts, compression, vibration and abrasion/erosion.

Causes of climatic or environmental damage include water (rain, humidity and condensation, sea water), excess dryness, extremes of temperature, corrosion, changes in pressure/vacuum (eg aircraft), light, solar radiation, odours from other products, and exposure to air.

Other possible causes of damage or deterioration include infestation (insects, vermin), contamination by other materials, fungi, bacteria and radio activity.

Control of the environment is, therefore, important in maintaining product quality. The following factors apply:

- temperature control where relevant;
- segregation of incompatible goods;
- cleanliness and hygiene; and
- exclusion of weather, eg rain.

In addition, appropriate packaging, and the right type of unit load can help to reduce damage.

Stability is important during movement, storage and distribution, and there are various ways of achieving this.

Packages can often be laid out so that they interlock and build up to a self supporting unit load. An example of this is alternating layers of bags or boxes on a pallet (see Figure 23.1).

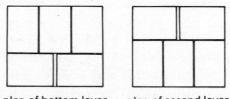

plan of bottom layer   plan of second layer

Figure 23.1 Stacking pattern for pallet loads

There are computer packages which, for different sizes and mixes of cases and boxes, will work out near optimal layouts to make best use of space.

Plastic or steel bands and even large re-usable ('jumbo') elastic bands can be used to restrain and stabilise loads, and also reduce pilferage. Reinforcing can be used at edges to prevent the strapping cutting into boxes. There are also special glues to stick cases together, but the adhesion can be broken, without case damage, when the time comes to 'break bulk'.

Shrink wrapping consists of covering a load in plastic film, and heating so that the film softens and takes up the shape of the load. On cooling it shrinks and clings to the load, providing a weather and dirt proof 'outer', which also binds and stabilises the load, and acts as a deterrent against casual theft. The heating can be either by passing the whole load through a heat tunnel, or by hand held gas gun.

Typically, polyethylene film is used, supplied in reels, with a film thickness in the range 50 to 100 microns. A ventilation system to remove the unpleasant fume from the heated plastic may be necessary.

The stretch wrapping technique involves wrapping an item or a collection of items in a film of tensioned plastic film. It is used widely for palletised loads and is generally less expensive – equipment and running costs – than shrink wrapping.

Fire

Fire is an ever-present risk in warehouse and depot operations, and recent years have seen major losses through this cause.

As early as possible in the design and setting up of a distribution warehouse, depot or store, the local fire officer, and the insuring company, should be consulted for advice, and to establish what facilities or provision have to be incorporated in terms of escape routes for personnel, fire doors, fire fighting equipment and access for fire appliances.

Certain flammable materials may require special storage facilities. They may be limited in the total quantity which may be held in one building or location, and indeed may have to be kept completely apart from main buildings.

Fire prevention and minimising risk depend on people. Staff should be trained so that they are familiar with what to do in the event of fire, where the fire escape routes are, and to have a responsible attitude to eliminating waste materials – rags, paper, scrap packaging – which could feed a fire. Proper metal waste receptacles should always be provided.

There are now regulations which dictate the provision of fire resistant doors, and the provision of illuminated fire escape route signs with independent power supply.

Transport security

Anyone attempting to steal a vehicle or its contents will generally look for an opportunity offering speed, quiet and non-violence. The goods will be attractive in terms of value and ease of movement and disposal, ie a minimum risk situation.

Theft can involve taking a complete vehicle and load, removing the load in the absence of the driver, or other more devious measures such as bribery or threats of physical violence, collusion with a driver, or even impersonation.

The driver is clearly the key person in vehicle security. He/she should be selected carefully, vetted and trained in the security measures appropriate to the vehicle and type of business. The use of driver identification cards is a valuable measure in vehicle security. When vehicles have to be parked overnight, secure commercial vehicle parks should be used.

Security measures also include physical protection of vehicle loads such as sheeting, door padlocks, door seals and van doors wired to an alarm system.

Vehicle and trailer protection include various mechanical and electrical devices to immobilise the vehicle, and/or activate alarms.

Safety

The handling, movement (manual and mechanical) and storage of goods is potentially hazardous and risks include collisions, collapses, falls of materials, strains, trips and falls. There are also risks of 'short-cuts' – moving excessive loads, driving too fast, poor stacking, manual lifting of excessive weights, stretching too far to pick up loads, etc.

Accidents are usually caused by a mixture of technical and human factors; technical to do with the capacity and condition of equipment to carry out the required job, and human to do with abilities, attitudes and training of managers, supervisors and operators concerned with the job and their working environment.

One way of classifying accidents is:

- accidents involving transport, moving machinery and equipment; and
- accidents in manual handling.

There are more accidents in total arising from handling activities, but there are more fatalities associated with transport, movement and equipment. There is more concentration on the training of fork lift truck drivers than on correct techniques of manual handling.

Safety in the use of equipment

The Health and Safety at Work Act requires, amongst other things, that, so far as is reasonably practicable:

- Employers shall provide and maintain plant and systems of work that are safe and without risks to health, including the provision of information, training, etc.
- Every employee shall take reasonable care for the safety and health of himself and of other persons.
- Any person who designs, manufactures, imports or supplies any

article for use at work should ensure that it is designed and constructed so as to be safe when properly used.

These requirements influence the design, use and maintenance of equipment, and place direct responsibility on management, and on equipment suppliers, users and maintainers.

Safety in using equipment depends on such things as:

- company/management commitment;
- safe systems of work;
- the right equipment for the job; and
- training and supervision and attitudes of operators/drivers.

Fork lift trucks

Powered trucks operate in or near areas where people work and where there are often large quantities of goods and equipment. Powered vehicles are involved in many of the more serious warehouse accidents. In one sample year accidents involving fork lift trucks accounted for 8.5 per cent of all industrial fatalities.

Accidents can be caused by a number of factors, eg fork truck coming out of an aisle into a cross aisle may collide with a pedestrian because of one, or a combination of the following factors:

- no horn used – driver error/discipline/training/supervision;
- brake failure – inadequate maintenance;
- driver's view obscured by load – driver error/discipline/training/ supervision;
- no separation between pedestrian and fork truck routes – planning; and
- pedestrian should not have been there – discipline/training, etc.

Points to watch in areas where trucks operate include:

- visibility, eg the need for lighting;
- condition of floor;
- separate routes and doors for pedestrians and trucks;
- sufficient overhead clearance – door lintels, service pipes;
- housekeeping, no floor spillages;
- obstructions (protruding pallets); and
- adequate and marked access aisles.

Points for driver performance include the following rules:

- Load within truck capacity, stable, secure, symmetrically positioned on forks, not on front of forks.
- Load should not obscure driver's view. If it has to, vehicle should be driven in reverse.
- Pallets should be in good condition.
- No speeding, especially when cornering.
- Drive with forks lowered and mast not tilted forward, and use horn, flashing lights as appropriate.
- No passengers on the truck.
- Drive in reverse if going down a slope, and forward if ascending a slope.
- Never lift with the mast tilted forward, Only tilt when load is in position.
- Forks should be down when truck parked.

Points relating to trucks include capacity adequate for required tasks, fitted with overhead guards and warning lights, tyre pressures regularly checked (daily), fork widths adjusted to suit the load, and truck well maintained.

Proper training is vital to safe truck operation, and although formal training is directed towards the driver operated trucks, there is a need for some basic training for anyone who uses any powered trucks.

Pallet racking
Safety in racking design, construction and use is covered in the Code of Practice of the Storage Equipment Manufacturers association (SEMA).

Relevant factors in the use of racking include:

- racking damage which can reduce beam or stanchion strength, or joints, by overloading and over straining (excess deflection);
- using damaged or wrong sized pallets;
- badly loaded or badly positioned pallets;
- loose floor fixtures, missing connectors; and
- poor floor condition

   - broken up, soiled, bumpy or sloping surface,
   - excess slope/bumps.

In some cases corner stanchions are protected by fitting guards to prevent trucks damaging the structure, or by fitting guide rails to lead trucks into the aisles.

Pallets
Damaged pallets can cause accidents such as slipping, or unstable loads or stacks. They can also cause injury from protruding nails, etc. Pallets are damaged by such things as overloading, being struck by forks, incorrect fork width and being thrown about or dropped.

Conveyors
Various types of conveyor are used in distribution applications, and hazards include:

- nips between rollers and belts, and at transfer points;
- moving parts generally;
- guarding removed; and
- unauthorised crossing of conveyors by operators, or removing items from the conveyor.

Safety measures should include guarding wherever possible, authorised crossing points, potential 'nips' at transfer points (eg belt or slat to rolls) fitted with jump out rollers or be bridged, and emergency stop buttons or trip wires. Conveyors in series, which feed from one to the other and so on, are often fitted with interlocks so that up-stream conveyors cannot feed forward unless the downstream ones are operating. Warning devices (lights, sirens) should be used when starting up conveyors.

Manual lifting and handling
A large proportion of all accidents in distribution activities come into this category, and despite the availability of literature, courses and training aids on correct methods of manual lifting and handling, it is probably the most neglected area. We all know that fork trucks out of control are lethal. The results of back injuries and other consequences of bad manual handling are less obviously dramatic, but account for a high proportion of all reportable accidents.

The principles of good manual handling practice are well established:

- use leg muscles rather than the weaker back muscles;
- use body momentum and weight to initiate movement;
- correctly position the feet to spread and envelop the load;
- straight (natural curve) back – not necessarily vertical;
- arms close to body for lifting and carrying;
- correct hold and grip;
- chin in; and
- use body weight.

Short training courses are available for teaching the proper techniques, but the main problem is gaining acceptance that such training is of value, or necessary. The accident statistics show clearly that the need is there.

CHAPTER
24
Trends in Logistics and Distribution

Introduction

In recent years, the logistics and distribution industry has experienced quite revolutionary developments in a number of different fields. Many of the developments have been associated with information technology, while others have been concerned with new organisational and management ideas as well as advances in equipment and operational methods. In addition to these changes from within distribution and logistics there have also been developments from outside the industry which have had an effect on the structure and management of distribution and logistics.

It is possible, therefore, to identify many activities both within the broad scope of logistics and in areas associated with logistics that have seen important recent changes. Some of these changes reflect fairly short-term developments whilst others can be seen to form a pattern of long-term trends that have, and will continue to have, very significant effects on distribution and logistics planning and strategy. Any attempt to view the future must necessarily take into account the major trends in recent years and this approach is adopted as the basis for this final chapter of the book.

Where any major factor has already been identified and discussed previously in the text, a brief summary of the main points is given here.

External factors

One of the trends that has been given a great deal of attention over the past decade is the rise in costs of distribution. In the UK, for example, since 1980, while the retail price index has risen by about 20 per cent to 1987, costs related to transport have increased by approximately 50 per cent, storage costs by approximately 70 per cent and labour costs by nearly 100 per cent. These increases have had a significant influence in identifying logistics and distribution as a major area for concentrating effort in improving efficiency and controlling costs.

It is interesting to note that the statistics indicate a very good response to the drive for efficiency and improved productivity. In the same period, 1980 to 1987, distribution costs, expressed as a percentage of sales turnover, have dropped from an estimated 16 per cent to 6.5 per cent. Although this reduction is partly due to increased sales volumes which have allowed for a greater spread of fixed and overhead distribution costs, a significant proportion of this reduction is undoubtedly due to increased efficiency and better control.

An indication of the breakdown of these costs amongst the major elements of distribution is given in Chapter 1 (pp 8–10).

It was indicated in Chapter 13 (pp 151–4) that this is a particularly exciting period for the European logistics and distribution industry because of the advent of the Single European Market in 1992 and the planned opening of the Channel Tunnel in 1993. Both of these events should have a significant effect on the structure of distribution and logistics systems and add weight to the trend towards the internationalisation and integration of logistics systems. A detailed discussion of these implications is given in Chapter 13 under the heading 'European perspective'.

There have been a number of important developments in the retail sector in recent years that have had very direct consequences on the distribution of goods to the high street. The retail sector continues to be an area of industry where innovation and change are the norm, and this imposes a continuous challenge for the distribution and logistics manager.

The major retailing patterns and developments that impose on distribution can be summarised as follows:

- The sustained importance of the food sector, and in particular the large food retailers. In addition, other mixed retail businesses, such as variety stores, have maintained an important position in the market place.
- Static sales, particularly of food, and the corresponding problems of maintaining profitability.
- The maximisation of selling space at shops and stores, together with a general policy of stock reduction throughout company systems.
- The acquisition of other companies in order to bolster market share.
- A significant growth in the market share of multiple organisations, and the corresponding decline in independent shops. In a very dynamic market, the current (1988) 'big five' grocery retailers (Tesco,

Sainsbury, Argyll, Dee and Asda) have 54 per cent of the total sector sales.

- A significant decrease in the number of shops falling from well over half a million in 1970 to a quarter of a million in about 15 years (grocery shops from about 100,000 to 48,000 in the same period).
- A substantial increase in the average size of shops. This is emphasised by the growth in numbers of superstores, hypermarkets and discount stores. This is indicated by the growth in superstores in the UK from 47 in 1972 to 315 in 1982 and 457 in 1987.
- An increase in the product range to be found in supermarkets, superstores and variety stores. This indicates a clear policy by the food retailers to diversify into other food (delicatessen) and non-food (clothes, DIY) products, and the variety stores into food and other product ranges.
- The growth in the number of out-of-town shopping centres and shopping malls.
- The introduction of date coding and age control, shorter life products and additional temperature controlled products. This has necessitated much stricter stock management and control.
- Linked to the reduction in shop storage areas has been the movement of a number of activities away from the retail environment and back into the depot. Examples include labelling, cost mark-up, unpacking and other break-bulk activities.

Clearly, these changes have had effects on, and implications for, distribution and delivery systems. Some of these are fully recognised while others will have a significant part to play in the future. The power and importance of the multiple retailers has certainly been established, particularly with respect to their distribution requirements. The distribution policies of the large retailers, however, vary quite considerably, indicating that the 'optimum' distribution strategy has yet to be found, some companies run their own systems and, among these, strategy may differ between central and regional stock-holding points. Policies related to direct or via depot deliveries may also vary. Other companies use third party operators to run their entire distribution system.

The decline in the market share of independents, and the associated reduction in the number of independent retail outlets has had a major effect on distribution. This has made it uneconomic for many suppliers to run their own urban delivery fleets (due to the reduced overall demand by independents), and has created the need for wholesaler/cash and carry facilities to be established for the independent retailers to make their own collections.

The policy of maximising selling space in stores has been achieved by a corresponding reduction in stock-holding space. This, allied to the general trend of reducing inventory levels to cut costs, has accentuated the need for retailer, supplier and third party distribution systems to provide a greatly improved service. These trends correspond directly with the acknowledged need for distribution systems to respond more quickly and more effectively to reflect increasing service demands.

The ability to provide this better service should be made easier with the growth of new shopping centres. This is because demand should be consolidated into a limited physical area, and because these centres should be purpose-built for both shoppers, retailers and deliverers. Unfortunately, this is not always so. Some of the new centres provide very poor facilities for the goods delivery vehicle.

How will it be possible for distribution systems to react to these increased demands in terms of improving and maintaining response times? One answer will certainly lie with the development of information technology. For many retailing and retail supply systems these developments are already well under way. The key is the ability to collect, collate and transfer data with great accuracy and great speed. A number of advances have been made:

- Many shops use sophisticated electronic cash registers (ECRs) and electronic point of sale (EPOS) equipment which can collect and store data related to sales information as well as provide ticketed information for the customer.
- Article numbering is now well advanced in the UK. The Article Numbering Association estimates that well over 80 per cent of the goods sold through grocery outlets are bar coded.
- Scanning is now in use at the check-outs of many outlets. Recently there has been a significant growth in EPOS scanning systems.
- The scanning of product numbers on shelving takes place using light pens with portable data entry terminals (PDETs) for restocking purposes.

The next stage in the retailing story may well be a very dramatic one, as the possibility of *non-store shopping* becomes very much a reality. Indeed, there are already a number of examples of non-store shopping opportunities both in the US and the UK. The technology required to support a significant change of this nature is currently available:

- Non-store shopping in the form of mail order from catalogues is already a feature of existing shopping patterns. The goods are

despatched directly to the consumer 'on approval' and are retained or returned as required.
- Product advertising and demonstration is very common on television.
- The use of home computers linked to television screens is now well established.
- Teletext news and information services (Cefax and Oracle) are in use, and the two-way Prestel viewdata service via a telephone link to television and computer is in operation. There are already a wide range of goods which can be ordered via the system.
- The introduction of cable television will provide permanent links for these systems.
- Credit card 'instant' payments are in common use and the development of electronic funds transfer systems (EFTS and EFTPOS) providing automatic account debiting is now available.

Taken together, these developments could play an important part in creating new shopping patterns. If this is so, then the current channels of physical distribution may be drastically altered. What effects might be expected? Some of the possibilities are as follows:

- There may be a significant increase in direct deliveries to the home.
- A new type of distribution system may be required which can cater for many small drops in residential areas.
- Different vehicle types may need to be developed, possibly smaller and quieter than those currently used.
- Transhipment centres may be necessary outside large towns and cities where large loads can be broken down for smaller local deliveries.
- Special community depots may be required as pick-up points for parcels.
- Some existing distribution systems may get a new lease of life. The postal service and milk delivery rounds may become the basis for a much larger distribution system.
- Sophisticated information systems, linked to the ordering facility, may be developed to support the new distribution networks.

Trends in logistics and distribution

With respect to overall *distribution and logistics strategy*, there are several important trends that have become apparent in recent years which may well continue to determine company policies in the future.

There has been a quite distinct move towards the *centralisation* of distribution. Many retailing companies have, for example, undertaken significant rationalisation programmes which have led to large reductions in depot networks. The aim has been to cut total distribution costs by concentrating stock-holding in a limited number of centralised depots. This has led to quite substantial savings in inventory costs and storage costs, more than compensating the corresponding increase in transport costs which is necessary to support these new networks. It seems likely that this trend to centralisation will continue.

One major trend in distribution is discussed in detail in Chapter 6 (pp 61–7). This is the significant growth in the use of *third party distribution services*. The type of service offered can range from the occasional delivery of a few parcels to a total distribution system run by a third party contractor. It is this latter type of exclusive, complete service that has been of particular significance in recent years, and has led to the growth of third party distribution to its current level of well over a quarter of the UK road freight distribution market. This trend will undoubtedly continue for several years.

A very important feature in determining distribution strategy and operations is the emphasis now placed on *customer service*. It has been clearly shown that distribution is one of the most vital elements in providing a competitive customer service policy. Markets have been undergoing an interesting change whereby specific products are becoming less easy to differentiate – the 'brand' image is not so strong. The result is that availability is becoming the dominant feature – rather than wait for a particular branded product, the consumer will purchase any alternative that is available. Thus, the distribution function is becoming the key element in customer service strategy.

The move towards more *integrated systems* of distribution and logistics is another important development that can be expected to have a big impact in the future. Many of these systems rely on quite sophisticated computer techniques, and they have their origins in manufacturing and production management. Integrated systems such as Materials Requirements Planning (MRP), Distribution Resource Planning (DRP) and Just-in-Time (JIT) are outlined in Chapter 2 (pp 21–3).

The basis of these systems is the concept of stock reduction allied to the availability of the required material when and where required. Goods are supplied just in sufficient time and quantities to meet operational requirements. This approach necessitates careful planning, and highly controlled and disciplined operations, from both the user and his suppliers. The results can be impressive in terms of reduced inventories (for the user) and greater flexibility, although this is offset by the requirement for smaller and much more frequent deliveries of goods.

Trends in *warehousing* are closely related to advances in equipment and information technology. A number of these issues are related to developments in overall distribution strategy. Strategic considerations have influenced a number of companies to go down the path of rationalisation of their distribution networks, and to invest in large new centralised warehouses and distribution depots. The conception, design, construction and commissioning of such large projects, which can be in the capital expenditure range of £10 million to £20 million, require sophisticated and effective project control, with close liaison between planners, equipment suppliers and operators. The penalties of failure, or of less than effective achievement of objectives, increase with the size of the project.

Success in such major ventures depends not only on having the right equipment and other resources available at the right time, but upon a well-conceived and designed facility, and a well-planned project programme. Equipment suppliers are increasingly involved in the scheme design, planning and management of large projects.

The operating and control systems for effective management need to be carefully designed and integrated into the total system concept.

The adoption of technically advanced systems in the UK – automated storage and retrieval systems (AS/RS), high speed mechanised case picking systems, automated guided vehicle systems (AGVS) – has shown only a modest rate of growth, but growth nevertheless.

This is shown in Figure 24.1 with the number of high rise AS/RS systems in the UK, and in other countries, as at the years 1976 and 1982. These systems require not only the appropriate engineering design and manufacturing skills, but also understanding of control systems, and the total design and supply capability to provide the customer with a complete package. The enhanced power of computers enables better use to be made of advanced systems, and better utilisations to be obtained from them.

In the UK there has been some caution in adopting advanced systems. Generally they involve a high capital outlay, and certainly in earlier years they were perceived as having problems with reliability, and to an extent, control. It is interesting that in recent years established manufacturers of 'traditional' handling and storage equipment have added high rise stacker cranes, carousels, etc, to their product ranges.

It is important that special care should go into the conceptual design of advanced systems. They tend to be less flexible than more conventional systems and less easily modified to accommodate any future changes in operating, product, or market variables.

The ways in which storage and handling systems are evolving can be presented as two main streams of development, ie technically advanced systems, and improved performance through advances in information technology.

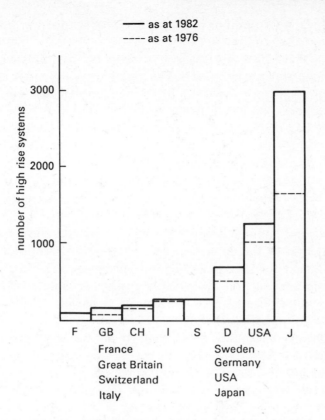

———— as at 1982
---- as at 1976

Figure 24.1 Number of high-rise warehouse installations in major industrial countries

The term 'advanced' in this context is not very specific. It encompasses a range of systems and techniques for storing and handling which use mechanisation and automation to reduce or eliminate manual movement and control, to increase the speed of response of the system, with high levels of reliability.

Computers enable rapid and effective control of mechanical and electrical systems. Current practice is for local independent control of individual functions using mini computers to give operational flexibility, although probably linked back to the main frame computer for information purposes.

The types of system which are included under the heading of 'advanced' include AS/RS for palletised goods, for long loads, and for completed products (eg motor cars), as well as systems for small parts storage, for automated order picking, for goods sortation, and automated movement systems. Advanced systems are also firmly established as components of manufacturing technology, eg the automated movement of work in progress between work stations using AGVS, and at the interface between production and distribution.

There are no hard and fast decision criteria for deciding when to use advanced storage and handling techniques, and each potential application should be examined on its own merits, in the light of its own particular needs, circumstances, and objectives.

However, it has to be remembered that advanced systems tend to be inflexible for future change, so the system design should be thorough. Relevant factors to consider include product range and value, total and individual product throughputs, market stability and short- and long-term fluctuations, costs of labour and land, and working patterns – normal day, 24 hour working etc.

One of the most important developments to affect freight transport in recent years is that of the application of information technology and the use of the computer for both planning and operations. The impact of IT is discussed in the next section. Many of the other notable transport issues and trends have been considered previously in earlier chapters, but the main points are summarised below.

In the UK, the overall importance of road freight transport continues to be a major feature of freight movement. In the last ten years, there has been a steady increase in the use of road transport (92 billion tonne-kilometres moved in 1975 compared with 104 billion tonne-kilometres in 1985). This has occurred at the same time as the decline in the use of rail for freight movement (21 billion tonne-kilometres to 15 billion tonne-kilometres over the same period). It seems likely that this trend will continue, with water transport and particularly pipelines steadily increasing in usage. The advent of the Channel Tunnel and the Single European Market in the early years of the next decade may change the fortunes of rail freight transport, but it is not yet clear how significant an effect these events will have.

It is always difficult to forecast any future changes in government legislation that might affect road freight transport. Based on recent history, however, it seems likely that environmental and safety issues will continue to be important, particularly those affecting the movement of hazardous goods and the safety features required for road vehicles. One paradoxical issue concerns the question of vehicle size. It is probable that at some stage the maximum permitted gross weight for an articulated combination will be increased from its current limit of 38 tonnes to 40 tonnes. While this will bring the UK more into line with the rest of Europe, any additional increase in maximum weights would be seen by the environmental lobby to be particularly detrimental to the environmentalist cause, with the attendant problems of additional damage to bridges and old buildings, etc.

Although there have been some significant improvements in the strategic trunk road network in the UK, notably the completion of the M25 London Orbital road, traffic congestion continues to be a problem, especially for the free flow of trunking and delivery operations. For some years, average speeds appeared to be improving due to better roads, more powerful vehicles and apparent reduced traffic congestion. This led to a longer average haul for vehicles, with changing distribution strategies and delivery patterns as distances became 'shorter' due to reduced journey times. In the years from the mid-1980s onwards, however, there has been a very distinct increase in the number of vehicles on the road. The major increases have occurred with cars and light vans, with the number of heavy goods vehicles remaining fairly static. The overall effect has been a very severe increase in traffic congestion, with vehicles on many motorways suffering long delays both during and outside the usual peak periods. Department of Transport forecasts for vehicle numbers to the end of the century show a continuing upward trend in car ownership and the number of vehicles on the road. With 1986 as the base year, the forecast is for an expected increase of 26 per cent of cars, 27 per cent of light vans and 9 per cent heavy goods vehicles. Should these forecasts be realised, it seems certain that road congestion will once again become a major issue for transport and distribution.

There has been a notable increase in the use of certain 'new' vehicle systems in the past few years. These 'new' systems – basically old systems that have taken on a new lease of life – are the draw-bar trailer combination and the demountable or swap body. These systems were described in Chapter 14 (pp 159 and 167). It seems likely that the use of systems such as these will continue to increase in the future and that, particularly the demountable style of operation, will play an important role in the introduction of satellite or stockless depot operations. Other developments that will undoubtedly retain their importance are the various special vehicle bodies and on-vehicle handling aids that are now in use. These include compartmentalised vehicles for moving frozen, chilled and ambient products, and railed bodies used for the carriage of hanging garments.

A feature of these systems is that they have all been developed as a part of an integrated concept of viewing the respective distribution operation as a whole. Thus, an expensive transport option can provide the least cost system overall through trade-offs elsewhere in the system.

One main area of concern associated with the ability of distribution and delivery systems to supply the retail sector is that of the problems that occur at the interface between retailing and distribution. This is often known as the urban delivery problem.

The major issues have been identified as:

- lack of adequate on-street unloading places;
- queuing to deliver;
- inadequate building design;
- time actually taken to physically unload;
- lack of rear access facilities;
- blocked rear access facilities; and
- local authority and retailer time restrictions.

Various solutions to these problems have been put forward over the years. Some have been of limited success, others not so. The use of appointment systems at the larger stores has certainly helped to alleviate the more serious queuing problems. The consolidation of small deliveries via third party operators has cut down the number of drops that need to be made. The use of roll cage pallets by most of the grocery retailers has helped to speed the physical act of delivery and improve vehicle turnaround at many stores. The possibility of out-of-hours or night deliveries has been tried, but this was not successful.

In terms of policies for the future, it seems likely that the recent improvements made will continue, and the question of out-of-hours deliveries will be asked again. The longer opening hours of large stores may now make this more feasible. One long-term solution for large stores may be the use of demountable units dropped overnight by trunking vehicles and unloaded by shop staff during the day.

Trends in information technology

A recent study undertaken by the Council of Logistics Management in the USA attempted to identify the major issues and trends that were likely to affect business logistics decisions by the mid-1990s. The study was based on the Delphi method of forecasting whereby various 'experts' in their field are asked to predict the importance and likely impact of certain events in future years. It is interesting, though perhaps not unexpected, to note that of the 20 major events that were tested, the top three that were identified as likely to have most impact were all directly concerned with issues related to computer/information technology. In looking for the major future trends in distribution and logistics, the area of information technology will clearly provide a ready supply of suitable contenders.

This section is again divided broadly into three main areas, the first covering the use of computers and information technology for determining distribution and logistics strategy.

A limited number of computer packages have been developed to represent or simulate the overall distribution and logistics structure of a company. Some of these models also provide an optimising routine whereby, for example, both the optimum number and location of facilities can be identified for a given demand and flow of goods. Typical features of models such as these were outlined in Chapter 20 (pp 251–2). These types of model will undoubtedly continue to play an important part in logistics planning in the future.

A very significant innovation in recent years has been the *integrated distribution information system*. The major features of such systems are to unify the many functions and components within a distribution organisation, and to provide ready access to data and information at all levels of the organisation. The most recent developments, and the likely impact for the future, are described on pp 261–3.

The use of computers and information technology for a number of differing warehousing applications has been and will continue to be very important. This represents the area of most significant change and development in very recent years, consequent on the evolution of computer power. The significant benefits of computer information logging and processing include speed of response, clerical effort reduction, accuracy, immediacy of information, and better management control. These apply across the range of distribution and logistics activities.

Warehouse management, operations and order processing computer packages are well established, but recent developments include the provision of portable terminals for sales staff which can be connected on line via a telephone link to the base computer. This allows interrogation of stock levels, and the on-line placing of orders from customers' premises. Some large suppliers have installed fixed terminals in the purchase offices of major customers.

The use of on-line mobile terminals in the warehouse, eg hand held or mounted on a fork lift truck, enables instantaneous up-dating of stock level and location files, and enables better utilisation of handling equipment and storage capacity.

One company introduced hand held terminals for recording quantities and locations of incoming palletised goods in order to reduce paperwork, improve accuracy, and get better fork truck utilisations. The virtually instantaneous communication on stock location status – full or empty – resulted in empty locations being refilled more quickly, and gave an effective increase in warehouse storage capacity of about 5 per cent.

There are schemes and packages which use the resulting data as a base for calculating such parameters as truck utilisations, and payment schemes for the operators.

Warehouse management computer packages, in addition to recording stock balances, can incorporate routines for:

- order picking to optimise pick quantities and routes;
- calculating picking stock replenishment requirements, based on goods issues;
- stock rotation;
- selection of optimal locations for stock; and
- reports on staff productivity and equipment utilisations.

Recent developments in warehouse management and communication include the use of mobile terminals, and bar code techniques, which give faster and more accurate handling of data and help to reduce or even eliminate paperwork from parts of the system.

Many established computerised order processing packages still require the order pickers to work from a paper picking list, and recent developments have been towards 'paperless' picking. Approaches to this include the use of truck mounted or hand held remote terminals, picking by lights and automated and robotic picking.

Remote terminals

Truck mounted or hand held terminals communicate with a supervisory computer by radio link, on-line anywhere within the signal range. Operators receive instructions via the terminal, and can 'talk' to the computer by key operation with messages such as: pick complete, stock-out, or what is next location to visit. Developments are also progressing with voice recognition systems in which the operators can literally talk with the computer.

One application had the computer issuing instructions to the operator, and also controlling/driving the ride-on picking truck, leaving the operator free to pack and label the goods during truck travel. This so de-skilled the job that there were problems of motivation and boredom, so the truck driving was returned to operator control – with beneficial results.

Remote terminals, hand held or truck mounted, can be on-line, or can be independent, holding data in a memory which can be cleared and recharged periodically.

Picking by lights

This is for case and unit picking by zones. At each picking location there is a light, a digital display, and typically two push buttons – 'pick complete' and 'stock-out'. As an order is entered, lights come on at those locations where picks are to be made, and the digital displays show the quantities to be picked. On completion of the pick, the relevant button is pressed, and the light goes out. When all lights are out the next order can enter the zone. Users (USA) report a very low error rate.

A further development to increase accuracy, is a system with load sensing devices under the picking trays at the front of the racking. These 'count' the number of items removed by the operator and show the balance on a digital display.

'People-less' picking

Despite problems with automated case or item picking, there are now systems for picking, or 'dispensing' under computer control.

In one such, banks of gravity roll live storage lanes feed on to powered take-away conveyors, and a computer controlled gate at the end of each lane, coupled with sequential conveyor control, ensures order integrity.

A similar concept, suitable for regularly shaped articles held in vertical magazines, dispenses on to a take-away conveyor which feeds each order as a discrete block to packing. Replenishment of this type of equipment is potentially time consuming and takes on greater significance than with manual systems.

An alternative to dispensing, is the development of case picking robots. In one design, a palletising, four axis robot, is mounted on a horizontal rail, in an aisle. The robot picks cases from shelving on either side of the aisle, up to about two metres high, using a vacuum gripper head, and puts them on to a pallet. Mixed case sizes can be handled.

Another system uses a gantry robot with four axis movement, with AGVs and live storage input conveyors. An AGV carries picking pallets, and moves along an aisle with stock pallets on either side sitting on the input conveyors. The gantry robot moves along the aisle, picking cases and putting them on the picking pallets on the AGV, which moves in parallel with the robot. Full pallets are taken to a transfer station and exchanged for empty ones. Another AGV feeds replenishment pallets to the input conveyors.

Developments are also in hand for robot picking of single items from a tote pan which has been retrieved from a mini-load system. Video cameras on the robot are linked to a computer which analyses the received images, determines the item centre point, and guides the pick up arm to it. This system can handle layers of randomly placed objects, but not a jumbled heap.

Computers can provide effective control of stocks, with accurate and up to date information. This depends on accurate data input which can be created by automatic identification.

As an example, it has been common practice for the goods-in function in a warehouse to forward batches of advice notes to a VDU operator, possibly at the end of the working day, for entry into the computer. This leads to inherent delay between goods receipt and stock record updating, VDU entry is a fairly slow process, and inaccurate advice notes and keying errors can lead to inaccurate stock records.

Faster and more accurate data entry can be achieved by transferring information directly into the system without human interpretation, eg using bar coding. (Some research results suggest that the error rate for keyboard data entry is about 10,000 times greater than for bar code systems.) Instead of the receiving clerk checking the goods against an advice note, bar code labels attached to either pallets or cases, are scanned using a laser scanner.

Bar coding is not limited only to data entry applications, and sortation and automatic control of material movement, which depend on some form of automatic identification, lend themselves to bar coding.

Bar coding is not suitable in environments where the label can be damaged or obliterated by, for example, heat, paints or solvents. For such situations it may be possible to use a programmable tag, which contains a micro-chip with a capacity of between 6 and 32 bits of data, which can be attached to pallets or other containers. Using microwave technology, the tags are read by interrogation units at various points en route, providing continuous feedback on the position and status of the unit. The interrogation unit can also reprogram or update the tag as it passes from one process to the next. For example a pallet load could be re-routed if it failed a particular quality assurance test. The tags may also be used to control AGVs.

In recent years, research has been carried out on the potential for using visual interactive simulation as a tool in the design, or improvement, of warehouse systems. Simulation enables a handling or storage system to be modelled on a computer and tested under various conditions.

Using computer graphics to show a continuous moving representation of the system, has a useful visual impact, presents a diagnostic facility for identifying where and why problems may occur, and can be a valuable training medium. For major capital projects, the ability to simulate different possible systems and configurations, before committing any capital, can give confidence in design and reduce the risk of serious design errors.

The large number of IT applications related to road freight transport were discussed in some detail in Chapter 20 (pp 256–61). Three distinct categories of application were identified: fleet management, fleet planning and operations, and vehicle-based systems. It is probable that all three will continue to be important in future years, but it is in the third area of vehicle-based systems where the most far-reaching implications seem most likely to occur.

Fleet management systems cover aspects including vehicle parts control, fleet administration and fleet costing. There are many well established packages available and the use of packages such as these is already quite common.

Systems for *fleet planning and operations* include tachograph analysis as well as various types of routeing and scheduling packages. This latter classification of packages covers three main types of use – strategic, tactical and day-to-day. In addition, packages are available for single vehicle routeing.

There are several different areas where innovations are taking place, and these all provide useful illustrations of the current trends in package and program development. Many packages now have a *computerised road database* to provide the basic road network. This makes routeing both more accurate and more realistic. Detailed computerised road databases are also available for many parts of continental Europe.

One of the most recent developments in day-to-day/operational routeing and scheduling packages has been the introduction of the facility which allows the scheduler to intervene and alter completed routes as he requires. This move to *interactive scheduling* makes these operational packages much more 'user friendly' and thus more acceptable. The scheduler can use the package to produce the basic routes and can then adapt the routes to take account of any localised problem or emergency order.

A number of routeing packages have now been designed using very sophisticated *colour graphics techniques*. Very detailed coloured screen maps are produced indicating the specific roads used for individual routes. These packages are menu-driven and combine the use of split screens, colour graphics, zoom facilities, etc, so that the visual output is easy to interpret and easy to use.

The other major applications of information technology to transport occur with various *vehicle-based systems*. These systems are generally aimed at monitoring vehicle and driver performance, and include data loggers for monitoring fuel, etc; local monitors for monitoring vehicle security; weight, etc; and various diagnostic facilities for measuring the condition of the vehicle – bearing wear, suspension, etc.

One of the most exciting developments is the 'computer-in-the-cab' whereby a vehicle-based computer can provide the driver with a wealth of information to assist him in his work. This information can be received from external sources and can include such details as localised road conditions, preferred routes, etc. Tests are already under way using computerised maps on screens in the cab whereby congested areas can be highlighted and alternative non-congested routes suggested.

Conclusion

Distribution and logistics are now accepted as being important and integral parts of the total range of industrial activities which are necessary in order to supply customers with the services or goods which they require in the most effective way. This is a fundamental change compared to 10 to 15 years ago, and the realisation has come that these functions have to be expertly and professionally managed in order to achieve their primary objective, which is to provide effective customer service.

As it has become apparent how important are effective planning and control in making efficient use of what are now recognised as being very expensive resources, and in providing good customer service, so have customers come to expect more from their suppliers. We are now in a climate where second class service is no longer acceptable, and unless these functions are effectively planned and managed, the customer will go elsewhere. He wants and expects speed and consistency of delivery, quality and completeness of order, accurate and timely information about the goods and services provided, good communication with his supplier, and flexible response to his demands. It has to be said, of course, that the ability to achieve improvements in resource utilisation and customer service, have been greatly enhanced by the continuing explosion in our ability to handle and analyse information quickly, and accurately.

In this chapter, the most recent trends have been discussed and an indication has been given of what the future may hold for the distribution and logistics industry.

A number of external factors were identified as having a current or potential impact. These included the rising costs of distribution, the major importance and consequential effect of trends and patterns in the retail sector, the introduction of the Single European Market and the Channel Tunnel and the possibility of non-store shopping and the potentially dramatic affect that this might have on basic distribution systems and structures.

Some of the major trends in distribution and logistics strategy included:

- the move towards the centralisation of distribution systems;
- the growth of third party distribution services;
- the importance placed on customer service; and
- the development of integrated systems.

Important warehousing trends were:

- the increased size of warehouses and depots;
- the move towards technical sophistication in materials handling; and
- the adoption of advanced, automated storage and retrieval systems.

The main issues concerning freight transport were:

- the continued dominance of the road freight transport mode in the UK;
- the importance of government legislation, and environmental and safety issues;
- the problems of traffic congestion;
- the increased use of 'new' vehicle systems – draw-bar trailer combinations and demountable bodies; and
- urban delivery problems.

The effects and implications of information technology on the future of distributon and logistics were seen to be of major significance. Factors included:

- the increasing use of computer models for strategic planning;
- the recent development of integrated distribution information systems;
- the growth in the use of computers for logging and analysing information for operational warehouse purposes;
- 'paperless' picking and 'people-less' picking;
- automatic identification – bar coding and sortation systems;
- warehouse simulation;
- the continued use of road transport vehicle routeing and scheduling models;
- computerised road databases;
- interactive scheduling;
- colour graphics techniques; and
- vehicle-based computers.

The current period is one of rapid change, and there is a growing awareness of the importance of distribution and logistics systems, both in their own right in terms of making the best use of resources, and also in terms of the need for integration with production and the total supply chain.

All this is going on at a time when the impact of technology in general and information technology in particular is growing at an ever increasing rate.

Alongside this change, and partly occasioned by it, industrial management attitudes and expectations are also changing. Expectations of what can be achieved are rising, and are being met, and this is the climate in which the distribution and logistics professional has to work. One major, and perhaps fortuitous trend has been the recent move to a much more professional discipline for distribution and logistics management. This is a trend that will undoubtedly continue into the future as new challenges are faced and are successfully overcome.

Selected Bibliography

Ackerman, K B (1983) *Practical Handbook of Warehousing*, The Traffic Service Corporation, Washington, New York.

Ansoff, H I (1986) *Corporate Strategy*, Sidgwick and Jackson, London.

Apple, J M (1977) *Plant Layout and Material Handling*, John Wiley & Sons, New York, London.

Argenti, J (1981) *Systematic Corporate Planning*, Nelson, Walton-on-Thames.

Arthur Andersen & Co (1988) *Guide to Distribution Software*, Institute of Logistics and Distribution Management, Corby.

Attwood, P R (1971) *Planning a Distribution System*, Gower, Aldershot.

Balou, R H (1973) *Business Logistics Management*, Prentice-Hall, New Jersey.

Bassett, R G (1974) *Road Transport Management and Accounting*, Heinemann, London.

Benson, D (1985) *Elements of Road Transport Management*, Croner Publications, New Malden.

Benson, D and Whitehead, G (1985) *Transport and Distribution*, Longman, London.

Bowersox, D J (1978) *Logistical Management*, MacMillan, New York.

Brown, L (1987) *Law for the Haulier*, Kogan Page, London.

Bugg, R and Whitehead, G (1984) *Elements of Transportation and Distribution*, Woodhead-Faulkner, Cambridge.

Carter, R J (1982) *Stores Management*, MacDonald & Evans, London.

Christopher, M (1985) *Strategy of Distribution Management*, Gower, Aldershot.

Christopher, M, Walters, D and Gattorna, J (1977) *Distribution Planning & Control*, Gower, Aldershot.

Christopher, M, Walters, D and Wills, G (1982) *Effective Distribution Management*, MCB Publications, Bradford.

Concise Oxford Dictionary (1964) Oxford University Press, Oxford.

Cooper, J ed (1988) *Logistics and Distribution Planning*, Kogan Page, London.

Croner (1988) *Operational Costings for Transport Management*, Croner Publications, New Malden.

Croner (1988) *Road Transport Operations*, Croner Publications, New Malden.

Davies, G J and Gray, R (1985) *Purchasing International Freight Services*, Gower, Aldershot.

Davis, B G and Olson, M H (1984) *Management Information Systems*, McGraw-Hill, New York.

Drury, J (1981) *Factories, Planning, Design and Modernisation*, Architectural Press, London.

Eastman, R M (1987) *Materials Handling*, Marcel Dekker Inc, New York, Basel.

Eilon, S, Watson-Gandy, C and Christofides, N (1971) *Distribution Management, Mathematical Modelling & Practical Analysis*, Griffin, London.

Falconer, P and Drury, J (1975) *Building and Planning for Industrial Storage and Distribution*, Architectural Press, London.

Freight Transport Association (1983) *Designing for Deliveries*, Tunbridge Wells.

Gattorna, J (1983) *Handbook of Physical Distribution Management*, Gower, Aldershot.

Greene, J (1976) *Production and Inventory Control Handbook*, McGraw-Hill, New York.

Hesket, J L, Glaskowsky, N and Ivie R M (1973) *Business Logistics*, Ronald, New York.

HMSO (1978) *Materials Handling. An Introduction*, London.

HMSO (1979) *Materials Handling. Packing for Profit*, London.

HMSO (1982) *Materials Handling. The Systems Approach*, London.

HMSO (1982) *Materials Handling for Senior Managers*, London.

Hodge, B (1984) *Management Information Systems*, Reston Publishing Co, Virginia, USA.

Hollier, R ed (1987) *Automated Guided Vehicle Systems*, IFS (Publications), Bedford.

ILDM Cost Survey (1988) Institute of Logistics and Distribution Management, Corby.

Jessop and Morrison (1986) *The Storage and Control of Stock*, Pitman Publishing, London.

A T Kearney (1981) *Distribution Cost Survey*, A T Kearney, Chicago.

A T Kearney (1988) *Logistics Productivity: the Competitive Edge in Europe*, A T Kearney, Chicago.

Keen, J S (1987) *Managing Systems Development*, John Wiley & Sons, Chichester.

Kulwiec, R A ed (1985) *Materials Handling Handbook*, John Wiley & Sons, Chichester.

Lee, R (1988) *Unit Load Handling Technology*, Woodhead-Faulkner Ltd (in association with Dexion), Cambridge.

Lewis, R L (1986) *Information Technology in Physical Distribution Management*, Technical Press, Aldershot.

Lindkvist (1985) *Handbook of Materials Handling*, Ellis Horwood Ltd, Chichester.

Lowe, D (1989) *The Transport Manager's and Operator's Handbook*, Kogan Page, London.

Lowe, D (1989) *Goods Vehicle Costing and Pricing Handbook*, Kogan Page, London.

Lucas, H (1984) *The Analysis, Design and Implementation of Information Systems*, McGraw-Hill, Tokyo.

Lucey, T (1982) *Management Information Systems*, D P Publications.

Martin, A (1983) *Distribution Resource Planning*, Prentice-Hall, Englewood Cliffs, New Jersey.

Muller, Thomas (1983) *Automated Guided Vehicles*, IFS (Publications), Bedford.

Parkin, A (1987) *Systems Analysis*, Edward Arnold, London.
Ratcliffe, B (1987) *Economy and Efficiency in Road Transport Operations*, Kogan Page, London.
Robeson, J and House, R (1985) *The Distribution Handbook*, Collier Macmillan, London.
Rodwell, P (1985) *The Road Transport Industry's Guide to Software*, Frances Pinter, London.
Rushton, A S (1980) *Materials Handling Information Systems*, NMHC, Bedford.
Rushton, A S (1983) 'The Cost of Materials Handling to the Economy', *Material Flow*, 1, Elsevier, Amsterdam.
Stone, C A (1968) *The Logistics Review*, Vol A, No 16.
Sussams, J E (1971) *Efficient Road Transport Scheduling*, Gower, Aldershot.
Sussams, J E (1983) *Vehicle Replacement*, Gower, Aldershot.
Thornton, R S (1988) *Goods Vehicle Operators' Licencing*, Kogan Page, London.
Wentworth, F & Christopher, M (1979) *Managing International Distribution*, Gower, Aldershot.
Whalley, B H (1986) *Production Management Handbook*, Gower, Aldershot.

Relevant periodicals
Commercial Motor, Reed Publishing Co, Sutton.
Distribution, Trinity Publishing, Middlesex.
Focus, Institute of Logistics and Distribution Management, Corby.
Freight Management, Fairplay Publications, Coulsden, Surrey.
Industrial Handling and Storage, Trinity Publishing, Middlesex.
International Journal of Physical Distribution and Material Flow, MCB Publications, Bradford.
Journal of Business Logistics, CLM, Columbus, Ohio.
Logistics Today, Highwood Publications, London.
Material Flow, Elsevier Science Publishers, Amsterdam.
Materials Handling Engineering, Penton Publishing, Cleveland, Ohio.
Materials Handling News, Reed Business Publishing, Haywoods Heath.
Retail and Distribution Management, Newman Publishing, London.
Storage Handling and Distribution, Turret-Wheatland, Rickmansworth.
Transport, Highwood Publications, London.

Index